PRACTICING VIRTUES

PRACTICING VIRTUES

Moral Traditions at Quaker and
Military Boarding Schools

KIM HAYS

UNIVERSITY OF CALIFORNIA PRESS
BERKELEY   LOS ANGELES   LONDON

University of California Press
Berkeley and Los Angeles, California

University of California Press, Ltd.
London, England

© 1994 by
The Regents of the University of California

Library of Congress Cataloging-in-Publication Data

Hays, Kim.
    Practicing virtues : moral traditions at Quaker and military boarding
schools / Kim Hays.
        p.   cm.
    Includes bibliographical references (p.   ) and index.
    ISBN 0-520-08237-0
    1. Moral education—United States—Case studies.   2. Society of
Friends—Education—United States—Case studies.   3. Military
education—United States—Case studies.   4. Boarding schools—United
States—Case studies.   I. Title.
LC311.H39   1994
370.11′4′0973—dc20   92-42858
                                                                              CIP

Printed in the United States of America
9   8   7   6   5   4   3   2   1

Contents

Preface

This book is about learning to be good. It concentrates on two traditional methods for defining goodness, one liberal and the other conservative, and describes how these moral traditions are part of the everyday lives of students and teachers at six boarding schools. Three of these schools are run according to Quaker principles, and three are private military academies. None of the six high schools is exclusively for Quakers or the children of military professionals. In fact, students and teachers who are members of the Religious Society of Friends or have close connections with the armed forces constitute a minority at the two sets of schools. In addition, few of those who attend Friends schools later convert to Quakerism, and few cadets join the military upon graduation. Nevertheless, key administrators at all six schools are either Quakers or former military officers, and people come to work or study at the schools because they (and, in the case of students, their parents) are attracted to the values that the two traditions represent: either the liberal values of Quaker schools or the conservative values of military academies.

During the 1987–88 school year I lived at each of the six schools for two or three weeks, observing school activities, talking informally with staff and students, and interviewing over 400 people, almost half of whom are quoted at least once in the following pages. Quotations from interviews are accurate but not always verbatim. Occasionally, I interviewed without a tape recorder and later reconstructed people's comments from notes. In most cases, I taped and later transcribed the interviews but edited out the false starts and confusing syntax that make normal speech so hard to read.

I use pseudonyms for both schools and individuals and have changed unimportant details about places and people in order to further disguise them. Sometimes, however, the fact that a speaker is the headmaster, head of the religion department, or commandant of cadets is important, and to disguise this would be to distort the significance of his or her words and actions. In these cases, I use the person's real title. Proper names are used sparingly, to refer to a few key adults and adolescents at the different schools whom I quote repeatedly.

I am neither a Quaker nor a military professional; my connections to both groups are limited to a few Quaker friends and an uncle who is a career naval officer. Although I consider my values more Quaker than military, I am not a strict pacifist. In researching and writing this book, I have found much to respect about the military moral tradition, and I have met many cadets and military-school faculty members who impressed me. Nevertheless, if I had to choose between sending my child to the best Quaker school or the best military school in the country, I would choose the former. My personal preference for the Quaker moral tradition makes it all the more important that I attempt in this book to do justice to the military moral tradition and its representatives. To the best of my ability, I have done so.

The purpose of the book, however, is *not* to recommend one tradition or one type of school over the other, but rather to show what both sets of schools are like. By analyzing the words and actions of faculty and students at Quaker and military boarding schools, I have tried to portray morality as a living thing—a process of virtues conscientiously practiced or deliberately rejected, duties undertaken or avoided, decisions debated, and dilemmas faced or ignored. I have shown how membership in a particular moral tradition can affect the traits people value, the problems they perceive, and the words they use to describe apparently similar situations. On the surface, the six schools are not very different from one another, except in size and location. But because of the influence of the moral traditions on everything from student discipline to administrative decision making, the two sets of schools present a striking contrast to each other. Yet Quaker and military boarding schools, by their efforts to communicate a strong moral code, a desire to serve others, and sense of responsibility, stand out in contrast to the average public school, where few teachers have the time, opportunity, permission, or training to teach such lessons. Thus all six schools, despite their differences, are deliberate moral communities.

This study was made possible by the six headmasters who allowed me to live on their campuses, ask difficult questions, and be part of the day-to-day running of the schools. I thank them, as I do the hundreds of teachers, staff members, and students who invited me into classrooms, offices, and dormitories, permitted themselves to be observed, and shared their thoughts and feelings with me. I was sustained throughout the fieldwork by their interest and generosity.

This book began as a dissertation under the supervision of Robert Bellah, Neil Smelser, Ann Swidler, and Hanna Pitkin, who gave advice, encouragement, affection, and thoughtful criticism during the research and writing process. I am deeply grateful to them. Others read all or parts of the book (or related essays), and I want to thank them very much. They are Douglas Bennett, Michael Bess, Martin Gilens, Angela Grosso Ciponte, Karen Hansen, Arlie Hochschild, Eleanor Hodges, Kimball Kramer, Robin McElheny, Ruth Meyer Schweizer, Lyn Spillman, Sally Williams, and Deborah Valenze. The comments of two anonymous readers for the University of California Press were also helpful.

Among those who helped me to collect information about Quakers and Quaker schools were Adelbert Mason, then executive director of the Friends Council on Education, and Kenneth Miller, then associate secretary of the Friends General Conference (FGC). I am also grateful to members of the FGC staff, who facilitated my conducting interviews at their 1987 meeting in Oberlin, Ohio. Most of all, I thank the seventeen people who agreed to be interviewed during the gathering.

My best source of military training materials was the Berkeley Department of Military Science. I thank Lieutenant-Colonel Richard C. Ashley, Lieutenant-Colonel John C. Goertemiller, and Captain James D. H. Bacon for their advice. Colonel H. Rance Farrell and Major Ken Talley also kindly provided information. My warmest gratitude goes to the nine army officers I interviewed during the summer of 1987, whose anecdotes and descriptions of moral dilemmas helped me to understand the military moral tradition better than any reading could do.

The initial stages of my research were supported by a scholarship from the Northern California Association of Phi Beta Kappa, a Josephine de Kármán Fellowship, a National Graduate Fellowship from the U.S. Department of Education, and a grant from the Chancellor's Patent Fund of the University of California, Berkeley. During two years of fieldwork, transcribing, and writing, I was a Dissertation Fellow funded by the Institute on Global Conflict and Cooperation (IGCC). For the last year of thesis-writing, I had a Charlotte W. Newcombe Dissertation Fellowship, and I revised the manuscript while working at the Institute for Sociology of the University of Bern. I am indebted to these organizations for their support.

Many offered other kinds of support along the way, including Elsa Tranter in Berkeley and Susi Oesch in Bern. My parents and sister, Joy, Tom, and Natasha Hays, were the kind of loving readers every writer should have to boost their spirits. The person who has made the greatest difference to me during the years I have worked on this book is my husband, Peter Stucker, who has had great confidence in me and my work and has sustained me with his love. I thank him for making me so happy.

Introduction

Teaching and Learning in a Moral Community

Schools with a Moral Purpose

Americans talk about a crisis of morality in the schools, about a failure to teach character. Public schools are perceived to have relinquished moral responsibility. Actually, anyone who has studied schools—for that matter, anyone who has gone to school—knows that American schools are not morally neutral. One of their primary goals is moral socialization.[1] From kindergarten on, teachers reward certain kinds of speech and behavior and punish others, and studies show that these patterns of reward and punishment usually reinforce differences in class. Middle-class children whose parents have brought them up to answer questions, give reasons for what they do, and demonstrate self-control and self-confidence are called "good"; children who have not learned these skills are called "slow learners" or even "bad." Through these labels, schools prepare children for the dominant or subordinate position that, because of their parents' occupations, they are often destined to assume in the adult world of work.[2]

This is not the kind of moral socialization that parents mean, however, when they talk about a crisis of morality in the schools. Parents complain that the public schools "aren't teaching kids right from wrong," and it is true that today's public-school teachers do not see themselves as providers of a moral education. The faculty at the average high school, if they think about it, may assume that they are passing on American values, but they do not communicate those values in a systematic way.[3] Although teachers may want their pupils to grow up to be good adults, they are more concerned with trying to help them graduate and get a job or go to college. They are wary of encouraging discussions of moral problems among pupils and of expressing strong views about political or social issues, for fear of reprisals from parents and school-board members. Whatever moral messages teachers may impart, they are not self-consciously teaching their pupils the vocabulary and virtues of a particular moral tradition. In fact, at many schools the teaching of morality is decried as indoctrination; children are treated as "adults capable of choosing their own morality as long as they do not commit crimes."[4]

Public-school administrators and teachers may also be unsure of how to go about teaching a child to be a good person, since philosophers, psychologists, and sociologists offer conflicting advice. One important subject of conflict is whether morality is universal or particular. Can goodness be expressed in the form of a few universal principles, which are accessible to people of every nationality and culture simply by virtue of their being rational human beings, or can it be described and experienced only in the context of a particular community and tradition?[5]

This book comes down squarely on the side of the particular. Whether we like it or not, whether we even acknowledge it or not, we are all part of groups, each with its own history and its particular ideas of morality, and it is in the context of these groups that we learn what it means to be a good person and that we practice what we learn. As Alan Wolfe has said, "[W]hat gives [individuals] the ability to create moral understandings in the first place are all the things they share in common with others, from language to stories to practices to laws. Because morality is a socially constructed process, no individual, standing alone, can ever be moral—or immoral."[6] Yet when it comes to talking to children, not about getting good grades or sitting quietly, but about living a good life, teachers are—with good reason—reluctant openly to advocate a particular moral code. This leads them to dilute the moral instruction they offer or else to provide young people with a smorgasbord of values from which they are expected to choose their favorites. Such methods rarely offend, but they also rarely instruct. Thus, though teachers often make their pupils feel good or bad about themselves, they rarely teach them—at least, not deliberately— what it means to be a good or a bad person.

The six schools portrayed in this book, three Quaker and three military boarding schools, take a different stance. They are self-consciously moral. They advocate two distinct traditions, one religious and the other professional, that have a long history in the United States. They are places where adults deliberately attempt to practice a certain way of life and teach adolescents to be certain kinds of people. Both Quaker and military moral traditions clearly spell out virtues by which adherents are expected to live, and the schools' brochures state plainly that these virtues are meant to be part of adult and adolescent life at the schools. In summary, these are schools where moral socialization is the acknowledged goal rather than the hidden by-product of education.

Morality is much easier to teach in a small private boarding school with fewer than 500 pupils than in a large public high school with more than 2,000. The Quaker and military schools described here are certainly not presented as models; no public high school would ever want to try to reproduce their way of life. What is interesting about these six schools is that they help us to understand the process by which a moral code is made available and sensible to those who are trying to apply it to their lives. They show us how ideals can be translated into manageable goals for teachers and students, how lessons about goodness can be given a moral context or narrative to make them meaningful.

These schools are, unabashedly, communities that uphold particular traditions, and *tradition* is a loaded word. From the political platform, the pulpit, the press, and the university, as well as in everyday conversation, many people are calling for a return to "traditional" values. These demands are countered by those who remind us that the guidelines of tradition easily become fetters, constraining individual freedom of choice. This debate about the value of tradition is a version of the debate over whether morality should consist of universal laws or particular precepts; it restates the dilemma about the relative merits of freedom and attachment. This debate seems to be a quintessential part of the modern condition, and in particular the American modern condition, of feeling torn between being a member of a traditional community and being a "free" individual in society. As John Hewitt has put it: "Modernity in the American context is typically marked by a sense of life as confronting the person with difficult and painful dilemmas—whether to stay in a community or to leave it, whether to conform to its expectations or rebel against them, whether to build an autonomous and independent self or to construct a self dependent upon (and depended upon by) others."[7]

Even those who live and work in traditional communities face this dilemma. At the six schools portrayed here, being an individual is as highly valued as being a member of the group. The schools are not utopian communities or cults, nor is their primary purpose that of fundamentalist Christian schools—to recruit students into lifelong service to a single, absolute truth.[8] More than anything else, the schools resemble regular high schools, where students enroll and graduate, most going on to college; where teachers come and go; where principals are answerable to school boards and parents. Like any American public school, these schools teach academic subjects and try to prepare students to be independent adults in society. But unlike most high schools, they also try to teach students to live in a close-knit community and to adhere to certain clearly prescribed values. Their purpose is to teach autonomy in the context of structure, independence in the context of tradition.

Public-school teachers feel they must focus on the basic skills that will help their pupils to get jobs. But young people need more than job skills; they need clear-cut moral goals and help in learning how to meet those goals day by day. The core source of values for any child is the home, but that does not absolve educators of their responsibility to endow their schools with a moral purpose and to address important ethical issues in the classroom. There is a disturbing lack of well-defined moral purpose in many American schools today. Neither Quaker schools nor military academies have all the answers, but they are not afraid to raise moral questions. We should look to these schools, not necessarily to tell us how to educate our children, but to remind us that morality can and must be taught and to help us think about ways to teach it.

The Practice of Virtues and the Acceptance of Conflict

Most of those who call for a return to traditional values do not explain how to live according to those values. Strict moral codes are not easy to practice; a process of translation must occur if a tradition is to become accessible on a daily basis. This book shows in detail how that process of translation operates at the six schools, where faculty members try to live, teach, make decisions, and organize student life in accordance with the Quaker or military moral tradition, while students try to understand the tradition and adapt it to fit their needs. The description of life at the schools focuses on two aspects of the translation process that determine the effectiveness of the moral traditions in teaching young people what it means to be a good person not only in school but in society as a whole: the practice of virtues, and the acceptance of conflict.

The moral weight of each of the two traditions is carried by a set of key virtues; these are the vehicles by which the ideals of Quakerism or the military are made accessible. Administrators at each set of schools have incorporated these virtues into the fabric of school life, and students and teachers are expected to try to live by them. Thus, the moral traditions are passed on primarily in the form of character traits—one becomes part of the community by becoming a particular kind of virtuous person and by helping others to become virtuous in the same way.

Virtues are taught at the schools by means of language as well as example, and moral language plays a crucial role in making sense of the traditions and keeping them alive. A common language of virtue allows the tradition to be shared by insiders. Special words and phrases that carry moral weight in the communities are shibboleths: they separate the initiate from the outsider and, in so doing, draw the insiders closer together. The Quaker and military moral traditions have a vocabulary for identifying virtues and vices, for classifying people as good or bad, for defining actions as right, wrong, or morally neutral. Both groups have what was called in *Habits of the Heart* a "second language" of commitment that they use among themselves.[9] Within this language are many important, value-laden terms that encourage both devotion and debate—debate over their true meaning, proper application, and relationship to one another. In this book these terms are called *magnet words*, because, like magnets, they attract or repel, depending on how they are used. Without the magnet words, language at the schools would be much less stormy and intense, but it would also be much less effective in sustaining and strengthening the moral tradition.

The idea of a moral tradition as the common virtues, duties, history, and language shared by a close-knit group suggests a life of order. But life in these thriving moral communities is not orderly. Instead, it is full of conflict. "A living tradition . . . ," wrote Alasdair MacIntyre, "is an historically extended, socially embodied argument, and an argument in part about the goods which constitute that tradition."[10] As the following chapters show, the Quaker and military moral traditions are, even in their ideal forms, fraught with tensions, and, at the schools, arguments about elements of the traditions and how to apply them for the good of the community are everyday occurrences. Conflict over the meaning of the magnet words strengthens the tradition's importance at the school and the feelings of attachment among administrators, teachers, and students. Members of the school communities would not be so devoted to the traditions and so familiar with their values and vocabularies if they did not argue about them.

Quaker and Military, Liberal and Conservative

Quakers, or members of the Religious Society of Friends, belong to a sect founded in seventeenth-century England by George Fox.[11] Persecuted in England, many Friends emigrated to the American colonies, especially to Pennsylvania, which belonged to the English Quaker William Penn; later, Quakers went West along with other Americans. Today's 120,000 North American Quakers do not dress, live, or speak differently from other Americans,[12] nor do they live in separate communities, like the Amish. Their religion is highly decentralized, and different forms of worship are found in different parts of the country. The majority of Quakers, however, are organized into local Monthly Meetings and regional Yearly Meetings, emphasize silence in their religious services, make decisions by consensus, and advocate pacifism, equality, strong community ties, and a simple way of life. The United States Armed Forces, by contrast, is a profession with an active, current membership of over 2,000,000 people, who are organized in a strict hierarchy, minutely regulated by laws and codes of behavior, and trained to plan and fight wars.

A study of Catholic or fundamentalist Christian schools, radical schools-without-rules, or famous New England preparatory schools would also offer insights into how moral traditions are taught and practiced. The Quaker and military traditions were chosen because they are representative of two characteristic American ways of thinking, one of which emphasizes tolerance and the other, discipline. This dichotomy in mainstream American society has been portrayed by social scientists under many different labels, with emphases that vary according to the scholars' special interests. The authors of *Habits of the Heart*, for example, might suggest a parallel between the two traditions and "expressive" and "utilitarian" individualism;[13] Ralph Turner might draw comparisons between Quakers and military professionals and what he has called "impulsives" and "institutionals."[14] Joseph Amato has written about "an elemental ethical antimony for all modern people" that he perceives as a choice between future and past or between guilt and gratitude: guilt that "demands the universal realization of human potential" and gratitude that "requires obedience to a specific established order."[15] James Davison Hunter might explain differences between members of the Quaker and military moral traditions using the concepts "progressive" and "orthodox."[16] Features of this same dichotomy can be found in Carol Gilligan's two styles of moral decision making and in Deborah Tannen's two ways of speaking: one emphasizing care and equality in relationships, the other emphasizing justice and hierarchy.[17] A case has been made for calling the Quaker moral tradition feminine, while the military, with its 89 percent male membership and its code of honor, is stereotypically masculine in its concerns.[18] But the dichotomy that I find most useful in talking about Quaker and military ways of thinking is that of liberal and conservative.

The Quaker tradition, which advocates the importance of individual conscience, openness to many different opinions, and benevolence toward those in need, is essentially a liberal tradition, while the military, which stresses firm standards, hard work, and competition, is essentially conservative. A teacher at a Quaker school describing how important it is for pupils to be "made to feel uncomfortable about their wealth" and learn "that some people are trapped in their poverty" is articulating typical American liberal sentiments, while a retired general turned headmaster, who praises military schools as places in which the young learn that if they work hard they will be rewarded and that "if they don't obey the rules and regulations they pay a price," is speaking as a classic American conservative. To understand the Quaker and military moral traditions, to examine their virtues and their ways of portraying the good, to study the dilemmas and conflicts to which the day-to-day practice of these traditions gives rise, is also to gain insight into the typical American liberal and conservative virtues and conflicts. By analyzing the difference between Quaker and military visions of what it means to live a good life and be a good person, this book helps us to understand why liberals and conservatives in the United States have such a difficult time finding common ground for discussion and problem-solving.

Surprisingly, dedicated Quakers and military professionals do have some things in common, as the following chapters show. They share a desire to live consistently and with integrity, in service to certain strongly felt truths; a willingness to make sacrifices; and a belief in the sacred nature of their responsibilities. They also share the need to find a middle way between individualism and conformity, both of which are part of their moral traditions. This tension between individual autonomy and communal solidarity is part of belonging to any group; membership in the Religious Society of Friends or the military brings its own version of this dilemma. The Quaker, or liberal, philosophy of tolerance assigns enormous worth to individual freedom of judgment; as a result, it runs the risk of becoming so all-embracing that it abdicates judgment altogether.[19] The military, or conservative, philosophy of discipline places great emphasis on obedience to authority, and as a result it runs the risk of becoming authoritarian. At its best, however, the Quaker tradition can encourage both tolerance and strong moral conviction, while the military tradition at its best can teach both discipline and individual initiative. One of the purposes of this book is to identify and analyze the mechanisms that exist within Quakerism and the military for easing the tensions between individual and community, and to show how these mechanisms are applied at the six schools. Insight into the ways the two traditions handle the individual/group dilemma and try to avoid the extremes of tolerance or discipline to which they are prone sheds light on the problems of liberals and conservatives, who tend toward the same excesses but lack the traditional resources, such as the Quaker concept of "concern" or the military concept of "leadership," to find a middle way between freedom and constraint.

Constructing Morality at the Schools

All of the relationships and events that make up boarding-school life can be studied productively. Classroom interactions, student cliques, teacher factions, problems of discipline, tensions between administrators and teachers, pressure from parents and school-board members, dormitory life and roommate problems, team sports, such school ceremonies as assembly, alumni weekend, and graduation: a sociologist could focus on any of these and learn a great deal about school life and the process of moral socialization. I have chosen to look at the way adolescents and adults interpret their responsibilities at the schools and use the Quaker or the military moral tradition to form an understanding of what it means to be a good student or teacher and a good person. The dining hall, English classroom, and dormitory are some of the places where they put their understandings into practice. Although the schools I studied are too small and homogeneous for the typical adolescent cliques to play a central role, students can easily identify the different groups to which their peers belong, and these friendship circles contribute to a sense of belonging at the school. The book does not focus on these cliques, however, but, rather, on students and teachers as a whole and on their interactions.

It is hard to understand the impact of a moral tradition on school life without some sense of what it is like to go to boarding school. Chapter One talks about boarding schools in general and shows how Quaker and military moral traditions influence even the smallest details of daily life. It introduces the three Quaker and three military schools and describes the traits they share. Chapter Two steps back from the schools to talk about the Quaker and military moral traditions in their ideal forms. It outlines their similarities, including an emphasis on service, and then analyzes their differences, which stem above all from the Quaker belief in the Inner Light as a source of goodness and the military emphasis on external standards. These central concepts are not enough to maintain the moral traditions on an everyday basis, however. "What sustains and strengthens traditions? What weakens and destroys them? The answer in key part is: the exercise or lack of exercise of the relevant virtues," according to Alasdair MacIntyre. These virtues are dispositions that support us in our particular tradition's quest for the good.[20] The Quaker moral tradition and that of the military have different quests for the good and therefore different virtues, which are described in Chapter Two. Practicing virtues is never simple; to try to do so is to encounter dilemmas and become embroiled in debates. The chapter shows that these tensions are different for the two traditions, but they are also similar, in that they grow out of the basic tension between the group and the individual or between conformity and autonomy.

The process by which moral traditions are translated into everyday behavior is the focus of Chapter Three, which explains how each virtue is interpreted in the context of school life and applied by students, teachers, and administrators in classrooms and dormitories. The practice of virtues at the schools takes place as part of an ongoing Quaker or military project, a quest for the good that focuses on self-discovery at Quaker schools and on responsibility at military schools. John Hewitt has pointed out that a shared culture does not just provide a model for conduct; it also provides things to worry and talk about.[21] At the six schools, the moral traditions have their own vocabularies and their characteristic tensions and dilemmas. Chapter Four shows that attempts to understand and practice the virtues give rise to disagreements among administrators, teachers, and students. As MacIntyre has said, "Traditions, when vital, embody continuities of conflict."[22] At the root of many of the conflicts at the schools are the continuing tensions between individual freedom and communal solidarity that are part of any attempt to live a good life within the context of a tradition.

The continued existence of an organized group depends on its solving the problem of authority or legitimate social control. A school cannot function unless it establishes methods for maintaining order.[23] Rules, whether official or merely understood, are part of school life, and it is in the making, enforcing, and obeying or disobeying of those rules that conflicts are most likely to arise. Chapter Five addresses adults' and adolescents' attitudes toward authority and the role that the Quaker concept of concern and the military concept of leadership play in determining teachers' and students' treatment of school rules and involvement in the process of self-government. Chapter Six focuses on the adolescents' needs as they work to form a sense of identity at boarding school. It shows how they draw on certain aspects of the two traditions to help them develop and live up to an ideal image—of sincerity and kindness at the Quaker schools, of courage and forbearance at the military academies. Even as they identify with these ideals, however, most of the adolescents reject another important aspect of the traditions—their quality of sacredness. Chapter Six explains how the schools try, and why they seem to fail, to teach teenagers about the sacred nature of the two traditions.

The book concludes by reviewing what it means to belong to a moral tradition and why the acceptance of conflict, as well as the practice of virtues, must be part of a moral life. Conflict is crucial to what Alan Wolfe has called "the social construction of morality." Morality, wrote Wolfe, "is neither a fixed set of rules handed down unchanging by powerful structures nor something that is made up on the spot. It is a negotiated process through which individuals, by reflecting periodically on what they have done in the past, try to ascertain what they ought to do next." [24] At the Quaker and military boarding schools, among faculty and students, it is possible to observe this process.

Chapter One

School Life Through the Lens
of Moral Tradition

The Common Characteristics
of Boarding Schools

Mott Friends School is sheltered from the busy streets nearby by a belt of trees. The campus is designed for pedestrians; walkways across the lawns lead to student center, dormitories, classroom buildings, library, auditorium, Quaker meetinghouse, sports fields, and gym. On fall afternoons the fields are full of students playing soccer and field hockey; a few teenagers—but not many, because sports are mandatory—sprawl on the lawn near the main building or stroll to the pond, and some manage to find a chance to slip into a thicket and smoke illicit cigarettes or a joint. To a visitor, the beautifully maintained grounds, the attractive brick dormitories, the modern student center with its brightly colored armchairs, and the meetinghouse with its dark wooden benches all speak of privilege and stability.

With some variation in details, this could be a description of any of the six boarding schools. For all their differences, the three Quaker and three military schools have much in common with each other and with elite counterparts such as Choate, Groton, and Exeter.[1] First, there are the impressive physical plant and the grounds, which include not only fields for sports but also buffer zones—woods and meadows that surround the school to create a sense of haven and isolation. The atmosphere of wealth communicated by the grounds is echoed by the interiors of the main administrative offices, with red leather and heavy wood prevailing in the military schools and a more austere, Early American style in the Quaker schools. Portraits of headmasters, group pictures of past classes—some dating back to the previous century—and, at the military schools, sports trophies, old-fashioned weaponry, and plaques commemorating alumni fallen in war decorate the corridors of the main buildings. The message that the schools convey to parents through these furnishings and decorations is that here, in this environment, their child will be enveloped in security, restraint, and tradition.

It is not clear whether the schools' decor is also intended to communicate an environment of luxury. On the one hand, parents paying between $8,000 and $13,000 per school year for their child's education expect him or her to live well.[2] On the other hand, a commitment to simplicity among Quakers and to austerity among the military, coupled with the traditional prep school "pride of deprivation"[3] and a shortage of funds for repairing old dorms and dining rooms, reduces the comfort of student life-styles. Even at Pershing Military Academy, by far the wealthiest of the six schools, the male students still return at night to sparsely furnished barracks with linoleum floors and bunk beds.

Another quality that Quaker and military boarding schools have in common and share with other boarding schools around the country is their regimentation. In her description of St. Paul's School in New Hampshire, Sara Lawrence Lightfoot commented on "the supreme orchestration of events and people" that wealth and tradition make possible.[4] This kind of planning is a necessity if boarding-school students and teachers are to be kept productively occupied throughout their waking hours. Students' time is structured from the moment they wake up until they go to bed: meals, classes, assemblies, religious services, sports, study periods, even "free time" are all scheduled. A typical day at one military school begins with Reveille at 6:30, but in fact students often get up much earlier in order to be showered and dressed in faultless uniform, shoes shined and brass polished, for the pre-breakfast military formation at 6:45. Even at the Quaker schools, which are more flexible, there are not many minutes during the day when a student is not supposed to be somewhere doing some specified thing. At Mott Friends School the faculty agree that, in the words of one teacher, "the kids' schedules are exhausting." Said another, "Besides classes there's the service requirement, arts, phys ed, and now we've got computer skills, and that's all good, too. But we keep adding on and adding on, and we don't subtract anything." For Mott students, whose favorite brand of one-upmanship involves comparing how little they've slept the night before, the regimentation also means that, as one senior said, "there's just not enough time to be alone."

Boarding schools, in other words, are to a large extent what Erving Goffman called "total institutions." Studying mental hospitals and prisons, Goffman identified certain characteristics that these organizations share with more benign residential communities such as schools, monasteries, and old-age homes. At total institutions, work, play, and sleep occur in the same place, under the same authority, in the company of a large group of others, according to a tightly scheduled regimen and as part of a rational plan imposed by a higher authority. Some other characteristics of total institutions are constant surveillance, separation of inmates and staff into different social strata, and the loss of personal autonomy even in such small matters of personal choice as hair style or food.[5] All of these qualities are found to a greater or lesser degree in boarding schools. In the six examined here, the degree of constraint varies, in part depending on the number of open weekends, when students may leave campus to visit friends or family. Even the strictest school permits students to visit the nearby town on Saturday and Sunday afternoons, while, at the most lenient, students with officially recognized good standing and no prior commitments can come and go essentially at will until bedtime. The fact remains, however, that boarding schools are places where a small group of adults try to control the lives of a larger group of adolescents. Like convents, boarding schools are also a type of total institution in which the restrictions of institutional life are shared by staff and inmates alike.[6] Thus, in spite of their greater authority, the lives of the adults, especially those living in the dormitories, are almost as regimented as their charges'.

A third characteristic of boarding schools is that their financial health depends on attracting and keeping students. Administrators must offer parents the two commodities they seek for their children: academic training and character-building. The quality of the academic program varies greatly among the six schools, but all six consider themselves college-preparatory institutions and list in their admissions brochures some of the colleges attended by their graduates. The graduates' acquisition of good character is not so easily demonstrated, but the schools' intention to impart to their students what one admissions director called "moral fiber" is clearly expressed in their catalogues, where qualities such as leadership, orderliness, and self-discipline (at the military academies), social responsibility, spiritual development, and trust (at the Friends schools), and responsible decision-making and accountability (at both) are touted. The desire to help young people to become better adults—however one defines that "better"—is shared by many of the administrators and teachers at the schools. To the head of Pershing Military Academy, for example, the military structure of the school is "simply a framework to give [the cadets] responsibility":

What's quintessentially Pershing is knowing that there is something beyond the intellect, and it has to do with character and honor and a sense of responsibility and commitment, and we're going to work very, very hard to make sure that [a student] doesn't go through here untouched with regard to those traits.

At Mott Friends School, an administrator described the two things he most wanted to impart to young people: "the Friends' attitude of seeking that of God within every human being" and a "responsibility to the world as peacemakers. . . . If we don't teach those kinds of things, . . . if all we do is help the wealthy recreate themselves in their children, then we should let someone else do it."

The Moral Meaning of Necessities

An imposing campus with a distinguished history, a system for regulating the lives of staff and students, a determination to educate young people not only academically but morally: sharing these basic traits, boarding schools share a certain similarity of appearance, structure, and mood. Students must be found, admitted, fed, housed, educated, and kept amused in their spare time through participation in sports, clubs, theatrical performances, and other adolescent activities traditionally considered character-building. Their comings and goings must be monitored, and they must be discouraged from lying, cheating, stealing, hurting each other and themselves, drinking, using drugs, and having sex. Teachers must be hired, paid, fed, (usually) housed, and evaluated; at a minimum they must teach classes, develop curricula, coach sports, and discipline and counsel students. Administrators must make decisions about major curriculum and program changes, supervise staff, soothe parents, court alumni, handle board members, raise funds, and try to meet admissions quotas. At the larger and richer schools a small army of secretaries, bookkeepers, cooks, food servers, gardeners, maintenance personnel, launderers, and cleaners tend to the more mundane side of running a school.

All of these activities must take place if a boarding school is to function. But such an ordered existence is not possible without a shared sense of moral purpose. In most formal organizations, people carry out the responsibilities assigned to them because they consider themselves part of a legitimate moral order: a business that manufactures a useful product, for example, or a government that serves the public.[7] All such organizations are regulated by moral traditions, in the sense that their members share assumptions about the purpose of their activities, as well as patterns of speech and behavior, that are reinforced by a particular conception of what it means to live a good life and be a good person. Moral traditions are especially prominent at boarding schools, which try to teach and exemplify a character-building way of life. Quaker and military boarding schools, in their allegiance to two clearly defined and historically significant American systems of belief and behavior, have explicit traditions that unmistakably influence everyday life. Because a school is Quaker or military, daily activities assume meanings they would not otherwise have. Moral tradition serves as a kind of lens through which the necessities of boarding-school life—meals, classes, dormitories, staff meetings, and so on—are viewed, and under this special scrutiny their significance is enhanced, reduced, or altered beyond the merely pragmatic. The everyday is transformed in service to the moral order.

Dress

Clothing is one of the necessities to which the different moral traditions have imparted special meanings. It is not enough to say that at military academies students wear uniforms whereas at Quaker schools they dress with extreme casualness. Rather, at military schools an enormous amount of importance is assigned to how students dress. The uniform is the most visible symbol of the school's military nature and is therefore charged with moral significance. The neatness of one's trouser creases, the shininess of one's shoes and brass insignia, the proper angle of one's hat are all outward signs of inner conviction—of a student's acceptance of the legitimacy of military authority. To wear one's uniform well is also to demonstrate a potential for leadership, the preeminent military characteristic.

The moral significance of clothing at Quaker schools is much more complicated. Friends' emphasis on equality and simplicity suggests that clothes should have no importance at all. One should dress functionally and acceptably and then forget about one's clothes until it is time to take them off at night. Thus, the majority of students and many faculty members wear jeans, T-shirts, comfortable old pullovers, and sneakers or brogues. However, since Quakers' belief in the importance of each person's Inner Light[8] translates, at the schools, into a respect for adolescents' right to express their individuality, students are also permitted to dress in costume, whether that means spiked hair and safety pins among the "punkers," tie-dyed shirts and ponchos among the "Deadheads," or hair-sprayed coiffures, makeup, and high heels among the "mall rats." [9] Adding to the complexity of the moral message carried by dress is the fact that although all students' clothing choices are supposedly respected by their peers and teachers, the choice to dress in a conventionally fashionable way is considered evidence of a lack of independence. *Trendy* is an insult at Quaker schools.

Classes

Quaker and military boarding schools share a desire to teach students enough of the formal secondary curriculum to enable them to graduate from high school and attend college. Beyond this minimum, however, goals differ. Passed through a Quaker filter, classes became places for learning self-expression, independent inquiry, and social responsibility. One Quaker teacher at Mott explained that he thought the purpose of his classes was to teach kids "to be critical, to be skeptical, to question—particularly authority." Part of his obligation as a teacher was to present different points of view, so as to create "moral dilemmas" for the students: "They have to confront them, and evaluate them, and decide where they come down." For example, in teaching American history, he makes sure that students "don't assume that everything moved . . . effortlessly and without controversy," since they "need to know that this country was built out of moral dilemmas . . . and [that] we made a lot of mistakes and . . . bad decisions."

But fortunately we are a country that has the possibility of learning . . . from history. . . . For me, the ultimate patriotism is that capacity to be self-critical. . . . Otherwise we become complaisant and spineless. . . . I tell the kids from day one that . . . nobody has a monopoly on truth, and . . . I try to give the impression that I'm not the great authority . . . with all the answers.

Another Friend, a science and mathematics teacher, believes that "the most important value that Mott can teach someone is the sense that they can make a difference." Important social issues, like space exploration and global water use, are raised in his classes, so that students will have "a sense of participating, not just in science class but in the world." He sees class as an opportunity for students to discuss "their responsibilities as residents of the earth. . . . They should think about science in the context of asking, 'Who am I?' and recognize the responsibility we have not to destroy."

At their best, Quaker-school classes are places where students talk more than teachers, discussing the Monroe Doctrine in the light of American involvement in Nicaragua, for example, or criticizing different historians' interpretations of the causes of the Russian Revolution, or role-playing a hearing to assess the ecological impact of a proposed dam. In these classes, teachers gently guide the discussion, ask provocative questions, supplement students' presentations with more detailed information, and help the class draw conclusions. At their worst, too, Quaker-school classes are places where students talk more than teachers: they interrupt discussions with irrelevant questions, gleefully try to confuse teachers or steer them off the educational track, and argue among themselves pointlessly. At Fox School three sophomore girls described with relish how their class had driven a young teacher into a frenzy of yelling and then reduced her to tears. "Some teachers deserved being tortured," said one, "but some teachers can take it, too." This particular teacher, they explain, is easy prey, because "she's scared of us."

In contrast to the liberal Quaker vision of classes as a forum for self-expression and questioning, the conservative military view defines the ideal class as a ground for self-development and disciplined absorption of knowledge. Whereas the Quaker-school student is encouraged to invest himself in his studies, the ideal military-school student invests his studies in himself and his future. Learning is seen as a conscious and competitive effort at self-improvement, and faculty members want to set standards for their pupils. One teacher at Jackson Military Academy, who combined a firm, no-nonsense manner with a robust motherliness that led many students to call her Mom, was glad that her classes provided an opportunity for religious discussions—something she felt would be impossible in a public school— since they gave her the opportunity "to let [students] know what my values are and really be a model" for them:

For this generation, everything is grayed out—they don't know what's black and what's white any more. We euphemize everything. But I guess I'm old-fashioned in that I teach right/wrong, black/white. We discuss all the gray areas, but I show them that even in looking at the gray, it will always be a shade darker or a shade lighter, toward the right or toward the wrong.

A Pershing teacher also saw himself as a standard-bearer, although of a different kind: he felt that his main responsibility was to make sure that students learned self-discipline. "We're not being mean or cruel when we say, 'If [your paper] comes in late, you're going to get an F,' because they need to learn, not just in class but in life, what it means to meet obligations":

They have this feeling: "Here I am, see, now entertain me if you can." I . . . take care of that attitude on the very first day. . . . I compare an instructor to a physician—you come here because you have a problem, you need strengthening in something, and the pills I give you may seem bitter, but I can tell you that in the long run you are going to feel better about the whole thing.

He is proud of the fact that so many of his students who were not very good scholars do well in college "because they were disciplined here . . . and can compete with all those people who were allowed to do whatever they wanted in high school."

The best military-school classes are places where a large and often complicated body of information is being conveyed, in lecture form, to a classroom full of interested pupils taking notes. Teachers keep students engaged and on their toes with frequent questions to which short, precise answers are expected: "If you were Catholic when Martin Luther posted his Ninety-nine Theses, would you have called that 'revolution' or 'reformation'?" "What does exponential growth mean?" "How did the Winged Hussars of Poland get their name?" The worst classes are also lectures: teachers talk to a totally non-responsive audience of students who sleep, stare out the windows, whisper, openly do crossword puzzles, or finish their homework in other subjects.

Meals

Three times a day, at both sets of schools, students and teachers pour into a dining hall and sit down to eat. In both kinds of schools the physical purpose is nutrition, but the moral purpose is quite different. At Quaker schools, meals are regarded as a time for promoting school-wide feelings of fellowship and closer relations between teachers and students and among adolescents of different ages. At two of the three Friends schools, one meal each day is served family-style: several teachers preside at each table and engage students determinedly in conversation. Even at the other meals, it is not uncommon to see teachers and students sitting together, although separation is more usual. No special tables are set aside for teachers, and they stand in the cafeteria line alongside the students.

At military schools, where cadets are organized into companies of twenty to fifty students, meals are a time for promoting unit integration. For at least one meal a day (at Sherman Military Academy, for all three), cadets gather in formation by unit outside the dining hall, march in under the watchful eyes of their student sergeants and officers and the adult military personnel, and sit down to eat with their fellows from Troop A, Battery B, or Company C. Usually the unit that has excelled that week at drill or barracks inspection is allowed to eat first, and units that are being punished eat last; this leads to a lot of competitive banter among cadets as they wait in line. Adults sit separately and are given priority in the food lines. At Sherman, the strictest of the three academies, dinner is a military performance. After an evening formation in the quadrangle, students are expected to enter the dining room in total silence and stand at attention behind their places while grace is said, announcements are made by the student officers, and the list of students to receive punishments is read aloud. As each unit's cadets line up to get their food, the others sit in silence at their places, waiting to be called. Teachers at this school eat in a separate room; only the "tacs" or tactical officers (one adult for each unit, who is responsible for military discipline in that unit) eat in the same room as the students, at a centrally placed table that allows them to keep an eye out for misbehavior and intermittently to shout orders at cadets.

Dormitories

At Quaker schools, dormitory rooms, like clothes, are seen as a means through which individuals can express their personalities; at military schools, dormitory rooms, like uniforms, are a vehicle for expressing self-discipline and loyalty to military expectations. At Fox Friends School, for example, many of the boys had lavished time, deliberation, and carpentry skills on decorating their rooms. Amid the ubiquitous Indian bedspreads, one set of roommates had constructed a basket chair that hung from the ceiling, another duo had built platform beds, and a third pair had papered the walls and ceiling completely with humorous pictures cut from magazines. Some of the rooms in Quaker-school dormitories look as though they had been hit by a tornado, with students wading through clothes, papers, and half-eaten sandwiches to get from bed to desk. At the military academies, students took pride in showing me how perfectly their spartan rooms—with utilitarian metal furniture, one poster per roommate, and a rug permitted only for officers—conformed to regulations. At Sherman, shoes are lined up under the bed, clothes hung in the closet on hangers spaced a regulation two fingers apart, books displayed in graduated order from largest to smallest, and beds made with precision. Even the objects in the top desk drawer—scotch tape, pencils, pens, and so on—are arranged in a specified way. At all three military schools, daily inspections by unit sergeants and weekly inspections by senior student officers or adults emphasize the importance of orderliness, and companies win points or acquire demerits based on the state of their members' rooms.

Quaker-school dormitories are settings where teachers and students can make friends. Teachers live in the dorms—at least one teacher for every twenty students; more often, one teacher for every ten. Their primary duty is disciplinary: keeping things quiet during evening study halls, making sure that students are in their rooms at bedtime, and trying to prevent misbehavior in general. Many of these adults also see themselves as filling the role of surrogate parent or older sibling to the students in their charge. One young married couple in a girls' dormitory said:

Other dorm people have told us to put up a sign saying "Do not disturb" when we want to be alone, but we like them to feel they can disturb us. We want them to knock if they need us. . . . And we also like to be out there [in the hall] at least an hour or an hour and a half a night, just so they know we're here.

At military school, dormitories are the primary arena where student officers are expected to exercise their authority; resident adults should be superfluous as either disciplinarians or confidants. (Here a distinction is made between the girl students, who at all three academies have some form of dorm mother, and the boys, who have no such figure.) The degree of adult supervision for boys varies from school to school. At two of the schools, each unit of approximately fifty boys has a tactical officer or counselor who stays in the dorm each evening until the official bedtime. Once he leaves, the Sherman cadets are completely on their own in the dorms, whereas the Pershing cadets are nominally in the charge of a resident teaching intern, hired right out of college for a term of only one year. Jackson was the only one of the three academies where an adult lived in each dorm, but teachers' apartments were sufficiently isolated from the students' rooms to allow the boys a large degree of independence.

Cadet behavior is the responsibility of the "commandant of cadets," the faculty member to whom tacs or counselors report; along with the senior army instructor and his staff, the commandant and the tacs are in charge of the military side of cadet life. The general attitude expressed by teachers was that it was not their job to discipline cadets outside the classroom or become too friendly with them. Said one Sherman teacher, "If we were asked to live in the barracks, there'd be a major strike. It's not appropriate. . . . Even the thought of having to eat with them: not me!" This attitude was reinforced by the Sherman policy manual, which cautioned that "there should, at all times, exist a professional abyss between faculty/staff members and cadets. Being 'one of the boys' is detrimental to discipline, and undue familiarity breeds contempt."

Senior Students

At most boarding schools, a few senior students are given official authority over their fellow pupils. There are at least four reasons for this policy. First, adolescents constitute free labor and can be of tremendous help to adults in counseling and maintaining order; second, some of the students are going to tell their fellows what to do anyway, so their spontaneous leadership might as well be recognized and regularized; third, adolescents are more likely to look to their peers for advice than to adults, and the schools keep a greater degree of control if they appoint the advice givers; and fourth, it is considered character-building for adolescents to be held responsible for one another. At Quaker schools, however, it is not expected that student authorities (called prefects or proctors) will act as disciplinarians; they are seen, rather, as troubleshooters and confidants. Only occasionally do the prefects assign demerits. The adult in charge of a girls' dormitory at Mott explained that unless the prefects could convince the other girls of their ability to keep information confidential, they could not be effective. It seemed appropriate to her that the prefects should know "a whole lot of things that we [adults] don't know":

Girls may come and talk about their roommate problems with a prefect, or about drugs or pregnancy. And that's how it should be. . . . The prefects can even come to a hall teacher and say, "There's a girl on the hall who told me this-and-this," and the teacher isn't going to try to worm out of her who it is, unless it has to do with suicide.

A senior prefect at Mott in a dorm for sophomore, junior, and senior boys didn't consider himself to be a disciplinarian:

I love these guys on the hall . . . and it's sad that it's all supposed to be over at 11 o'clock. I feel like a hypocrite when I tell people to get in their rooms. . . . We do enforce rules, because [the kids on our hall] are mostly younger. But your friends who are the same age just don't take you seriously.

In contrast to the informality of Quaker student authority, student leadership at military schools is taken extremely seriously. Indeed, all three academies emphasize that their primary purpose is to promote leadership qualities among students, and this claim is not merely admissions-catalogue hype: almost every teacher or student, when asked what lessons the school wanted its pupils to learn, included the word *leadership* in their answer. From their first day at school, male and female cadets' primary goal is intended to be—and usually is—to achieve the highest possible rank. Their ultimate aim is to become the head of the entire corps of cadets (the BC, or battalion commander), but promotion to the rank of platoon lieutenant, first sergeant, captain or executive officer of a company, or staff captain is also highly desirable. At all three schools many students compete fiercely for leadership through their academic and military performance, extracurricular involvement, and personal charisma. Rank gives some privileges, such as later lights-out and more comfortable quarters, but primarily it means power and responsibility. A popular Pershing company captain named Kyle Bennett said he thought he'd "go crazy" if he didn't have high rank:

It's not so much the power of telling people to go shine their shoes. . . . [Rank] gives me a chance . . . of being respected by peers as well as faculty. . . . When I say, "Let's attempt to change this rule," I can sit down with some people, write out a recommendation and submit it, and have people think it's valid. . . . I enjoy being in charge so I can get things done.

Being a leader, however, also means giving up personal freedom. One of the top prefects at the Pershing girls' school was grateful that she'd learned "how to run a meeting, speak out, get things done," but complained about the pressure on her to "be reg" (obey regulations, especially the dress code) and set an example:

I want to be me and totally free, but at the same time I like the responsibility of . . . getting things done. You just can't do both at this school. Either you don't have leadership, and then you don't have any responsibility and you can be non-reg, do anything you want, and people won't have a very good attitude about you. Or you can have all the responsibility, and then you leave behind personal freedom. . . . It's really hard and frustrating sometimes.

One of the hardest aspects of student leadership at a military academy is, as one captain put it, that "everything that ever happens in the company comes back to you, . . . [from] a broken window to a guy doing poorly in a class." In the spring of senior year, "when you have everything else coming down on you," the pressures are intense. Problems in the companies create moral dilemmas, since adults expect leaders to keep them informed, while an age-old loyalty code demands that each captain keep disciplinary matters "within the unit" and, ideally, away from adult ears. A student leader who wants to please peers as well as adults is expected not only to keep trouble in his unit to a minimum but also to protect his subordinates from adult wrath.

New Students

At any school, newcomers are put through a testing period and usually endure times of isolation and misery. When a sophomore tells me proudly, "This year I have friends," it is not hard to imagine how lonely freshman year must have been. At Quaker boarding school, the official emphasis is on kindness: new students are to be drawn gently into the community. That community, however, can be daunting. One senior boy at Mott worried about a freshman "who is just so petrified of going into the dining room and dealing with so many people that he's not eating dinner. . . . We've talked to him, and he just won't go. Walking into that dining room—it's a terrifyingly empty feeling." At Mott, and to a lesser extent at the other two Quaker schools, the responsibility for helping new students to adjust and feel welcome falls on a select group of prefects. Four senior boys are chosen to live in the male freshman dormitory, and they are treated as staff by the adults in that dorm, who meet with them weekly and consult them about most disciplinary and counseling decisions, sharing information with them as they would with members of the faculty. The teacher who heads the dorm considers the four seniors responsible "for the smooth running of the . . . dormitory." Although this means "they can't be as free-wheeling as they'd like," he thinks they "willingly make that sacrifice because of the good feeling they get doing this kind of service work and being treated like adults by us."

One of the members of this team of four is probably the most popular boy at Mott, Mike Dugan, a wiry athlete with a gift for witty remarks. He recognizes that many of the younger boys idolize him but says he tries to play down their hero-worship:

I hate power trips, especially in myself, because I don't feel I want to uphold that image. So [when] we [prefects] go out there and wrestle with the guys in the hall, . . . I always crawl into Freddie Fetus position and just sort of let them beat on me, to let them know that I'm human. . . . Sure, some kids look up to me just because I've got myself organized and I know basically where

I'm going. Then there are other kids that don't really need it. . . . I'd much rather be their friend.

Although the ninth-grade girls at Mott live in the same building as most of the other girls, they have their own corridors and prefects assigned just to them. One senior girl said, "Freshman year my prefects were so amazing; they were a big part of why I wanted to be a prefect, I wanted to do the same thing for these freshmen." And a freshman girl said, "I think the prefects are good to talk to, especially if you don't want to talk to your hall teachers. . . . And if they weren't there, we'd never get to bed on time. . . . I thought they were going to be mean, but they aren't."

At military school, the "plebes" or "new guys" must go through a period of initiation that officially lasts anywhere from six weeks to six months and unofficially, the entire first year. A plebe has to stand at attention whenever an officer walks by, may not address older students by first name, must run errands and carry out older students' orders, and is usually responsible for the most onerous dorm duties, such as cleaning the bathrooms and sweeping the halls. New cadets have a more difficult task than new Quaker-school students, since the former must not only get used to being at boarding school but also learn military drill. However, they have the advantage of being part of a military unit, a company of boys or girls with whom they will probably eat, sleep, march, fight, share secrets, and get into trouble for the rest of their time at the school.

The moral purpose of the plebe period is to teach a new cadet endurance, respect for authority, and loyalty to his or her unit and fellow plebes. Most of the cadets, freshmen and upperclassmen alike, believed in the value of a strict plebe period. "The plebe system is there for a purpose," explained one junior:

> It serves as a learning device. Otherwise . . . if you were just left to run around, you wouldn't learn any discipline, you wouldn't learn any military bearing—in other words, acting in a military manner and showing respect for people who deserve it. I think it's an excellent way of putting someone new into this environment.

While cadets are proud of surviving this traditional period of enforced suffering, they are eager to be accepted into the ranks as full-fledged members. In the spring of his first year, with the worst hardships of his newness behind him, a place on a varsity sports team, and the hard-earned rank of private first class, a sophomore at Pershing expressed his ambivalence about his plebe experience:

My father went here, my uncle went here, my brother and sister went here. . . . But I don't think there's anything that can prepare you [for the plebe system]. . . . When you look back on it you say it wasn't that bad, but when I was going through it, I thought it was really, really bad. The marching in the hallways, the stuff you have to do with no purpose. But I thought it did bring some sense of unity to the plebes, and it showed some leadership qualities in certain kids. So overall I would say it was a good experience.

These sketches of clothes, classes, meals, dormitories, and student responsibilities and initiations in the light of the two traditions have introduced themes that are familiar, not because of their Quaker and military associations, but because they are part of the classic American liberal and conservative worldviews. At Quaker schools, as among liberals, we find the desire for self-expression and inquiry, social conscience, openness, and relations of equality. When this combination works, the result is harmony, warmth, and mental challenge; when it fails, there is chaos, cynicism, and a deep sense of betrayal. At military schools, as among conservatives, we find a desire for self-improvement, high standards, hard work, strict accountability, and relations of mutual loyalty. When this set of expectations works, the result is order, affectionate respect, and lively competition; when it fails, there is tyranny, fear, and violence. In addition to sharing these key goals, each of the six schools has its own specific aims.

The Three Quaker Boarding Schools: Mott, Fox, and Dyer

Mott Friends School

Mott is the largest of the three Quaker schools, and it has the biggest endowment, the best academic program, and the most stable faculty. In 1987 the headmaster had been there for eight years, the academic dean for over fifteen years, and a third of the hundred-member administrative and teaching staff for at least a decade.[10] Mott was founded in the nineteenth century and has always been under the care of a Friends Yearly Meeting (a regional Quaker association). A large committee, made up of Yearly Meeting members and a few non-Quaker parents and alumni, oversees the running of the school with its

$5,000,000 operating budget and $15,000,000 endowment. Although Mott's beautiful grounds give an illusion of countryside, the school is located in a town not too far from a big city. In the fall of 1987, 500 students were enrolled, half boys and half girls; just over half were boarders, and the rest were day students or faculty children. That year 14 percent came from Quaker backgrounds; almost a third were the children or grandchildren of alumni; and 14 percent were classified as members of minority groups (about half of whom were black). At least 20 percent of the administrative and teaching staff were Quakers, and another 17 percent had attended Quaker colleges. Well over half the faculty were housed in dormitories or other on-campus housing.

Apart from its wealth and stability, what distinguishes Mott from the other two Quaker schools is the social and political engagement of many key administrators, faculty members, and students. History, geography, English, and science classes are treated as places for discussing the world's problems, usually from a liberal Quaker perspective. Charlie McDowell, head of the religion department, was eloquent about the political nature of his role as a teacher in a Friends school, which required him to challenge "the status quo," because "that's basically the way the world gets better":

I see everything as political, and for me, it's more a question of whether we accept things the way they are, or whether we support the things we agree with and question what we disagree with. That's what I believe is part of the [Quaker] tradition, and it's tied up with who I am and what I teach and how I live my life and how I try to affect students.

McDowell believed it was his and the school's responsibility to "build on what seems true and just" and challenge what seems wrong. For him, the idea of teaching "in a morally neutral way" is irresponsible; he cited John F. Kennedy's conviction that "the hottest fires in hell are reserved for those who in times of moral crisis just remained neutral."

Fox Friends School

Fox is the smallest of the three Quaker schools, with only fifty students in the winter of 1988 and a total staff of thirty, over half of them Quakers. A rural school, it has been educating the children of local Quakers since the early 1800s and did not admit a non-Quaker child until the 1940s. In 1988 the student body was about one-third Quaker; many of the students were related to each other and to the faculty and had well-known Quaker names, and several had ancestors who had attended the school before 1850. Fox is under the care of a small but dedicated Yearly Meeting; it has been running in the red for years but manages by supplementing tuition payments out of its substantial endowment. Although it has a core of long-term staff members—most of them alumni who belong to the Yearly Meeting—Fox has high turnover among its younger staff and headmasters. When I was there, the fourth headmaster in a decade had already given notice of his departure.

Fox is more concerned with spiritual matters than are the other two schools. Many of the staff and most of the school board are troubled because they do not seem to be communicating a Friends Christian vision to their diverse and chiefly irreligious student body. One board member, a Quaker minister and a woman of great presence, talked about her faith and its role in her life:

I was born and raised very much a quiet Friend. . . . I found that Quakerism had given me a real deep sense of belonging, a deep sense that God loved me and would commune with me, when I was open to commune with him. This sustained me through some difficult times and sustains me today. And I really feel that if Quakerism is anything to me, it is that real, personal, one-on-one relationship with the Lord.

To her it seemed crucial that students should come away from Fox confident of the special place "that each of them holds in God's eyes," and convinced as a result that "they, in turn, should hold each living creature in a special place in their eyes." She did not pretend that this love of one's fellow creatures was easy but called it, rather, "an ideal to grow to and work toward" throughout one's life.

Dyer Friends School

Dyer has for many years been known as a "last-chance" school. Most boarding schools in the United States attract a certain percentage of troubled kids—those who have been expelled from public school, for example, or have been heavy drug or alcohol users, or come from families with problems—but in 1988 Dyer had more of these difficult teenagers than either Mott or Fox. Located in a medium-sized city, this third school is also under the care of a Yearly Meeting. In 1988, 20 percent of its 160 students were day pupils and the rest five- or seven-day boarders; 15 percent came from foreign countries and about that same number from Quaker backgrounds. The staff was over one-third Quaker. In the fall the headmaster was preparing to turn over his job to a successor; the fall was also to bring a new development director, admissions director, and business manager.

What seems to make Dyer distinctive, apart from its facilities for special students, whether foreign, mildly learning-disabled, or in need of psychological counseling, is its emphasis on the importance of togetherness among faculty and between adolescents and adults. All three Quaker schools consider themselves communities, but at Dyer this word is used with passionate frequency by everyone. Interestingly, community was almost always equated less with cooperation than with tolerance for individual difference. The departing headmaster tried to explain this apparent contradiction by identifying Dyer as a community that encouraged dissent, because it allowed "the negative adolescent emotions" to surface and be expressed:

Yes, we talk about community; yes, we want it; yes, we achieve it on some level. You will see very close, genuinely affectionate relationships between students and faculty. But you also have the complexity of adults and adolescents dealing with each other. . . . The drive and thrust for independence, the need to be questioning, is part of being a healthy adolescent.

For this headmaster one of the most important roles of a "progressive, or liberal, or humanistic community" like Dyer was to tolerate not only diversity of opinion and life-style but also "ambiguity" and "emotions that have been suppressed." He acknowledged that other institutions might "see a lot less anger, or confusion, or really deep sorrow," but he felt that Dyer had a responsibility to allow those feelings to surface. "Schools like this," he explained, "become safe [places] for a level of turmoil, conflict, struggle, that is . . . part of the process of growing up and learning about oneself and becoming a broader but more self-aware person."

What do these three schools have in common? As representatives of the same moral tradition, they are united by the shared quality of concern, in both its Quaker and its common meaning. The word *concern*, according to a glossary of Quaker terms, "should be reserved for weighty matters that disturb the conscience and impel a person toward action";[11] the devout Friend experiences concerns as God-sent. The commitments of key staff members to social and political engagement at Mott, spiritual education at Fox, and intense communal experience at Dyer are in the nature of Quaker concerns at those schools, not only because they carry a powerful meaning for their adherents but because they excite heated debate within the communities, as Quaker concerns have done for the past 300 years. As part of a Quaker education, concerns help students "enrich and clarify their sense of moral values," "be of service to the world," and "make responsible decisions and find the courage to stand by them," not only at school but in later life.[12]

More commonly, the word *concern* is a synonym for care, a virtue that all three schools attempt to promote in both students and faculty. Teachers pride themselves on caring for their pupils, which means giving them the benefit of the doubt, sometimes repeatedly. At Mott, a teacher remembered that when she was new, it impressed her that a colleague sought her out to tell her that he was worried about one of her student advisees. "The longer I was here," she said, "the more I realized that that was standard practice.... There's real depth of concern that people have for one another, in a personal way.... We go out on a limb a lot of times for kids." Sometimes, she admitted, "the kid goes from bad to worse," and the faculty end up "with egg on [their] faces," because they got "carried away and lost perspective." Other times, however, "we go out on a limb and it does work out. And I think that's a ... Quakerly thing to do.... We're still willing to keep trying."

In their interviews, students at the three schools volunteered care as one of the main lessons not only taught but learned. A defiant senior, back at Mott after an expulsion during his junior year and already teetering dangerously on the verge of another major disciplinary action, criticized the school at length and then suddenly praised the faculty for having put up with him as long as they had and for finally expelling him when he broke the disciplinary contract he had made with them. "If they didn't care," he explained, "they wouldn't have kicked me out when they did, because they wouldn't have said, 'We have this deal and we're going to hold him to it.' [It] shows that they expect me to be a real person, and they're not just baby-sitting me for four years and then shipping me off to college." A senior girl at

Dyer said, "I love this place so much. . . . It teaches people compassion and caring for one another, so your whole value system switches over a little bit. I think the faculty feel it, too, and the more they put out for us, the more we put out for each other and for them."

The Three Military Boarding Schools:
Pershing, Jackson, and Sherman

Pershing Military Academy

Pershing is a rural school. With its 650 students (60 percent boys, 40 percent girls, and 95 percent boarders), its 100 teachers, its 60-odd administrators, counselors, coaches, and supervisors, and its large staff of hourly employees, it is the largest of the six schools and also the wealthiest, with an endowment of about $50,000,000 and an enormous campus. Although boys and girls attend the same classes, eat in the same dining room, and live in neighboring dormitories, only the boys are cadets who are part of a military system. In 1988 few of the students were black; about 20 percent came from foreign countries, chiefly Mexico. Pershing's adult community is highly stable. In 1988, the headmaster had been there for six years, the academic dean for more than thirty years, and over a third of the administrators, faculty, and staff (excluding the "faculty interns," whose tenure is always one year) for ten years or longer. Unlike the other two academies, where military skills are taught through the U.S. Army's Junior Reserve Officers Training Corps (JROTC) program under the guidance of one or more active-duty sergeants, Pershing has developed its own leadership program for boys and girls, taught by a mix of former servicemen and civilian teachers. In 1988, 38 percent of the school's thirteen top administrators were either retired career officers or active in the reserves, or both; among the faculty and staff, 11 percent were either retired military professionals or members of the state National Guard.

Traditions, which are important at any boarding school, are particularly revered at Pershing. A teacher complimented the school by saying, "It's like stepping across a time-line to come here." Students almost never talk about changing the school but, rather, about recapturing a golden past, when adult interference in military discipline was—supposedly—minimal, and student officers had more control over their units. Many teachers pride themselves on having taught courses the same way for thirty years, using the same tests and handouts. For other teachers—often the younger ones—the emphasis on continuity is both comforting and frustrating. One said with rueful amusement:

When you have a school that's so entrenched in traditions, it's hard to make changes. . . . Some of these traditions are like albatrosses hung around our necks . . . and if you do something two years in a row, you'll be stuck doing it forever. . . . This is a problem you have in any institution, that change is very difficult. And yet in a place that doesn't have traditions, you lack loyalty and continuity.

Pershing faculty, students, and alumni are, indeed, extremely loyal. "Our alumni are more loyal to their secondary school than they are to their colleges," an administrator said. "Being away, being on your own, having to do it yourself without Mom and Dad looking over your shoulder . . . I think there's a pride . . . about having been part of that that is unique."

Jackson Military Academy

Jackson, like the other schools, was founded in the nineteenth century; although small towns surround it, it lies in the country. With 150 students in grades seven through twelve and a senior class of only 25 in the spring of 1988, it is the smallest of the three academies. Girls constituted 20 percent of the student body and were completely integrated into the military program. Ten percent of the cadets were black or Asian; there was also a small contingent of Central Americans. The headmaster, a retired general, had been there for ten years, during which time he had saved the school from fiscal catastrophe and had begun to build an endowment. In addition to the headmaster and the active-duty sergeant who taught the JROTC courses, four members of the thirty-member faculty were retired from military careers, and at least one other had served in the armed forces. Another 50 percent of the faculty were women. The students at Jackson were almost all five-day boarders, so only those who were being punished or who lived far away and did not go home with friends were left at the school every weekend, in contrast to the other two academies, where most weekends were closed.

Jackson cadets live a kind of double life. During the school day they are in uniform, drilling, holding parades, forming up outside the main building for inspection and announcements, and generally living under a military system, while on weekends those who remain at school are in civilian clothes and free to come and go more or less as they please unless they are being punished. Only eight faculty members live on campus, and most of them are off-duty on the weekends, so supervision is limited. In fact, Jackson might be said to have a relatively relaxed air about it, even during the week, were it not for the dedication of the headmaster, whose office lights burn late every night and whose presence is felt at all times. More than the other two military schools, Jackson is dominated by one man. "The general is very quiet," said one of his staff; "we may go several weeks without speaking. But he always knows what's going on and where everyone is, and if he wants something done, he sends me a memo."

The American flag flies in front of the main building at Jackson, and patriotism is seen as a natural part of school life. A popular teacher called himself "a very old-fashioned, wave-the-flag American . . . [who] presents the United States [to students] in a positive light when comparing it to any other form of government." Not that he believed in "cover[ing] up the warts. . . . Racism, discrimination against women, and the criminal justice system—that's where I think things are not as they should be." But the countries he saw during his years in the service—West and East Germany, Korea, Vietnam, Panama— convinced him that "we've got the best place":

I served three years in Vietnam, and I came back to the U.S. at the height of the anti–Vietnam War controversy and went to graduate school. And people were not only anti-military then, they were anti-American, I thought. Kids nowadays are exactly the opposite: . . . patriotic, pro-American, pro-military. In attitude they resemble me in 1950. So I really get on well with them.

Sherman Military Academy

Sherman is the strictest of the three military schools. Located about an hour from a large city, it was founded in the 1800s and had, in the fall of 1987, 350 students, almost all boarders and more than one-third of them African-American, Hispanic, or Asian-American. As at Jackson, the school's sixty girls were integrated into the military system. The teaching and administrative faculty included twenty-two women, one of them a former military officer; of the forty-two men, nine were retired from military careers, another eighteen had experience in the armed forces, and two were active-duty sergeants involved in the JROTC program. Thus Sherman had a much higher percentage of staff with military training (47 percent) than the other two schools. Although the headmaster and key administrators had all been at the school for over four years, there was a great deal of turnover among teachers and tactical officers and tremendous tension between the administrative staff and the board of directors, who wanted the school to generate more money.

No one at Sherman, from faculty members with thirty or more years at the school to the most enthusiastic cadet officer, describes the school as a happy place. Rather, it is a place where young people come to learn "discipline" and, promises the school's admissions material, to be turned into "winners." Another of Sherman's lessons is wariness; adults and adolescents alike talked about "being careful," "keeping to myself," and following the rules. However, while the adults lament the school's financial problems and low admissions standards, most of the cadets express loyalty to Sherman, because it teaches them tough lessons that will help them later in life. As one boy said, "They are trying to discipline you so you'll be a responsible person. . . . A lot of things happen here that are totally unfair, . . . which is good, because through life you are going to face problems a lot . . . so you've just got to get used to that."

Many of the adults, too, pride themselves on the school's toughness; in fact, there are those who yearn for a more "disciplined" past. A Sherman alumnus on the staff said:

These children have no fear. You can call it respect, but I call it fear. When a full colonel came by when I was a cadet, . . . [you said,] "Yes sir, no sir, thank you very much, sir," and you were thinking, "Let me out of here." You didn't look him in the eye and give him 50,000 excuses. . . . That's the only thing I give [today's cadets] credit for—they are such good liars. And they are so proud of getting away with things.

He reminisced fondly about his own algebra teacher at Sherman, who on the first day of class grabbed a boy by the collar and threw him down a flight of stairs—"desk and chair and all"—because he was still "yucking it up" when the teacher walked into the room. "From then on," laughed the alumnus, "no one talked out of turn":

Now we have lawsuits, so I guess that guy would have gotten fired. . . . We're the ones that are afraid now . . . afraid that the kids will leave the school, and we'll lose our jobs. . . . Every meeting we have, because we're under enrollment, everyone's saying, "Oh, we can't make the kids do that; they'll get mad, and they'll go to their parents, and then they'll leave the school."

Pershing, Jackson, and Sherman are all schools where the desire to impart character to young people is focused on the quality of leadership. The Sherman admissions brochure puts it squarely: "Leaders are not born, they are made, and the military program at Sherman Military Academy is designed to encourage all students to develop their full leadership potential." In its "Statement of Purpose," Pershing explains that its military program teaches not only "self-discipline and integrity" but also the "principles of leadership." One of the most important of these principles is service. The leader serves the people under him or her, creating "meaningful relationships with subordinates." More important, however, is loyal service to the organization, even when this means "placing the good of the organization above one's own needs and desires":

Such loyalty may include making or suggesting changes and improvements; in fact, one of the responsibilities of leadership *is* to make suggestions, with appropriate recommendations, to the proper authority. However, once a course of action is agreed upon or decided by that authority, even though it may differ from the leader's own preferred alternative, he or she gives his or her wholehearted support to such direction—without reservations that might subtly undermine it.

This is a clear statement of the classic military concept of leadership, with its complicated mix of initiative and obedience. At all three academies there are staff members who are familiar with leadership as a military ideal and who work to bring student sergeants and officers up to the taxing standards set by military moral tradition. One of their keywords is responsibility. For Lieutenant Duncan Graham, the Pershing commandant of cadets and a Vietnam War veteran, personal responsibility is the most important lesson that students can take away with them: "Yes, I did it. . . . I take credit for the things I've done well, and I accept responsibility for the things I didn't. And I'm not going to duck it." He admits that the kids may be right when they claim that some things just aren't their fault. But he wants them to know that "most times, . . . even those times when you can't control the situation, a lot of your choices, your decisions, your actions put you where you are. . . . Always remember you are responsible for what you do and how you handle the situation."

Graham and his fellow commandants at the other two academies care about the cadets in their charge, but that care is not protective. Unlike the Quaker-school system, which is nurturing, the military-school system, as Graham puts it, "is relentless":

It keeps making you take stock of how well you're doing at this whole business of managing your life and making wise choices and accepting responsibility for your actions and being honest. You can't duck it; [the system] just keeps 'em coming. . . . Whew! As soon as you get one thing out of the way, it pops another one right out in front of you. You can [say] . . . "I'm not going to do this, I hate this, I hate that," but you can't escape it, it's right there in front of you.

The qualities of responsibility and leadership that Graham describes represent the military ideal. Stripped of its idealism, the word *leadership* means rising to the top and having power over others. In this sense, too, it is a lesson taught by all three schools: how to compete for promotion, how to give orders, and how to get people to obey those orders. The majority of cadets want to be officers by their senior year, and they look forward with glee to having the power over subordinates that comes with superior rank. One Pershing freshman confessed that he could hardly wait till the following year, when he could "give [the plebes] a real hard time. . . . I'd like to say I'll relax after [the first week or two], but I know I won't. I know I'm going to enjoy getting called Mister and having them go to attention when I come in the room!" Leadership for the older students means a different kind of power. Student captain Kyle Bennett is proud of being "the choke point" in his company:

What I want to go to the faculty goes, and what I don't, doesn't go. That way, people can trust the person who's living next door to them, and if they have a problem they come to me or the first sergeant or any one of the [student] officers and say, "This is really annoying me; can you try changing this?"

Moral Tradition as Lens and Filter

Moral tradition transforms boarding-school life. Acting as a lens, the tradition magnifies certain aspects of life and diminishes or distorts others. At military school, for example, it magnifies the importance of clothing, while at Quaker school it minimizes the importance of formal courtesy. Acting as a filter, the moral tradition eliminates and discards certain options for speech and behavior, permitting others to predominate instead. For example, the military tradition filters out the idea of friendship between adults and adolescents, in order to emphasize respect for authority and rule enforcement. The Quaker tradition attempts to filter out classroom competition as a learning device, in order to discourage feelings of inferiority among students. When it comes to the key values of concern and leadership, both lens and filter are in operation. The Quaker lens reveals the feelings of concern present in the relationship between, say, the four senior prefects at Mott and their freshman charges, while paying relatively little attention to what is undoubtedly also a leadership experience for the prefects. The military lens focuses on the lessons in leadership taught by the officer-subordinate relationship and deemphasizes the affection that some officers feel for their younger charges. At the same time, the Quaker filter also eliminates some opportunities for practicing leadership: it is simply not a lesson that Quaker schools intend to teach, and if it is learned, it is learned in spite of and not because of the Quaker moral tradition. Similarly, the military filter eliminates opportunities for cadets to express deep concerns for political or social issues; such passionate commitments are actively discouraged by the military moral tradition.

The three Quaker and three military boarding schools are both similar and different. They are similar in structure and function: each is a privileged total institution designed to teach character as well as the usual high-school subjects. They are also similar in that their concepts of character are clearly defined, well-documented, and rooted in history. What it means to be a good person is something about which the Quaker and military traditions have a great deal to say, and, as the following chapter will show, the good Quaker and the good soldier have some important traits in common. Nevertheless, the two traditions have contrasting visions of the way the world should work, and these visions have shaped the Quaker and military boarding schools, making them, in spite of their similarities, extraordinarily different. In the following chapter, these two moral traditions, one liberal and the other conservative, are compared and analyzed. Understanding them is key to understanding what happens at the schools—and also to recognizing why American liberals and conservatives have trouble defining a common vision of a good society.

Chapter Two

The Quaker and Military Moral Traditions Compared

Similarities: The Call to Selfless Service

A comparison of the histories of Quakers and military professionals[1] in America reveals that both went through periods of ostracism from mainstream society, and both groups responded to this hostility by becoming consciously and outspokenly service-oriented. Quakers adopted what historian Sydney James calls a policy of benevolence in part as a response to the attacks made upon them because of their pacifism during the Revolutionary War.[2] The military emphasized their role as servants of the state to assuage public fears that the growth of a peacetime army meant a threat to democracy.[3] Both groups came to see themselves as serving the American people not only by their actions—social reform in one case and defense of the nation in the other—but also by the moral example they set.[4] Today, partially as a result of their emphasis on service, American Quakers and military professionals share at least four other important similarities.[5]

A Full-time Moral Identity

Social psychologist Ralph Turner has identified a phenomenon that he has called a "role-person merger," which occurs when "the attitudes and behaviors developed in an expression of one role carry over into other situations."[6] This is a good description of what many Quakers and military professionals experience. Being a Friend or an army officer does not just involve performing certain actions at certain times of the day or week; it involves being a certain kind of person. Committed Quakers and officers find that they cannot be that special person part-time. Instead, they incorporate Quaker or military values into everything they do, in order to maintain a coherent sense of themselves. As one Quaker explained it, "I find that if I compartmentalize any part of my life apart from Quakerism, I can't function. I have to have a sense of consistency." A military officer expressed a similar feeling when he said that the army was "a separate ethic" by which he felt compelled to live at all times. As a result of this shared need to live in a way that is consistent with their religious or professional tradition, both Quakers and soldiers exhibit a high degree of self-control and even austerity. They also value truthfulness and straightforwardness in speech and action.

Self-Sacrifice as a Way of Life

The Quaker who answers a concern to work in a prison or a mental institution and the soldier who guards a wounded buddy for hours until help can arrive have in common an impulse to subjugate the self for the sake of others. The devout Quaker experiences his or her own will as subsumed in the greater will of God and is thereby enabled to shoulder great burdens or suffer persecution. The soldier's will is swallowed up by the enormity of war, lost in an ecstatic mixture of comradeship, dutifulness, fear, rage, exhaustion, and detached incredulity that can sometimes lead to acts of great bravery. A Vietnam veteran who has searched for the quality of self-sacrifice in both traditions explained that before Vietnam he had "felt a strong calling for the army" and considered making it his career. His service in Vietnam showed him that what he was looking for—"an unambiguous feeling about the importance of what you are doing, and a certain ascetic quality"—was not to be found in the military. He then sought it among Quakers:

In the traditional military view of itself, an officer would lead . . . a life of devotion . . . a life of selflessness. . . . I think some of those same reasons are what attract people to Quakerism . . . the selflessness of a lot of Quakers. Following your Inner Light. I guess . . . the thing that attracted me to them was that they were not afraid to do what had to be done.

Perhaps the best statement about the importance of sacrifice and suffering to Friends and fighting men alike comes from the head of the Friends Relief Service in England during World War II. Shortly after the war he wrote that, although he was a pacifist, he had felt a great "spiritual unity" with many soldiers who, "detesting war as deeply as I did, yet felt that there was no other way in which they could share in the agony of the world":

We [Friends] could not engage in warlike activity in the hope of relieving the suffering of the Jews or of other oppressed peoples in Europe and Asia. We had, somehow, to try to participate in their suffering and to express the conviction that it is ultimately the power of suffering in love that redeems men from the power of evil.[7]

A final demonstration of the importance of self-sacrifice to both groups is their abhorrence of egotism—what soldiers call careerism and Friends see as a self-righteousness that excludes all viewpoints other than one's own. An army captain expressed his contempt for one of his commanding officers, who "gave a great deal of lip service to such things as honor . . . [but] would sell you down the river in a heartbeat if he thought it would save his career." A Friend described a co-religionist who "has such a strong sense of God speaking through her that she can't see that possibility in others." Such people are seen as threats to the integrity of the moral community.

The Sacredness of the Calling

The Vietnam veteran referred to an army career as a "calling," and, being a Quaker, he does not use the word lightly. "Mind the call; it's all in all" is a Quaker saying that expresses the sacredness and urgency of God's message experienced from within. For centuries, politicians and generals have declaimed the sacredness of military service, but even rhetorical exploitation cannot devalue the genuine devotion that many soldiers feel toward their country. Recognizing the presence of something holy in the military tradition, scholars compare the army to a religious order, see the hazing experienced by cadets and recruits as a rite of initiation into a religious cult, and describe the battlefield as a world "wholly other" and therefore sacred, imbued with an awesome religious power.[8] Both the Quaker moral tradition and that of the military have developed around a core concept of sacred service that calls for willing sacrifice—if not of life, then of luxury, leisure, and the self-centered pursuit of one's own goals. The good Friend or soldier seeks to devote his or her life to goals set by God or country, tempered by the Meeting or the military hierarchy, and experienced from within as a profound personal obligation—duty transformed into choice.

At each of the six boarding schools there is at least one adult who seems to view his or her job as a calling in this sacred sense. These are men and women whose lives are permeated with Quaker or military values, people who have in common a deep integrity and a willingness to make sacrifices for the sake of school and students. But the vision of goodness that inspires their sacrifices is different in the two environments.

Differences: Internal and External Sources of Morality

The central difference between the two traditions' visions of goodness lies in their images of the root of virtue. The Quaker tradition stresses the *internal* origin of moral conviction, while the military tradition emphasizes its *external* origin. For Quakers, virtue is obedience to the Inner Light: an inner sense of what is right and good that comes from God. However fallible, the individual Quaker's conscience is the best guide he or she has to whatever measure of Light has been revealed to him or her.[9] Members of the military, by contrast, see virtue as obedience to an external set of values, a code or standard of behavior that is clearly understood by all. Loyalty to this code and to the people with whom it is shared is the essential military quality.

A Quaker convert who had served six years in the National Guard compared the two types of commitment, one based on an individual interpretation of duty and the other on shared obedience to a set of standards:

[T]here's something we [Friends] sort of have to live up to. It's not necessarily a tradition, but[, rather,] the idea that you as a Quaker are supposed to identify with your calling and make a commitment. . . . [It's] something like a military idea of honor and duty, providing standards. But it comes from my own discernment of what my calling is.

The emphasis here is on choice, on the Quaker's obligation to determine his or her own moral commitments, with God's help. Friends are "very reluctant . . . to try to lay responsibilities on people." An army captain, a West Point graduate, considers choice less important than uniformly high standards. "People can be taught a higher code. . . . [They] can change if they want to . . . [and can] at least be forced to meet a set of standards if they do not embrace it for themselves."

This dichotomy between internal and external sources of morality is at the root of three clear-cut differences between the Quaker and the military attitude: their contrasting positions on violence, ceremony, and authority.

Violence

Since the modern American military regards itself as a peace-keeping force,[10] it would be incorrect to draw too absolute a contrast between Quakers' and soldiers' desire for world peace. The two differ markedly, however, in their perspective on violence. Quakers regard violence of any kind—whether warfare, fist-fighting, or hurtful speech —as counter to the teachings of Jesus. Since there is "that of God" in everyone, human life and the human spirit are sacred. Professional soldiers, by contrast, accept angry conflict as endemic to the human condition; their job is to become its master—in Huntington's much-quoted phrase, to be a "manager of violence." While the military tradition of self-control precludes displays of temper, it recognizes violence—whether occurring as part of warfare or between individuals—as a problem-solving technique. To be acceptable, however, violence must be sanctioned by the proper military authority. Private vendettas and Rambo-like rampages are anathema to the military professional.

The internal/external dichotomy offers insight into these different attitudes toward violence. Because every individual, in Quaker eyes, carries his or her potential goodness or Light within, no enemy can be distinguished: there are no external signs that establish one person as more deserving of hatred and violence than another. At their core, no matter what they have done, all people are good, because, as one

Friend said, "their essence is good"—that is a basic Quaker tenet. But to a military professional, goodness is demonstrated by adherence to certain standards of behavior. Those who break the code or do not accept it in the first place will be easy to identify, because they will act differently. In the military tradition, it is through their actions that people—or countries—make themselves targets for punishment. If a private disobeys a sergeant or an officer lies to a fellow officer, if a country breaks a treaty or invades a neighboring nation, then the rules of correct behavior have been broken, and retaliation should be expected.

Ceremony

The internal/external distinction also explains why Quakers have traditionally rejected all forms of ceremony, while the military promotes ceremonies as a matter of principle. In the Friends tradition, the outer show is sham; simplicity means "no facade," as one Quaker put it. The fewer trappings one surrounds oneself with, the more one's Inner Light can shine through. To swear an elaborate oath or receive an award for bravery is therefore superfluous: honesty and courage should be simply a part of daily life and are in any case God-given, rather than personal, qualities. But in the military tradition, appearance provides crucial evidence of standards. The officer with a dignified military bearing, the private with a positive attitude, the company with plenty of spit-and-polish are showing their loyalty to the army and its values. Parades and oath-taking ceremonies are important rituals that reinforce this loyalty by making it visible and public: if in front of your comrades-in-arms you swear to defend your country and the Constitution of the United States, you will be bound to that oath by pride as well as honesty.

Authority

Authority in the Friends tradition is vested neither in a person nor in a document but in a process, that of consensus. At its best, Quaker consensus represents a way of distilling "the Truth"—which to a religious Quaker means the will of God—from the various inner convictions and "leadings" felt by those Friends who attend what is called a Meeting for Business. "Out of this sharing of light may come a greater light."[11] This search for truth should be facilitated—but never dominated—by the "clerk" of the Meeting and certain "weighty Friends" whose leadings are especially valued. A decision to act that arises from the long, slow process of reaching consensus is a communal decision. It is, in a sense, the product of the combined contributions of the individual, the community, and God, and its source is profoundly internal.

Authority in the military tradition is distributed in more complex ways, as befits a much larger and more complicated institution. Its official source is the United States Constitution, from which the hierarchically distributed authority of the military, the Constitution's sworn defenders, is derived.[12] Also derived from the Constitution is the set of laws, regulations, and minor rules that governs the activities of soldiers, sailors, marines, and airmen of all ranks. In daily practice, however, military authority is vested in "the order," a concrete demand for action. Before an order is issued, loyalty demands that subordinates express their opinions; after it is issued, loyalty demands obedience. Whether an order must be obeyed depends not on the character of the one who gives the order but on the legality (or, more rarely, the feasibility or intelligence) of the order. The Constitution, laws, orders, and standard operating procedures: these are all external authorities.

Everyday life at the six boarding schools is deeply influenced either by the Quaker vision of morality as something felt from within or the military vision of it as something acquired from an outside source. At Quaker schools, the emphasis on self-expression and informality in classes, dress, and dormitory decor; the teachers' willingness to "go out on a limb" for students; and the friendly, nonauthoritarian relationships between older and younger students all stem from the Quaker belief that the inner self is more important than appearance, behavior, or differences in age. In military academies the neatly pressed uniforms and austere dorms; the well-regulated classes intended to strengthen and discipline; the inspections, parades, oaths, and honor codes; the heavy responsibilities that adults expect cadet officers to shoulder; and the sometimes harsh treatment of younger students by older ones all stem from determination to mold the visible self and impose high standards from without.

The neatness of this internal/external dichotomy should not be permitted to overwhelm discussion of the two traditions, however, since the distinction is far from absolute. Quakers recognize the importance of concrete communal standards as well as the demands of conscience (if they did not, they would not long survive as a group), and members of the military know that personal conviction, not just obedience to orders, leads to the kind of loyalty and integrity that make a good soldier. At times, too, individuals in both groups are confronted with moral crises, brought on by the clash between internal demands and external demands. Then Quakers and soldiers alike find themselves turning to their moral traditions for help in balancing the conflicting pressures of conscience and community.

The Individual and the Group:
Sources of Reconciliation

The conventional image of morality suggests that it is a social straitjacket constraining individual thought and behavior in order to ensure that communal obligations are met. In fact, morality is by no means so unambiguous in its demands on the psyche. It does not simply reproduce the rules of collective life, but instead attempts to reconcile the individual's desire for self-determination with the society's need for order. Far from being a simple set of requirements, morality offers individuals the means to understand and the chance to choose freely what is right. It cannot eliminate the clashes between individual choice and social duty to which daily life gives rise, but it can provide guidelines for handling these tensions in a productive way.

The Quaker and military moral traditions are complicated structures that address the conflicts between choice and duty. The Quaker's struggle to communicate the urgency of a religious conviction in the face of opposition from other members of the Meeting has something in common with the soldier's internal debate over how to respond to an order that seems stupid, unethical, or unnecessarily dangerous. In both cases, private conscience clashes with institutional demands, and in both cases, too, the tradition offers guidance to the person who is trying to do what is right. Within the Quaker tradition, with its emphasis on the internal, obedience to conscience must take priority over social constraints; within the military tradition, with its focus on external standards, loyalty to the group and its codes predominates. But both moral traditions do recognize a middle course between independence and control. In real life such dilemmas are not always resolved, but at least the two traditions provide a language in which to discuss them. Some of the apparent vagueness and ambiguity of this moral language is in fact a deliberate vehicle for compromise, opening up a middle way between the extremes of rebellion and submission.

The key concept of the Quaker moral tradition, from which all else is derived, is the Inner Light. It is the idea of "that of God within" that gives Quakerism its internal moral orientation, or, in the terms of the inevitable clash between the choice and duty, a distinct tilt toward choice. How, then, does the Friends tradition reconcile conscience and community? Here the keyword is *concern*. The Quaker concept of concern is deliberately ambiguous: it encompasses both the deep conviction of an individual and the sharing of that conviction with the Meeting:

A Quaker is never sure that [his concern] is divine until his meeting is in unity with him. He therefore shares his feelings with his meeting as urgently as possible. . . . This translation of individual sensitivity into group concern is one of the secrets of Quaker strength in the field of social action.[13]

The process of consensual decision-making, which is central to Quakerism, is dependent not only on the open expression of concerns in Meeting but also on the acknowledgment of those concerns by others. By subjecting the worth of private convictions to the scrutiny of the Meeting, the Quaker tradition, for all its emphasis on the individual, maintains the authority of the group.

The key concept of the military moral tradition is the mission. It is the ultimate importance of the job—which must be done according to "standard operating procedures" if it is to be done well—that gives the military its external moral orientation, its emphasis on duty over choice. Individual freedom is not abandoned, however; it is reconciled with group pressure by means of the ambiguous keyword *leadership*. The leader has the mission at heart, but he also has the right and the responsibility to make his own choices: to consider the safety of his men, the morality of his orders, and the dictates of his conscience in the context of the group's goals, and then to decide what steps to take. Where the Quaker emphasis on sharing a concern acts to check the impetuousness of the individual, the military emphasis on leadership acts to check the impersonality of the group.

In Chapter One, concern was already introduced as a force at the three Quaker schools, where it provides both a shared sense of purpose and a reason for trying to understand individual needs. The first chapter also explained how the teaching and learning of leadership underpin the activities of members of the military-school communities. Powerful as they are, however, these two concepts are insufficient as guidelines to moral practice, whether at the schools or among Quakers and military professionals in less defined communities. More detailed information about leading a moral life is needed. How does a person go about trying to live as a Quaker or a military professional? What guidelines exist to help someone know what it means to act in a Quakerly or soldierly way? If they are to survive from generation to generation, all moral traditions must answer questions like these. To show members how they should behave, the Quaker and military moral traditions provide a set of virtues (or, in Quaker parlance, "testimonies") that define a good life. These virtues are prominent in the lives of Friends and military officers, and, as is shown in the following chapters, they are also prominent in the lives of administrators, teachers, and students at Quaker and military boarding schools. The Quaker virtues—equality, community, simplicity, and peace— are prerequisites for a true experience of concern; Friends try to promote these virtues among themselves and, through service in the world, among others. The military virtues—loyalty, competence, selflessness, integrity, and pride—are the prerequisites of leadership. Only men and women who demonstrate these qualities will have the capacity to inspire them in others and so to forge that crucial bond between leader and subordinate upon which military success depends.

The Key Quaker Virtues

Equality

Equality was the first virtue to be practiced by the seventeenth-century followers of George Fox, who came to be called Quakers. Even before Fox began to preach pacifism, Quakers were dismissed from Oliver Cromwell's army because they refused to treat their officers as superiors.[14] The outer signs of this belief in the equality of all people were Friends' refusal to bow, use titles of honor and flattering greetings, or doff their hats to anyone, and their insistence on addressing people of all ranks using the informal *thou*. These behaviors, shocking at the time, rapidly became Quaker trademarks in England and, later, in America. Unlike their proto-socialist contemporaries the Diggers, the early Friends advocated an equality of respect, not of economic resources. They believed that each person, whether servant or master, had an obligation to follow his calling; they argued, however, that the servant was not the inferior of the master, since both were equal "in the Light." This is a classic Christian principle; Quakers simply put it to practice more frequently than did many Christians of their time. Friends also called for equality between the sexes, and Quaker women preached in Meetings for Worship all over England and abroad and ran their own Meetings for Business.

The primary fruits of the equality testimony in the United States came in American Friends' work to protect and educate Indians and in their efforts to abolish slavery. The American fight for women's rights was also inspired and partially led by Quaker women. Today, through their local Meetings for Worship or Yearly Meetings, and through the American Friends Service Committee, the Friends Committee on National Legislation, and other organizations, many Quakers continue to support volunteer projects and government programs that, in the words of a Friends Service Committee publication, are intended to express a "belief in this infinite worth and equality of each human being."[15] As one woman said, "Quakers believe that there is that of God in everyone: that if it is there in anyone, it is there in everyone." This is the root of the equality testimony.

Community

Friends' relationship to God is bound up with their relationship to one another. A statement frequently cited by Quakers to explain the spiritual value of community was made by the seventeenth-century Quaker Robert Barclay:

As many candles lighted and put in one place do greatly augment the light, and make it more to shine forth, so when many are gathered together into the same life there is more of the glory of God, and His power appears to the refreshment of each individual, for each partakes not only of the light and life raised in himself, but in all the rest.[16]

In the traditional Quaker Meeting for Worship, Friends sit together in silence, waiting and praying for the Spirit of God to be among them. If a worshiper feels compelled to speak by the voice of God within, he or she rises and delivers God's message to the assembled Friends. When "the presence of God is experienced by each person as part of a group experience,"[17] then the Meeting is described as "covered" or "gathered":

In the gathered meeting the sense is present that a new Life and Power has entered our midst. . . . We are in communication with one another because we are being communicated to, and through, by the Divine Presence. . . . He has broken down the middle wall of partition between our separate personalities and has flooded us with a sense of *fellowship*.[18]

The primary experience of community sought by Friends is a religious one: a feeling of being "joined in the Light." But community among Quakers also means a sharing of resources. During the first hundred years in America, Quakers limited their generosity to the members of their own Meetings, but the policy of benevolence that Friends adopted in the late eighteenth century meant extending care to those outside the Quaker circle.[19] Many modern Quakers take seriously this call to care.[20] One Friend is still haunted by her failure to respond to a woman who walked in front of her car at a crosswalk near a hospital many years ago:

She was holding a tiny baby and looked absolutely distracted. . . . The next day I read in the paper that a dead baby had been found nearby . . . and I was sure that it was the mother and baby I saw. It had flashed through my mind that the woman needed help, and I hadn't helped her. . . . This person in the crowd, begging with her eyes for understanding, with so much urgency that I couldn't help but see it . . . : the lesson is there.

Simplicity

The simplicity testimony is more complex than it appears, since it has as much to do with a state of mind as with shunning luxurious possessions. Friends are encouraged to exercise moderation in their lives and households so that they will be free to "answer a concern"—to go wherever they feel their services are needed.[21] More important, however, than this physical simplicity is a mental simplicity: "a right ordering of priorities" that facilitates one's openness to the Light, a "clearness" of thought, a congruence between one's inner and outer life.[22] Simplicity is a result as well as a prerequisite of a life of concern:

Quaker simplicity needs to be expressed [in] . . . a relatively simplified and coordinated life-program of social responsibilities. I am persuaded that concerns introduce that simplification, and along with it that intensification which we need in opposition to the hurried, superficial tendencies of our age.[23]

In an interview a Quaker expressed another aspect of simplicity: "basic honesty in human relationships." He felt that Friends' "lives and the things about them [should] be really what they seem to be. . . . They [shouldn't] need a facade on their houses or on themselves."

Peace

This fourth testimony is probably the one for which Quakers are best known. The majority of Friends are pacifists, and have been since the time of George Fox. In 1661 Fox wrote to Charles II, "We utterly deny all outward wars and strife, and fightings with outward weapons, for any end, or under any pretense whatsoever. . . . The Spirit of Christ, which leads us unto all Truth, will never move us to fight and war against any man with outward weapons."[24] Since the 1650s, when they first began to arrive in the American colonies, most American Quakers have refused to serve in the army or militia or to fight in wars. As conscientious objectors in the twentieth century, Friends have performed a variety of alternative services during wartime, in the United States and abroad. The American Friends Service Committee was founded in 1917 to provide conscientious objectors to World War I with the opportunity to do relief work in Europe or what the founders called a "service of love in wartime."

Many of today's Quakers are passionately opposed to war and violence. One man, who was drafted at age seventeen during World War II and later became a Quaker, thought that his pacifism began during basic training:

They told us that when you put that bayonet in a body, the involuntary reaction of the muscles is to clamp around the bayonet, so you have to put your foot on [the person] to get it out. And . . . everything inside me just screamed that this is so radically wrong, wrong, wrong. . . . I remember vividly.

Being opposed to violence, however, doesn't mean being passive. In his letter to Charles II, Fox emphasized Friends' refusal to fight "with outward weapons"; he himself and many of his followers for over 300 years have shown a great willingness to fight in other ways, chiefly through civil disobedience. As early as 1661, Edward Burroughs counseled his fellow Quakers: "If anything be commanded of us by the present authority which is not according to equity, justice, and a good conscience toward God . . . we must in such cases obey God only and deny active obedience for conscience's sake, and patiently suffer what is inflicted upon us for our disobedience to men."[25] Quakers argue that peace is not simply a lack of conflict but a way of life, an activity in itself, a process of peace-making in private and public life using the tools of consensus and guided by the Inner Light.[26] Friends who are truly able to follow this way of life are deeply respected by their fellow Quakers, as is evident in the following description of one woman Friend by another: "I think the thing about her that makes her most obviously Quakerly is the way she approaches conflict and deals with decision making, the way she listens and weighs and asks questions. . . . There's something in [her decision making] that makes room for other people's values. You are never run roughshod over." Another Quaker, describing how the clerk of his Meeting helped the members to reach consensus, attributed this skill to "nonviolence," which he called "paying attention to the Light within each person, reaching . . . for the best human qualities of that person."

The doctrine of the Inner Light, the process of waiting for the Light in Meetings for Worship and Business, and the practice of the four virtues constitute the essence of the Quaker moral tradition, supplemented by an insistence upon honesty and a distaste for ceremony. Friends' key virtues describe the kind of loving, egalitarian society that they would like to see made real on earth. The military virtues serve a more practical purpose: they represent the key qualities an individual must possess in order to meet the highest standards of the military profession. Like their Quaker counterparts, however, the military virtues also define a particular way of life.

The Key Military Virtues

Loyalty

Loyalty is the quintessential military virtue: loyalty to the country, the Constitution, and the president as commander-in-chief of the army; to the army itself and its standards and traditions; to the unit in which a soldier serves, and to peers, superiors, and subordinates. In theory the most important of these loyalties is to the United States Constitution; in practice the most important—to a soldier's morale and to his or her willingness to obey orders and assume responsibility—is to comrades. A study of American enlisted men during World War II found that soldiers fought not for ideological reasons but to defend their immediate companions, and forty years later a veteran of that war was still able to put this feeling into words: "The only thing that kept you going was your faith in your buddies. . . . You couldn't let them down. It was stronger than flag and country."[27]

Reflecting on his own World War II experiences, a philosopher tried to explain the extraordinary power of group loyalties in war:

Many veterans who are honest with themselves will admit, I believe, that the experience of communal effort in battle, even under the altered conditions of modern war, has been a high point in their lives. Despite the horror, the weariness, the grime, and the hatred, participation with others in the chances of battle has its unforgettable side, which they would not want to have missed.[28]

Another veteran recalled those emotions: "For the first time in our lives, we were in a tribal sort of situation, where we could help each other without fear. . . . It was the absence of competition and boundaries and all those phony standards that created the thing I loved about the army."[29] A darker side to this intense small-group loyalty is the fear of rejection: "Men will fight and die neither for ideologies nor for economics. They will stand and fight for one very simple reason: fear that their peers will hold them in contempt. There is no place to hide from such ostracism."[30]

In a good unit, loyalty to comrades includes loyalty up and down the chain of command—to superiors and subordinates, as well as peers. Essays on leadership emphasize the importance of an officer's or NCO's loyalty down, the obligation to "take care of the men." A *Military Review* article described a commanding officer as outstanding because "loyalty was the key to [his] style of command. He gave before he demanded anything in return. He demonstrated his loyalty and confidence in [his men] first, and only then demanded it back."[31] An army captain, when asked what he had done in his career that he was particularly proud of, answered, "Being able to stand up and do the right thing for the soldiers. . . . It gave me the greatest satisfaction I've ever had to be able to do right by another human being that was getting crapped on by the system." For another captain, one of the most important measures of his success at a particular post was "when . . . they call . . . two or three years later to find out how I'm doing— not my superiors or peers but my subordinates, the NCOs and soldiers. That means . . . I've done a good job."

For some officers, this responsibility for subordinates is simply part of a loyalty to the army itself. "When I've encountered bad officers," said a third captain, "I've sometimes taken their nonprofessionalism almost personally, because I thought they were messing up my army and my profession, . . . affecting the soldiers that dealt with them . . . and really [taking] a toll on their subordinates." And a major, after describing something he had done to help his men, vehemently denied that any kindness was involved: "I care about the army; I don't give a shit about people. . . . If I were to look back from the year 2000 and ask, 'What did I do with my time, and would I agree now with what I did?' the standard I would use would be, 'Did it benefit the army?'"

In this list of a military professional's loyalties, the most abstract is the loyalty to standards: to the duty-honor-country motto and to other, more subtle codes of right and wrong. A young West Point graduate explained that the U.S. Military Academy gave him "an absolute standard, an ideal of absolute honor through the Cadet Honor Code.[32] . . . The West Point idea of what's honorable and what's ethical is a very, very short statement of what you don't do. That's the letter, and you have to decide on your own what the spirit is." For many military professionals, it is the adherence to the letter *and* the spirit of the military code that constitutes what they identify as honor. Another officer explained:

Honor is kind of like a religion. It's a belief in the standards, values, morals of an organization and an adherence to them, [but] . . . it's not a mindless adherence. . . . Duty, honor, country: You have a duty, and by properly executing your duty you cause an honor to be associated with yourself and your profession and therefore, doing those two things, you serve your country.

Competence

Competence is the second crucial military value. In the words of an army colonel, it "undergirds all the other values of the battlefield." [33] There is a simple reason for this emphasis: an incompetent soldier is dangerous to his or her companions and a threat to their victory in battle. One captain, when asked to describe the best officer he had encountered in his military career, explained that the highest compliment he could ever pay an officer was that "if we had to fight a war, he wouldn't kill any of us through his own stupidity." Thus, the man he respected most was someone he hadn't liked, "but he was an in-charge guy, and he knew what he was doing." For a military professional, as for a doctor, competence is "an ethical imperative. . . . The willingness to serve . . . implies a companion factor, the competence to do so effectively." [34] Competence is related to trustworthiness: "You don't mind people depending on you," said a captain. "You don't mind people saying, 'We'll go to him because we know he'll do it.'"

But competence in the military tradition can sometimes mean a stoic willingness to accept the consequences of failure, for whatever reason, as this description of West Point training illustrates:

If . . . you should foul up a particular assignment, a sense of duty meant that your only reply to a superior who wanted to know why the task had not been accomplished to his satisfaction would be, "No excuse, sir." . . . For the military professional there should be no alibi—no "puny b-ache" [belly ache], as cadets would say. [35]

Selflessness

The cadets' stoic acceptance of blame illustrates the link between competence and the third key military virtue, selflessness. The selflessness expected of the military professional takes several forms. First, there is putting the common good before one's own. The soldier serves his or her country, and "all who serve the nation must resist the temptation to pursue . . . personal advantage . . . ahead of the collective good. What is best for the nation comes before personal interests." [36] A veteran remembers World War II as a time when he was trying "to do something that affected the lives of other people . . . to do something useful with my life." [37] The West Point graduate quoted above said he believed "that by being a member of this society, everyone has an obligation to contribute to . . . [its] maintenance. . . . That's why I'm where I am [i.e., in the army]."

Second, selfless service obliges the leader to take care of subordinates. This ideal is preached in countless training manuals and articles on military leadership, and contemporary officers look for it in their senior officers as well. "He will risk his career in order to protect his people," said a major in praise of a superior; similarly, a captain reminisced about an outstanding commander who "would draw a line and say, 'Look, I will take a chance of sacrificing my career if I feel that one of my subordinates is being unfairly penalized for something.'"

The third and ultimate selfless service expected of a military professional is courage in battle in the face of possible loss of life. At the very least, a member of the military should be proud to suffer whatever is necessary to accomplish the mission. "For the professional, . . . courage in performance of his duty is a shining ideal. Death will not be shunned if the interests of duty and honor require it, however unpleasant dying may be." [38] Patton called soldiers "privileged" to die for their country; MacArthur called their sacrifice "the noblest of human faiths." [39] Even setting aside inspirational speeches by famous generals, it is hard to overestimate the extent to which military training for enlisted men and officers emphasizes the importance of the capacity to suffer, particularly for the sake of helping others. A special army pamphlet on values, distributed to all members of the army, includes a collection of twenty-four true stories about soldiers who exemplify military values. The common theme in all these tales is an acceptance—even an embracing—of risk and suffering: the captain who turns a problem company around while fighting a losing battle with cancer; the private who, unable to swim, nevertheless dives into a rain-swollen, icy river and saves a man from drowning; the sergeant who takes command of a company when the officers in charge are critically wounded and organizes it to hold off the enemy until relief can arrive.[40]

In addition to selflessness expressed as service and sacrifice, soldiers experience another kind of selflessness that has to do with intense group membership. This is not so much the conscious performance of duty as it is the unconscious loss of individuality. J. Glenn Gray described the selflessness of soldiers in battle as an "ecstacy": "At such moments . . . we are liberated from our individual impotence and are drunk with the power that union with our fellows brings. . . . 'I' passes insensibly into a 'we,' 'my' becomes 'our,' and individual fate loses its central importance." [41]

Integrity

Army literature speaks more or less interchangeably of integrity, honesty, and candor as crucial military values involving absolute truthfulness and "steadfast adherence to standards of behavior." [42] In the words of former Secretary of War Newton Baker, "the inexact or untruthful soldier trifles with the lives of his fellow men and with the honor of his government, and it is therefore no matter of pride but rather a stern necessity that makes West Point require of her students a character for trustworthiness that knows no evasions." [43] Today, integrity for both officers and enlisted men has come to mean (at least on paper) not just truthfulness but standing up for what is right, even to the extent of defying commanding officers. "This does not mean that every order or policy is to be questioned, but if soldiers . . . truly believe that something is not right, they have the responsibility to make their views known. . . . We must achieve a balance between unswerving loyalty to our institution and healthy criticism." [44] One captain called the honesty of the military professional "the willingness to comply with the spirit of what is right, rather than constantly looking for a loophole."

Pride

Soldiers who are loyal, competent, selfless, and honest will take pride in themselves and their units: pride is a product of following the military moral tradition, as well as one of its requirements. Military pride is disciplined, not ostentatious; nevertheless, a certain amount of show is necessary. Members of the military are well aware of the importance of image, since the projected image can become reality. As one captain put it, "I like to project the image of someone who has the ability to face a crisis. . . . I guess ultimately . . . that's what they pay us for. . . . In a crisis environment, if I cannot control myself . . . then I could kill someone, and I don't want to have to live with that." The higher an officer's rank, the more important it is that he or she live the military moral tradition for all to see, since army studies have shown that junior officers look to their commanders to set standards of behavior.[45] Generals Patton and MacArthur were extremely conscious of the examples they set for their men; Patton in particular considered it his responsibility to project a warrior image for the soldiers and was so often to be found at the front that he was accused by his superiors of being too reckless for an officer.[46]

One crucial element of military pride is expressed in the much-used military phrase "a positive attitude," which means showing enthusiasm and self-confidence under almost any circumstances. "Forcing people is inefficient. . . . Conformity is not enough in combat. In order to win, there must be enthusiasm and initiative that can only come from 'willing and cheerful obedience.'"[47] This is a lesson cadets learn at West Point: as one graduate put it, "There is no worse crime than indifference."[48] The troops show a positive attitude "by smartness of appearance and action; by proper maintenance of dress, equipment, and quarters; by mutual respect between senior and subordinate; and by the prompt and cheerful execution of both the letter and the spirit of lawful orders to the fullest of one's comprehension."[49]

Traditionally, one way the military has instilled this pride in its professionals is through rituals of group suffering: the indignities of boot camp for enlisted recruits and of hazing for first-year cadets (plebes) at the military academies. The plebe systems serve "not only as a means of indoctrinating new members but also as a test of their worthiness and desire to join an elite community." Unfortunately, "the line between legitimized actions which serve to 'put a plebe through his paces' and unauthorized hazing has remained difficult to draw."[50] One of the best descriptions of hazing can be found in Pat Conroy's *The Lords of Discipline*, a fictionalized account of his experiences at the Citadel, a military college in Charleston, South Carolina. He shows that some young men are "violated" and "broken" by the plebe system, while others come through it "with a feeling of transformation and achievement" that is like nothing they have ever felt before or will ever feel again.[51] This experience of being transformed through suffering was put into words by a retired marine, describing the humiliations of his basic training during World War II:

It made me feel like a nothin'. But on the other hand, they did so many things that made me feel like I was a person, that I could tolerate that. . . . They humiliate ya, they make ya do things that you don't think are physically possible. At the same time, they're makin' you feel you're something. That you're part of something. When you're there and you need somebody, you got somebody. It was the high point of my life. . . . I was somebody.[52]

An army major echoed this perspective from the point of view of a commanding officer for whom discipline meant "thinking about the group rather than the self":

The bulk of our time [as commanders] is spent . . . trying to promote spirit and cohesion. . . . And some of the ways we do that [are] shaving their hair off . . . and dehumanizing them and making them identityless, so they can more relate to the group. If you strip the macho identity away, the evil away, and all the me-ism away, then they can start performing as a group. A lot of people think that's beating people down to gain control of them. I really don't think that's it at all. That's one of the great things American soldiers have over the bad guys: we instill, in the end, the feeling that each individual is special.

Conflicts Inherent in the Two Moral Traditions

The Quaker virtues have religious roots and are perceived to be generated from within, whereas the military virtues are based on the demands of a profession and are perceived to be learned. Nevertheless, both provide guidelines for living a life of service to a calling. Attempts to practice the virtues have shown, however, that they are not easy to follow. Indeed, they are not always easy to understand, since a quality like simplicity or loyalty can lend itself to many interpretations. Within the two traditions, most problems with the practice of the virtues lie in conflicts between personal and communal interpretations of what is right. In traditional Quakerism, both the individual and the Meeting as a whole are struggling to do God's will, but they do not always agree on what it is. In the military profession, service to the country should be of paramount importance to all, but individual soldiers may not agree that official army policy is in the country's best interest.[53] The concepts of concern and leadership can help members of the two groups steer their way between private conscience and the will of the group, but many dilemmas are still difficult to resolve. It is not only at boarding schools that the practice of Quaker and military virtues gives rise to conflict. Rather, many of these conflicts are rooted in controversies that have plagued the two traditions for years.

The Quaker Tradition: Conflict over the Inner Light

Traditional Quaker doubts and conflicts grow out of trying to determine what actions are truly prompted by the Inner Light. One of the most common dilemmas among devout Friends has been whether to speak out in Meeting for Worship. For a Friend to break the silence of Meeting, he or she should have a "leading." To speak because one has thought of something interesting to say or wants to be noticed is frivolous or even sacrilegious—it is called "going before one's Guide" or indulging in "creaturely activity." Friends' journals from the 1600s to the present record indecision about speaking in Meeting. If they were to speak, would they be outrunning their Guide? If they felt a call to speak but didn't, out of fear that the call was only imagined, might they actually be turning their backs on Divine Will?[54] These fears were heightened by the presence, in most eighteenth-century Meetings, of "elders," respected men and women appointed by the Meeting to support and encourage those who "spoke in the Light" and to discourage those whose messages seemed to be without Spirit. Even today, a person who speaks often in Meeting without having anything spiritual to say may be taken aside and "eldered" by a "weighty Friend." The risk of failure to respond to a "leading" also continues to worry Quakers today, although modern Friends focus more on their responsibility to speak in public than in Meeting. One Quaker told of her boss's cruelty to a fellow employee. She longed to confront the boss, but "I never did anything, I just sat there and listened to him humiliate this man. . . . Fear stopped me. God—a good leading—was pushing me to speak. . . . I have more strength now: I failed the test that time, but I will do better next time."

This Friend seemed to feel it was her duty to speak out in defense of her fellow employee, to do God's will. But *duty* is not a word that comes easily to modern Quakers. In the nineteenth century it seemed natural to a Quaker like John Greenleaf Whittier to hope that he might be able to do God's will "as if it were my own."[55] But many Friends have trouble reconciling this idea of being led with the Quakerly injunction not to "sacrifice one iota of the moral freedom of your consciences or the intellectual freedom of your judgments."[56] To someone who is completely confident of the Inner Light, duty and freedom of conscience are not contradictory concepts. However, this kind of religious assurance is less common today than it was two or three centuries ago. Modern Quakers struggle with the idea of duty, and many seem to have difficulty equating it with the will of God at all. A fifth-generation Friend, for example, said he was comfortable with the idea of having obligations only "as long as I realize that I'm the one making the choice, and I'm making it out of love rather than out of some rigid societal sense of [what I should do]."

One of the hardest decisions modern Quakers have to make is not when to act, but when not to act. Although Friends have a reputation as social activists who seek to "mend the world," their actions are constrained by the conviction that they should proceed only "as way opens": "We run ahead of our Guide and risk a calamitous outcome when we endeavor to force action on a concern by bowling over everything that stands in the way."[57] The fact that a group of Quakers should proceed to action only after consensus has been reached makes the prompt, decisive achievement of clear-cut ends unlikely. In relief work, for example,

the administrator with a wide range of information and experience before him may not have much difficulty in thinking out a line of action. . . . But if he lays it before the group he may very well find that . . . intellectual apprehension of ascertainable factors must give way before the sense that the Lord has not spoken, for without a sense of being encompassed by a cloud of witnesses, the Quaker relief worker or group cannot feel that the concerns of the Society are being truly followed.[58]

Although Friends may pursue specific political goals, they should not make the achievement of these ends all-important to their identity as Quakers. Often the fact that one bears witness—"an activity in which both ends and means are emergent"—is enough.[59] But for the Quaker living in our results-oriented Western society, and particularly for the activist, the need for concrete goals and achievements becomes a problem, which some Friends have been accused of trying to solve by putting peace-making activities—participating in demonstrations, organizing committees, lobbying, and so on—before "living in the Spirit." This problem is intensified by the fact that a growing number of people are becoming Quakers mainly because they are attracted to Friends' liberal political positions. Since the days of George Fox, Quakers have identified the Inner Light with Christ, yet today many Friends are not Christians or at least do not express themselves in Christian language. Instead, they talk about the Divine Presence or the universal force, and some do not mention God at all. These Friends are more comfortable discussing Quaker stands on political issues than Quaker religious beliefs.

For an eighteenth-century Friend like Thomas Shillitoe, religious faith and political action were inextricably linked. "If I remained willing to become like a cork on the mighty ocean of service . . . ," he wrote, "willing to be wafted hither and thither, as the Spirit of the Lord my God should blow upon me, he would care for me every day and every way; so that there should be no lack of strength to encounter all my difficulties."[60] Following his leadings, Shillitoe had audiences with George III and John Quincy Adams; he traveled to Germany to pray with prisoners and to America to preach to slaveholders. Throughout his travels, he allowed his faith in God to lead him to service. Many twentieth-century Quakers, by contrast, have become Friends in the hope that service will lead them to God. As one Friend put it:

We have gotten lots of new members, especially in recent years, who are attracted by our testimonies—peace, racial harmony, women's rights, and the like. But it seems to me that most of these people will eventually leave us unless they become turned on by our worship. . . . After all, we try to base our actions on divine leadings. And that means we're more interested in finding the divine than in any given cause taken by itself.[61]

In his study of the consensus decision-making process among Friends, Michael Sheeran finds that this tension over religious belief hinges on the capacity to experience the sacred. It is not the name one gives to "the Spirit" but one's ability to feel its presence that is all-important to the Quaker religion:

Quakerism has always been a community without creed precisely because it did not need a creed. Unlike other faiths, Quakerism builds on the experience of the gathered meeting. Together Friends experience something beyond themselves, superior to the human pettiness that marks ordinary life. . . . In the experience, [a Quaker] finds guidance, motivation to reconsider preferences, a sense of obligation to the decision reached by this special atmosphere.[62]

These experiences are denied to the person who does not feel a sacred presence in the gathered Meeting. No matter how devoted the person is to Quaker causes, he or she cannot act "in the Light" if the Light has not been felt. This problem gives rise to the question: What is the worth of action without spiritual inspiration? More disturbingly, members of the Meeting are forced to ask themselves: Can one be a Friend if one does not experience the Light? Many answer, Yes—but only if one is open to the idea of the sacred and willing to search for a spiritual capacity within oneself. Mere dedication to Quaker causes and testimonies is not enough.

These conflicts over silence versus speaking, duty versus choice, waiting versus acting, and faith versus politics come to a head when a Friend brings a concern before his or her Meeting. In an ideal situation, the members of the Meeting are fired by the concern, and the Meeting makes a consensual decision to offer it their full spiritual and sometimes financial support. In reality, unity over a concern may fail. The members of the Meeting may question the validity of the concern or doubt the wisdom of carrying it out. Or, despite the support of many members, the Meeting may fail to unite behind a proposed plan. Although anyone is still free to act on the concern without the Meeting's support, such community disapproval may lead the individual to doubt his or her own conviction.

The tension between private conscience and communal judgment is perceived by many Quakers to be healthy, since it limits both the excesses of the individual and the conservatism of the group:

Quakerism has always had within it a strong centrifugal force of individualism, but likewise there has always been a centripetal force of corporate life in tension with it; and from the fruitful interaction of these two have come the decisions of the Society. The visions and concerns of individuals prevent the Society from being over-traditional and static; the insights of the gathered group prevent it from moving over-hastily in unconsidered enthusiasm.[63]

Yet, a healthy balance between the individual and the group is easier to prescribe than to achieve. In the early 1800s, for example, the Meeting, with its "elders" and "overseers," was frequently dominant, and discipline rather than enthusiasm prevailed, giving rise to the stereotype of Quakers as strict and joyless. In recent years, by contrast, the emphasis on the primacy of private conscience caused a "weighty Friend" and educator to remind his fellow Quakers that "to heed the voice of Truth, 'the still small voice within,' . . . does not mean to accentuate and glorify a self-centered individualism . . . [because for] Friends, to live in Truth is to overcome the impetuous claims of self."[64]

The Military Tradition: Conflict over Duty

In 1960, *Military Review* printed an essay stating that "the only categorical imperative of military conduct is: A military body and every member therein must perform the duty assigned, whatever it may be."[65] Today, duty no longer carries the same implication of absolute and uncritical obedience to orders. Training materials for officers emphasize initiative, imagination, reflection, flexibility, and creativity instead of obedience, and enlisted men are taught that they are required to follow only legal orders. An army major is proud of this fact:

It's not just the Hitlers and the Eichmanns, it's the guys who lock the doors, it's the guys who turn on the gas: how did that happen? And we're not going to let that happen in this country—it's not going to happen! We're going to have lawful orders and unlawful orders. And if Captain Medina . . . gives an order to Lieutenant Calley to "take care of them," then that's an unlawful order and a guy like Calley has got to buck that order.[66]

In spite of the increased emphasis on initiative and questioning in today's army, however, obedience—the "can-do" attitude—is still the safest response to an order, or even a request, from a superior.

Officers' careers depend on regular performance evaluations from their superiors, called Officer Efficiency Reports, or OERs. "One bad OER and you're dead," explained the major. Many officers are afraid of discussing problems with their superiors, for fear of being branded "negative," so they answer "Yes, sir," to all orders and then either attempt the impossible, pass the buck to their subordinates, or, worst of all, engage in a cover-up to hide their failure.[67] This focus on results can also lead to an obsessive quantification of data to "prove" success or to "the energetic accomplishment of meaningless things."[68]

Officers think a great deal about the possibility of disobeying orders; the military has come up with a number of slang phrases for this behavior, such as "being hung," "going to the wall," or "falling on your sword." It is significant that all these phrases have to do with death: disobedience is still regarded as a probable deathblow to a military career. Nevertheless, wrote one officer:

there are things, should always be things, for which we must be willing to be hung. To forget it is to risk slipping into the unthinking obedience, false loyalty, and phony honor of "my country, right or wrong," or "my boss, right or wrong." And, of course, the tempting "me, right or wrong."[69]

One major felt strongly that "you don't do something because someone told you to; you do something because someone told you to and it's correct." He had made a point in his career of refusing bad orders and had been relieved of command four times as a result. So far he has always been reinstated, because "the higher authority would say, 'No, you can't relieve him for that, because you shouldn't have been telling him to do that in the first place.'" He argued that one should not carry disobedience to an extreme and "become known as a guy who goes to the wall daily. . . . What you should go to the wall over is something that is hurting the army: the organization or the people."

Another officer, who approved of soldiers' disobedience under certain circumstances, admitted that he himself found it extremely difficult to imagine saying, "Damn it, I don't want to do this, this is dumb. I've got a good mind to go into the general's office and just fall on my sword." He dreaded the "bad report card" that would result from being so "disrespectful and blatantly disloyal." The problem with this fear, he said, is that "you give up your integrity an inch at a time . . . and after a few years you look back and there's a whole football field behind you. And that's from having put off falling on your sword."

Few issues are more likely to raise questions about orders than mission-versus-men dilemmas. In the military, the mission is the goal that must be achieved, and the men are the primary means for accomplishing that goal. General Maxwell Taylor wrote, "The measure of the quality of the officer is his success in carrying out his mission, despite all obstacles. . . . He is a good officer professionally to the extent that he succeeds, a bad one to the extent that he fails." [70] Yet, in the words of an air force general, "Overemphasis on mission can lead to the age-old ethical problem of subordination of means to ends." [71] In wartime, this can refer to an unnecessary sacrifice of men's lives; in peacetime, to overworking subordinates or asking them to behave unethically or unsafely, by lying on reports or using faulty equipment, for example. A primary criticism of OERs is that "the standards of evaluation being applied have failed to penalize those who exploit their units to advance their own interests." [72] Still, many officers and NCOs believe that "taking care of the men" is their primary responsibility, and they will put their own career in jeopardy to defend subordinates or protect them from unreasonable demands. Indeed, the officer who described his fear of falling on his sword had in fact done so once for the sake of his men, refusing an order that he felt made frivolous and unreasonable demands on the troops.

This kind of loyalty within a squad, platoon, or company, either between superior and subordinate or among peers, is crucial to the cohesion of the army. It is also what makes men fight in war. "I hold it to be one of the simplest truths of war," wrote S. L. A. Marshall, "that the thing which enables an infantry soldier to keep going with his weapons is the near presence or the presumed presence of a comrade." [73] In theory, loyalty to the members of one's military unit should be compatible with loyalty to the army as an institution and to its values. But in fact the two loyalties frequently clash. To counteract this tendency to put the subgroup before the organization, cadets at West Point, Colorado Springs, and Annapolis, who take an oath not to lie, cheat, or steal, must also swear not to "tolerate those who do." This nontoleration clause means that cadets or midshipmen who fail to report their classmates' dishonesty may be punished as severely as the actual offenders.

Loyalty to peers or subordinates is one of the most common reasons for putting conscience before command and defying an order. But the most difficult situation for a military professional is when conscience urges him or her to go against both subgroup and organization, to do what he or she thinks is right even when it seems to work against the profession. In spite of the army's recent policy of "sensitiz[ing] individuals to ethical issues" and moral dilemmas,[74] the prevailing norm is that professional standards are more important than private conscience. "It is not acceptable for a person to act in ways contrary to ethical norms simply because he or she 'feels' it is right to do so. We must divorce ourselves from emotional responses to human behavior, and we must emphasize the role of standards in evaluating such behavior."[75]

These tensions between acting independently and acting with the group, between following one's "leadings" and accepting common norms, are inherent in both the Quaker and the military tradition. The two sets of virtues provide guidelines for handling some dilemmas, but they also raise dilemmas of their own. Concern and leadership are helpful as reconciling concepts that acknowledge the simultaneous validity of individual judgment and community standards, but they cannot be applied to every situation. Ultimately, these tensions are part of life as a Quaker or a military professional. They are part of life at the boarding schools. They are also part of modern society, perhaps especially among Americans, whom Hewitt describes as "torn between individualism and communitarianism."[76] He identifies several themes in our culture that involve "dilemmas of choice," one of which is conforming versus rebelling: "Should one go along with the constraints and demands imposed by others, or should one rebel against them, marching to the beat of one's own drummer?"[77] The liberal Quaker tradition favors the drum solo; the conservative military tradition, the marching band. But neither tradition is single-mindedly individualistic or communitarian. There is room for compromise in both.

At the boarding schools, where the traditions are taught and practiced, the virtues play a crucial role as guidelines for a good life and as centerpieces in the "dilemmas of choice" that arise during the school year. Concern and leadership are important forces in boarding-school life, but they need the virtues to make them intelligible. For Quakers or military professionals, the virtues represent the "specific skills" they need in order to live a life that is "faithful to [their] tradition's understanding of the moral project in which its adherents participate."[78] In their different ways, the Quaker and military moral traditions share a strong ethic of service; the virtues are simultaneously prerequisites, building blocks, and goals in each tradition's quest to serve. At the six schools, where the Quaker and military moral projects have been adapted to fit the requirements of classroom and dormitory, the conscious espousal and pursuit of each virtue by teachers and students impose order on the everyday. Chapter Three describes in detail how the virtues shape school life.

Chapter Three

Virtue as a Source of Order

Lives with a Purpose

Using their traditions' virtues as building blocks, two different ways of life are constructed at Quaker and military boarding schools. Chapter One has described what happens when classes, meals, styles of dress, and methods of supervising and orienting students are passed through the filter of moral tradition. Chapter Two has shown that the resulting life-styles grow out of carefully constructed and purposeful moral worldviews. Even someone with no previous exposure to Quakerism and only a layman's knowledge of the military can find much that is familiar in the two worldviews, because embedded within them are classic American liberal and conservative ways of thinking. Although liberals do not think in terms of the Inner Light, nor conservatives in terms of the mission, the former, like Friends, emphasize an ethic of openness that promotes tolerance and equal treatment of individuals, while the latter, like military officers, emphasize an ethic of personal responsibility that promotes discipline and successful accomplishment of tasks.

The Quaker and military moral traditions are different from everyday liberal and conservative ways of thinking, however, because they reflect a coherent sense of purpose. Quaker and military virtues are carried to their logical conclusions. Thus, a belief in the equal value of every person means that one cannot kill another human being, whereas a belief in personal responsibility for country and comrades means that one is ready to kill and die for them. Such single-minded adherence to a moral tradition, whether it is deemed constraining or strengthening, does give order to life. A tradition engages its members in a story with a plot they can follow, in which they have a clear-cut role to play. This chapter analyzes the Quaker and military stories as they unfold at the six boarding schools and shows how the virtues define adults' and adolescents' roles as teacher and student.

The Quaker Virtues at the Schools

Equality

A teacher in his late fifties said, only partially in jest, that he preferred Mott to a conventional prep school because he found it "revolting" to be called "sir." At Quaker schools, adolescents and adults call each other by their first names. Closeness exists in more than just this token form, however. As a senior girl at Mott explained:

Something I've really valued here is that there isn't a huge distinction between freshmen and seniors, or between faculty and students, or between employees of the school and faculty and students. The school says, "Yes, these people are teaching you, and yes, they are older than you, but they are also your friends and they are here for you to go to other than to learn about math or history."

Of course students and teachers are not equals in authority: teachers assign homework and enforce rules which they, and not the students, have established. But the easy dialogue in the classrooms, the exchange of opinions between prefects and adults at dormitory staff meetings, and the astute way that many of the older students talk about individual faculty members—without either knee-jerk hostility or unreflective adulation—show a lack of generational distance that is rare at the high-school level.[1] The three Friends schools promote another kind of equality by giving no prizes of any kind; students receive grades but are never publicly ranked. A teacher said that when he started at Mott he was convinced that "contests would be a good way to spark enthusiasm and get things happening," and he made an assembly presentation to encourage students to join in a bridge-building contest. After the assembly, "several teachers talked to me very informally and quietly and graciously and told me that contests really aren't the way we do things here at Mott. Who is best is not all that important, and ballyhooing who is best is definitely not a done thing."[2]

A similar emphasis on equality exists among the adults on campus. Teachers and administrators at the three schools meet regularly to discuss new policies, program changes, proposed budgets, and serious disciplinary problems, and teachers speak out at these meetings. One Mott department head said, "In no workplace before have I ever felt the equal of the headmaster. Here I am perfectly comfortable telling [him] exactly what I think." An attempt is also made to minimize the division between faculty and kitchen, grounds, and office staff. At Fox a cook is also a dorm resident and student advisor; at Dyer a maintenance man is a popular coach. The grounds foreman at Mott, who coaches and serves as an advisor, criticized a new administrator for telling him, "'You people in grounds are here to serve the faculty.' But that's not true. Nobody here is serving anybody—we are all here together in a community—the students, the faculty, and us. . . . I feel part of my job is helping to raise the kids."

Equality is also one of the important lessons that a number of the teachers say they want to communicate to pupils. Mott sponsors one-week work camps in Appalachia and Washington, D.C., where students paint houses or work in soup kitchens and shelters for the homeless. A teacher thought the students' essays about these trips were "among the best examples of what our moral education is about at this school," because they showed that the students were challenged to think about "whether or not we have a right to the wealth we have. For the first time they encounter the fact that maybe it's not that the poor are poor because they are lazy and don't have the motivation to take advantage of the American dream . . . that some people are trapped in their poverty." History, English, and religion classes also address the issue of equality between races and nations. In a discussion about the nineteenth-century American ideal of progress, a junior concluded, "When we tried to live up to our goals of expansion and progression, our principles suffered, and other people were victimized, especially working-class people." "When we try to protect smaller countries," said another junior, "it puts them in debt to us; it gives us control over them."

At military academies, by contrast, the emphasis is on hierarchy, not equality. Students are separated from each other by their ages and ranks and from most of their teachers by strong conventions that inhibit closeness. One teacher at Pershing complained, "They're so polite I want to shake them sometimes," and a senior girl, telling about her deep depression for most of the previous year, said, "I suppose I would have loved to talk to any adult, but I wasn't really sure how to approach them." A similar distance exists between teachers and top administrators at the three military academies. Occasionally people at the military academies complained about the hierarchical nature of relationships, but for the most part equality was neither expected nor sought.

Community

Two mornings a week, teachers, administrators, and students at Dyer Friends School gather together for "community meeting," a time when anyone who has anything to share can get up and speak, sing, or play music. Like a Meeting for Business, this gathering is in the hands of a clerk, a popular senior boy whose lazy manner hides a surprising amount of authority. There is no agenda. One Friday, a student opens the meeting by playing one of his own compositions on the piano; afterwards, team captains report on wins and losses in sports, a teacher urges students to attend an AIDS rally in a nearby city, and various members of the audience list events scheduled for the upcoming weekend: a hike, a dance, an open house hosted by the academic dean. Each of these announcements is accompanied by a background murmur of student commentary, affectionate rather than hostile, which is skillfully held in check by the clerk. A young teacher plays his guitar, then a girl with a remarkable voice gets up and belts out a song. A staff member asks students to look presentable for the upcoming alumni weekend—this generates a ripple of disapproval and mumbles about hypocrisy. Finally, the dean of students talks about the increase in theft in the school; he begs students to help him find the culprits, whose most recent booty was the school's video recorder. After this speech, the clerk closes the meeting, as he opened it, with a few moments of silence.

"Community meeting" is not a misnomer: at this informal gathering of 200 people there is a shared sense of belonging. This feeling is displayed by bookbags flung down in the halls, coats tossed over chairs, and student artwork on the walls; by the open office doors; and by the faculty children in the dining room. Dyer is not always harmonious—there are adolescents who make life miserable for their dorm mates and adults who make it clear they cannot stand one another.

But the school is home to teachers and students. It engages them profoundly: they think about Dyer, argue about it, and are constantly trying to improve it. To that extent it is exactly what so many of them want it to be—a community.

The concern to turn the school into a close-knit community of adolescents and adults is most clearly articulated at Dyer—perhaps because it attracts more emotionally needy students and adults—but it exists at the other two Friends schools as well. Fox is so small, and so many of its teachers and pupils are alumni or the children of alumni, that their strong sense of belonging is only to be expected. Yet at Mott, the largest of the three schools, students and staff also share a sense of being at home. One long-term teacher said:

This is not just a job, it's where I live. I don't see an end of my workday, I'm just here. I lived in a dorm my first seven years here, and the first two years I wasn't in a dorm I felt left out. So we chose to become dorm parents again. And I coach. So I feel constantly involved.

When a senior was asked what she thought Mott considered the most important lessons for her to learn, she answered immediately, "Community and equality. . . . Everyone who comes here—even friends of mine who don't go here but have come to visit—say there's such a feeling about this place. It's a feeling we have for each other."

Because of its political concerns, Mott goes beyond Fox and Dyer in promoting a sense of belonging in the world as well as in the school. A Quaker staff member thought that the most important value students should take from Mott was "a feeling of the total world as a world community." Other teachers expressed their desire to communicate to students something they called "responsibility to the world" or "a sense of world citizenship."

Students and, more rarely, teachers use the word *community* at military school, but it is almost always tied to the military virtue of loyalty, as when Pershing's Kyle Bennett said that people in his company who tattle on their fellow cadets "have no sense of community." In a technical sense, all boarding schools are communities, places where people live, eat, and work together, but the emphasis on building a shared sense of caring and belonging, either between students and teachers or among the faculty, is not present in the military environment. Quaker schools hold frequent meetings of adults—department meetings, dormitory staff meetings, and so on—and also assemblies, Meetings for Worship, and other gatherings for both adults and students. During my weeks at the military academies there were no full-faculty meetings, no school-wide meetings of teachers and students, and only two student assemblies. All three military school faculties include adults who care deeply about particular students, but the sense of togetherness and mutual affection shared by the adults and adolescents in Dyer's community meetings or in Mott's twice-weekly assemblies is not in evidence at the military academies.

Simplicity

Today's Quakers are not like the Amish; their simplicity is a matter, not of rejecting twentieth-century life, but of carefully weighing twentieth-century priorities. "In listening to the Inner Voice, [Friends] know that moderation is better than excess, that our lives should be centered, not dissipated, and that if we cannot live in voluntary poverty, we should not live in voluntary prodigality."[3] Moderation is not an easy doctrine for twentieth-century American adolescents, who tend to experiment with excesses on their way to developing a sense of identity.[4] One Mott senior, a non-Quaker, when asked about the lessons he thought the school taught, ran through an impromptu list of Quakerly virtues and dismissed simplicity out of hand: "Let's see. The cornerstones of Quakerism are simplicity, truth, nonviolence, and equality. Well, simplicity is out the window—people are extravagant here. I like to dress up—that Miami Vice look!" A long-term Quaker staff member also thought that Mott sometimes failed to convey the virtue of simplicity, although she considered it a very important value. She could not reconcile her belief that one should "live simply, so that others may simply live" with the wealth of many students and their "expectations of more and more and more."

Ellen Kahn, another Quaker teacher, was more hopeful about Mott's success in teaching simplicity. She felt that the required service programs—work camps or weekly volunteer work—helped students see that "it is good and noble to work in professions that don't necessarily make a lot of money, but which can be of use to other people in the world":

I think we help kids to see how a responsible person from an affluent society needs to relate to the world, and that implicitly discourages materialism. . . . I think most of our kids really *are* quite materialistic. . . . But the . . . faculty are role models, because I think there are very few of us who are conspicuous consumers.

Of course, she concluded with a laugh, it wasn't only Quaker-school teachers who were role models for simplicity. "Probably the same could be said of any independent-school faculty, since none of us get paid very well, and if we cared about getting paid well we wouldn't be here!"

Although the tendency toward informality, casual dress, and direct speaking encourages a simplicity of manner at all three schools, the virtue is most prominent at Fox. There students and adults live un-elaborately, sharing meals and chores. On many mornings students get their own breakfasts, chatting with the cook, who is already start-ing the noon meal, and after breakfast each student does his or her cleaning job around the school. The older alumni remember an even simpler time, when students also milked cows, helped with the apple-picking, shoveled coal, and did repair work around the school. A couple from the class of 1940 reminisced with amused affection about the strictness of the school in their day. One of the first ordeals of the new school year was a clothing inspection by the Yearly Meeting's dress-code committee. Students unpacked their trunks and laid their clothes out on the beds; then the women's committee would examine the girls' clothes and the men's committee, the boys', asking them to "lay aside . . . anything too flashy or gaudy for a proper Quaker." This meant, explained the woman, "nothing red. No bright colors, no big plaids. . . . Now, my senior year I had a dress that was dark red with a tiny flower in it, and they let me keep that." In addition, "we weren't allowed to show very much skin: we had to wear silk hose—that was before nylons—and long sleeves and high necks, even in the summer."

This dress code no longer exists at Fox, but the emphasis on frugal-ity and hard work remains, best exemplified by Andrew Henley, a Quaker in his early thirties who teaches several subjects, coaches sports, and runs the work program. The Fox headmaster had no hesitation in naming Henley as the person who best embodied the spirit of the school. First of all, "there's just plain old-fashioned heri-tage." Andrew Henley is descended from generations of local Quak-ers; his ancestors have been members of the Yearly Meeting and attended Fox School "for who knows how long." Yet, the headmaster insisted, "he's not an anachronism. He is in touch with the real world." Another reason Andrew embodies the Fox spirit has to do with his faith. "His spirituality has not been confused by a lot of the things going on in Christianity today: evangelical things, fundamentalist teachings. He has not been entrapped by that sort of dogmatic approach to spiritual growth." Finally, as leader of the work program Andrew is responsible for students' keeping the school clean:

So much of the experience of being a student here has to do with contributing to the community, and Andrew is extraordinary on that front. [The work program] works because it's such a given for him, not a big deal. He doesn't feel in the least awkward about insisting that someone do a better job cleaning a bathroom. . . . Andrew's greatest wish is to transfer to other people a simple love of work. He likes to work hard, likes to work up a sweat. He finds joy in that and likes to share it with other people.

During one of my weekends at Fox School, Henley asked for volunteers to help him mop and wax the floors; the first work crew was filled in minutes. "The kids enjoy working with him," explained one of his colleagues; "they get into discussions." One of his students said she respected Henley more than any of the other teachers, because "he's the most honest; he doesn't play games. . . . He's someone I can trust."

This dedication of Henley's, this combination of honesty, openness, and single-mindedness, is part of what Quakers mean by simplicity. There are some equally dedicated people at the military academies, but no one with Henley's serenity and emotional transparency. Austerity is an important part of a soldier's life, and members of the military profession cannot be accused of being materialistic, since they earn relatively little money compared to civilians with similar responsibilities. Nevertheless, simplicity is not a military virtue. At the military academies, the grandiose architecture, the ritualized exchanges of titles and courtesies, the importance of parades, ceremonies, and elegant uniforms, and, perhaps above all, the artificiality of the formal self-control cadets and adults are required to show all work against simplicity.

Peace

The Quaker schools are peaceful places in two senses. First, pacifism is a clearly articulated political stance adopted by many—although by no means all—teachers and students. It emerges in discussions of current events, world history, religion, and literature and often colors the statements of those who speak in assembly or in Meeting for Worship. A group of Mott freshmen in a social studies class discussing the national budget deficit want to know why the United States can't cut defense spending; in a Latin American history class, a Fox teacher expresses his distress at the U.S. government's support of the Nicaraguan Contras; and at Dyer students in an American history class listen to their teacher describe with obvious bitterness how in the late 1960s the Democrats split over opposition to the Vietnam War. Pacifism is not limited to talk: teachers and students participate in peace marches and demonstrations. One senior girl, a birthright Friend,[5] said, "I try to get to political gatherings off-campus. Last year I worked it out through the school to go to the peace march—I took off for a week and went down to Washington by train."

Peace-making was also the foremost lesson the head of Fox's school committee wanted students to take away with them. He hoped they would realize that:

The peace testimony is more than just refusal to go to war. It involves nonviolence in all confrontations . . . whether it's with your roommate or your girlfriend or someone you meet on the street. And it goes back to . . . how teachers interact with their students both in class and out. Because you learn from what you observe.

In other words, pacifism is not only a political stance but also a vision of how members of the school community should treat one another. Physical violence is strongly discouraged, and according to students it rarely occurs. Not everyone is kind, but at all three schools the expectation is that members of the community will try not to hurt one another's feelings. At a tiny place like Fox, such a norm is perhaps to be expected. But even at Mott, with its 500 students, teenagers insisted that no one was treated cruelly. A senior, Leah Brodsky, believed that "people at Mott have an interesting kind of tolerance," because they are polite to people they don't like. Not that people should dislike each other, she said, but when they do, "if everyone is at least civil, then your confidence isn't shot and torn apart, and you can go about your life and then go to other places where maybe people will like you." She compared Mott to her earlier school, an all-girls academy "where they absolutely despised me, and they ganged up on me like crazy. . . . They sensed my difference."[6]

Dyer had several obvious bullies; nevertheless, students thought of it as a nonviolent place compared to the schools many of them had come from. A junior boy who valued "the oddity and diversity of people at Dyer" couldn't imagine a person who wouldn't fit in "except maybe someone who was really violent and liked to be angry. And even those people usually fit in eventually, because they change, and you get to see what they are really like and get close to them." Another student echoed this vision of Dyer as "big on nonviolence." He thought that having "a Quaker philosophy at a high school" wasn't easy, since "it's hard to deal with people on a mature level when you're not that mature yourself." Nonetheless,

people who have been here for all four years learn that there are more ways to deal with people and situations than just with violence. That talking, explaining your side of the situation, is better than hurting. . . . People are suspended and expelled for violence, and I see that as a major thing.

At military academies a favorite classroom topic is war, not peace. In history classes, students came alive when particular battles were discussed, and several showed a surprisingly detailed knowledge of the facts behind such events as the charge of the Light Brigade and the bombing of Pearl Harbor. Many of the cadets fantasized about military careers (although only a small fraction of each graduating class goes on to a military college or enlists in the armed forces).[7] Peace is also not a word that describes relations between cadets. Hazing—mental or physical abuse, especially of the junior ranks by their seniors—is officially forbidden at all three schools, but a great deal of it occurs nonetheless.[8] At Pershing, for example, a cadet expressed his approval of a certain amount of force or at least intimidation as part of military training: "If you can get someone scared without hurting them, that's the idea; that teaches respect." Yet he drew the line at one method of scaring cadets: hanging them out of a fourth-story dormitory window. This had happened to him the year before:

They had me out the window head first, and then they started taking the strings out [of my boots], and I could feel my feet starting to slip out. When one of my boots came off they held me by [the other], and then when I started to fall they just grabbed my underwear and yanked me back in. . . . I was petrified.

The Quaker Story: Bringing Out the Inner Light

A Search for the Good

Equality, community, simplicity, and peace are all chapters in the Quaker story of fostering the Inner Light in every individual. In a peaceful environment where people feel equal to one another, share a strong sense of community, and live simply and single-mindedly, it is easier for that of God, or what is best in every individual, to emerge. That is, in essence, the moral project of Quaker schooling. A Mott dean believes "that there is that of God in all . . . kids, . . . something that is unique and spectacular and that deserves celebration" even in "the kid who comes in here with a peace symbol etched on the top of his head and reeking of pot smoke." This belief, he said, shapes his approach to advising and administering discipline. "We expect the best of kids, and I think sometimes when you look for that which is special in kids you are more likely to find it."

For most of the students at Mott, Fox, and Dyer, the Quaker project of bringing out the Inner Light translates into the desirability of expressing one's inner self—in other words, being different from everyone else, being a unique, special individual. In formal interviews and informal conversations with students in Quaker schools, the most common answer kids gave when asked what was distinctive about their school was, "This is a place where we can really be ourselves." A Mott sophomore explained that even if you stay in your room and are anti-social, "people are still nice to you," because "people respect the fact that someone is different." Of course, she added, "there aren't that many super-conservative people here." Asked if those few conservative students were ostracized, she answered, "Well, they interact with everyone. Actually, I don't know anyone here who's straight as an arrow. Mott is a good place to bring out the parts of you that make you different. This is a place for letting your Inner Light shine." A young Dyer student said the school had taught her to accept "nontrendy people" who "dare to be different." This emphasis on the importance of expressing one's inner self and "daring to be different" was not

confined to the students; teachers, too, stressed their school's tolerance for eccentricity. One young teacher, a Mott alumnus, said, "Here
you can be the person you want to be, and be safe. No matter where
you are in the Breakfast Club,[9] you're okay."

Students and teachers at the Quaker schools frequently use words
and phrases having to do with being receptive and expressive, such as
*openness, listening, speaking out, feeling comfortable, sharing, accept-
ing*. To some extent this is simply the fashionable "let's communicate"
vocabulary of the 1970s and 1980s, an outgrowth of what the authors
of *Habits of the Heart* call "expressive individualism."[10] But images of
opening oneself, sharing thoughts, and listening have been part of the
Quaker vocabulary for generations; they reflect the importance of
trying to get access to one's own and others' Inner Light. For some,
this emphasis on the internal is religious. A Fox administrator valued
the silence that is a key part of the Quaker experience because "it is
very important to live in a listening mode. I have a belief that God
really does communicate with us directly. . . . It's the responsibility of
each individual to make his or her own contact, to listen in his or her
own way . . . and seek to serve God." For others, especially students,
this emphasis on listening, feeling, and communicating has little to do
with God and a great deal to do with trying to understand oneself and
one's peers. When a boy in his second year at Mott was asked what he
had learned there, he answered, "I think you learn how other people
feel"—like punks, for example. "After speaking to someone, you get to
know why they want to do that, spike their hair or wear clothes that are
torn. . . . Unless you speak to them, you just think they are weird and
dirty, so you have to ask them how they feel." Different as their
viewpoints are, both the Dyer dean and the Mott sophomore, along
with many others at the three schools, believe that listening and
expressing feelings have to do with discovering an inner truth about
oneself or others. To be faithful to this truth is to acknowledge the
internal source of morality that is so important to Friends.

Flaws and Failures

The Quaker focus on the inner self has its negative aspects. One is that
it can be intrusive. A shy new teacher at Mott was afraid she would not
be able to handle the degree of openness required by the community.
I asked her, "If you had to tell an outsider one thing about Mott,

something the person ought to know before coming to work here, what would it be?" She answered that she would warn the person that "they could not expect to be able to hide anything about themselves from anyone else in the community." First of all, you are "exposed in everything you do"; second, she felt that you could not teach well unless you were willing to confide in other teachers and ask for their help. "You need to get their advice . . . and you can't do that unless you are very open about what you are struggling with and what you're successful with. Which is new for me. I'm a fairly private person and I like my privacy, but I couldn't get by here if I just kept to myself."

The faculty's desire to encourage the Inner Light can also lead to various forms of well-intended deception. One Mott teacher, although a strong supporter of the Quaker educational philosophy, described "the other side of the coin":

Because of this need for each person to feel good about themselves and feel important, we praise people who are really mediocre or poor. And sometimes the real education would be to say, "You really can't sing; you should give it up." . . . I think sending people out of here thinking that they are very, very special when they are really very ordinary—that's what nervous breakdowns are based on.

In handling students' misbehavior, another kind of deception can arise. A disillusioned young teacher at Fox who assured me that "Friends' philosophy is marvelous" nevertheless felt that its "spiritual, very positive, pro-individual perspective" led many Quakers to believe that "people just somehow accidentally do bad things—it's never intended at all." At Fox this "very liberal educational line" could become "the argument for why you never deal with anything." Much as he, too, respected the individual, he didn't think it was respectful "to deceive yourself or someone else. I'm not going to pretend I don't know what kids are up to."

At its worst, the Quaker concern with the inner self, the desire to care, and the tolerance for difference can lead to a show of favoritism toward the odd, the disturbed, and the loudly needy. A member of the Dyer community said bitterly:

This school . . . had a reputation of being a school for misfits, and I think that attracted faculty and staff who felt that they were misfits and that somehow by being leaders in a school for misfits they would work out their own feelings about [themselves]. . . . Some of the strongest teachers in the school, professionally competent people who don't bring their personal problems to the job, are poorly treated, whereas some people who are far less competent get a lot of TLC . . . because they seem to require it.

The Quaker Story at Its Best

The Quaker story of furthering the Inner Light can become an excuse for poor education, poor discipline, and poor management, but it can also bring out the best in school life. The Mott advisory meetings exemplify this value.[11] Held quarterly, they consist of a group of twelve faculty members discussing every student with academic or disciplinary problems. Other teachers besides the core twelve come and go during the discussion; some are present for the whole meeting, others only to talk about students of special concern to them. This is no gripe session, but a period of real knowledge-sharing, in which the adults, with an astonishing amount of humor and sensitivity and very little in-fighting, do their best to understand, but not to excuse, students' behavior and to come up with practical solutions to their problems.

Although the meeting is informal, the academic dean keeps it running smoothly. As each name on the list comes up, the student's advisor describes him or her, referring occasionally to notes. The presentation goes something like this: "Well, David is still a problem. He has an F in American history from not turning in his work, a D in Track II Math, a C- in physics. He seems to be doing okay in his other courses. This kid is just too easygoing. He has the capacity to do well in everything, but he can't seem to focus. We've talked about it, and he admits he doesn't study well. We had him in monitored study hall most of last year, and it helped. At least he didn't spend all his study time socializing. So I think we should put him back there again."

After the advisor's presentation, other people give their opinions about David. The academic counselor: "I think monitored study hall really was a big help to him; he thought so, too. He needs to have study guidelines laid down for him." David's dorm head: "He doesn't misbehave in the dorm, but he sure isn't working. His room is a real social center." Another dorm resident: "I've had a little trouble getting him to keep the noise down, but he was good about being quiet once I spoke to him. He's never rude." David's English teacher: "I want to say that he's doing very well in English, especially compared to last year. I don't think he's getting enough sleep, though; he's fallen asleep several times in class." Soccer coach: "You'll all be glad to hear that he's performing extremely well for me, and not just as a player but as a supportive member of the team."

Student after student is discussed in this straightforward, caring way, and their behavior is analyzed: "She's always testing the limits." "He's in his thirteenth year of school and sick of being institutionalized." "I find him brilliant, but he won't work because he's so afraid of failing." Frequently the conversations focus on students' relationships with their parents: a girl's mother didn't have time to come to Parents' Day and sent her secretary instead; a boy's mother just died after a long illness and his father is an alcoholic; kids' parents are divorcing; others are having problems with stepparents. There is much affectionate laughter, as well as exasperation, over some of the incorrigibles on the list. As sensitive to extenuating circumstances as the teachers are, however, their analyses contain little wishy-washiness. They tend to fall back on psychological counseling, sometimes rather desperately, but they do not offer this step as an excuse for ignoring reality. Teachers say bluntly that someone "hasn't cracked a book," "needs a swift kick," or "stinks of marijuana." The praise that balances these forthright comments sounds genuine: a kid may be failing but is good in chorus, helps her dorm mates, deals with adults more maturely than she did last year.

The academic dean moves the discussion along, pushing the group to make recommendations. "So we agree to keep him on the problem list and assign him to monitored study hall, and I'll write a letter to his parents saying that if he continues this way he won't graduate." Other specific follow-ups include notes to teachers, meetings with the headmaster, tests for learning disability, a stint in disciplinary study hall, a special tutor, therapy. The process falters only when the committee is faced with a student who has been officially threatened with expulsion. There is a moment of silence, a kind of collective holding of the breath, when the word *expulsion* comes up. Then several people dive in to try to find an alternate solution.

These sessions are like a Quaker narrative unfolding, with the story's protagonists working toward a common goal. In the teachers' and administrators' respect for each other and attempt to reach a consensual decision, in their shared affection for a student or sympathy with a dorm resident's problems, in the straightforwardness of the advisors' reports, and in the lack of animosity among committee members one can see the Quaker virtues of equality, community, simplicity, and peace being devoted to the search for that of God in every one of the teenagers under discussion.

The Military Virtues at the Schools

Loyalty

Loyalty is the preeminent military virtue because loyalty to country, commander, and comrades forms the basis of so many other soldierly qualities: courage, obedience, selflessness, pride. The military-school faculty envision loyalty as owed to the school and to the ideals it seeks to uphold. One administrator at Pershing called the feeling of deep attachment to the academy the "Pershing mystique." When asked what was expected of student officers, the commandant of cadets at Sherman answered unhesitatingly, "I expect them to be loyal to the policies of the school. By the time they are seniors in high school, if they can't support the school program, they should admit it and resign their command."

Students are tremendously attached to the military academies, and most are eager to preserve the traditions that they consider crucial to the success of the military program: the plebe system, the drills and parades, the JROTC classes in leadership, the uniforms. "The school is built on tradition, and all the tradition has to do with the military," said a Pershing sophomore. He admires the plebe system because it reinforces unit loyalty. "The Old Men . . . always told us, 'If someone picks on you from another unit, tell us, because that's not their job, it's our job.' They said . . . they were there to stick up for us. . . . I've never had any brothers or sisters, and now I have a huge family." Another Pershing cadet, a freshman athlete who was a member of Band—a separate military unit—said that many of his athlete friends had urged him to switch units, since Band members were infamously bad at sports. But he staunchly insisted that Band cadets were "the best" and had a lot of unity, too. "Even the meanest guy in the unit stood up for a Band freshman against a Trooper one time."

Another important kind of loyalty is that between subordinates and officers. The retired NCO who heads Jackson's military program said he expected student officers to earn the respect and loyalty of their fellow cadets. "It's easy to say . . . 'Let me tell you right now—I'm a company commander and you're going to respect me,' and that doesn't mean anything. You can never demand that anybody respect you; we would hope that the officers would command the respect of their subordinates through their own actions, whether off campus or on campus." Cadets at the military academies do indeed feel this kind of respect for the best of their officers. At Pershing many looked up to the top-ranking cadet, battalion commander Tom Hurd. A freshman rejoiced at finally being allowed to drop the "sir" when talking informally to student officers but admitted, "There are certain people I sometimes still hesitate to call by their first names, the people I respect the most. Especially Tom Hurd, because he's always setting a good example." Another cadet, a senior private with too many demerits to get any rank, would have had every reason to resent Tom's success, but instead he called him "the nicest guy," mainly because "he's fair . . . not a hypocrite at all." Tom "expects you to do stuff that he'll do—that's what I really like. Like he's always all shined up, and if he's got 'em shined, he'll expect you to be shined." Admitting that Tom is "a goody-goody," the private nevertheless respected him for living up to the rules and thought other students did, too: "I don't think you could go up to anyone on this campus who wouldn't say he's a nice guy."

When asked what he thought the school had taught him, this senior private said, "Responsibility and respect . . . respect for the system, respect for your fellow man, respect for people older than you. It can go on and on, the respect, but especially respect for discipline. You discipline yourself to know what's right and what's wrong." Clearly he himself, with all his demerits, would not stand as the school's best example of someone who had learned to discipline himself, but he felt he had gained a lot of self-control during his years at Pershing. This loyalty to standards and to the people who uphold them represents a devotion to the system as a whole that many students expressed, in spite of their complaints about a particular rule or teacher. Erik Bergstrom, a platoon lieutenant at Sherman who was busted to private for a hazing incident in which he said he hadn't taken part, was committed to the military system despite the injustice he felt he had suffered. He believed that people came to the school "to learn about discipline," and even details like shining shoes were a vital part of that discipline, because "shining shoes teaches you to take care of the whole job, instead of just part of it. Who cares if you're awesome at rifle drill, because if your shoes aren't shined . . . you're going to look really bad." Discipline was important at Sherman because it was important in life, since "eventually you're going to be at a job where the details are going to matter."

At Quaker school kids are fond of friends, teachers, and the community as a whole, but they do not have the same devotion to their school and its traditions that military-school students have. They also have no equivalent to the military units—Band, Company A, Troop, and so on—in which to invest their loyalties. The only similar subgroups in a nonmilitary high school are the different "hang-out groups" and, as a Mott senior put it, "You've got the preppies, punk people, trendy-wendies, and all the rest, but most people move from group to group. Only a few people are confined by it."[12] Quaker students also treat their prefects with much less respect than cadets do their officers. A good prefect is rewarded with the trust of his or her charges, but not with heartfelt loyalty.

Competence

When a Mexican junior at Pershing was asked what she had learned there, she answered, "How anyone that works hard enough can get what they want through hard work. . . . In America everything is pretty fair and straightforward—if you work for it, you'll get it." This quintessential conservative credo, that hard work will bring success, prevails at all three academies. Sherman bills itself as a place "that trains winners." At Jackson, the headmaster considered his school a strict meritocracy; since competence was rewarded, you had only yourself to blame if you failed. First you "learn what it takes, and then, if you really want it, . . . go for it." He thought there were "too many people—not just cadets but adults—who are always blaming external factors for what are their own failings. It's always the system or someone doing something wrong, when in fact they haven't met the requirements."

All three schools had a number of competent cadet officers and NCOs. Each company included sergeants who assigned clean-up jobs, distributed supplies, and inspected rooms; lieutenants who coached drills, organized hall activities, recommended people for promotions, and trained plebes; and a first sergeant, executive officer, and captain who were in charge of shepherding between twenty and fifty cadets through each day's activities, from reveille to taps. One of the most professional NCOs was seventeen-year-old Lamont Sandler of Sherman Military Academy. Lamont was considered such an excellent first sergeant that, three months into the school year, he was suddenly taken away from his own company and put in charge of another, the most difficult of all the units. He said that the change had been hard but not unmanageable. His approach, he explained, had been to "go in there with a positive attitude, be very optimistic. . . . Now we're striving to be the best in the corps." Lamont's "ideal in life" was "to be the best you possibly can and then try to be a bit better." He described the care with which he handled company meetings, writing down what he was going to say beforehand and keeping his remarks as short and to the point as possible. He was proud that, although "I've not used my hands to discipline people this year" (a fault for which he had been put on probation the year before), cadets knew he was "tough." "They know I play football, they know I do 100 pushups a night, and when I drop them [discipline them by making them do a specified number of pushups on the spot], I go down with them, and I do twice or three times as many as they do."

At military school the desire for competence shades easily into an emphasis on competition. According to the headmaster, "Pershing is about initiative and striving and constantly seeking to be better." In other words, said another faculty member, "the youngster must thrive on competition." A similar point was made with less optimism by a cadet captain at Sherman. Asked what lessons the school had taught him, he said, "This will sound negative, but I think the main thing you learn is a sad lesson—that people are in a rat race, always competing with each other. This school has taught me the importance of cut-throat competition." At Jackson, the retired NCO in charge of military promotions encourages strenuous competition for rank among the students: "Junior and senior year are really tough because it's the old pyramid; you're getting closer to the top and those positions are getting fewer and fewer, up to the battalion commander who is sitting on the top." Ideally, there should be lots of cadets who are good enough to be considered for BC, "making it rough on us selecting someone." From the first day at Jackson, a cadet's primary goal should be "to wind up being battalion commander in his senior year, and to demonstrate that through the ninth, tenth, and eleventh grades—that he feels he's the best qualified and should be BC."

For the unit counselors at Pershing, who oversee companies of about fifty students each, the relationship between competence and competition, when well handled, is the best aspect of the military system. The students' desire for rank, said one counselor, "is an incredible motivating machine":

> You tell a kid that unless he gets his grade-point average up, he's never going to get a promotion and be an officer, and if he cares about that—and most of them do, even if they won't admit it—he will become a better student. It's just incredible how badly they want that stuff.

No matter how hard cadets work, however, not everyone can get to the top of the hierarchical pyramid, and several counselors regretted cadets' distress when they didn't achieve the rank they had worked for—and sometimes deserved—because someone else got it first. At military school, learning to live with failure is an important lesson. In the words of Sherman's commandant, "I'd like [cadets] . . . to learn disappointment: that life isn't just a bowl of cherries."

In Quaker classrooms and art rooms, on sports fields and stages, there are talented young people working hard and performing well, and the academic standard at Mott is higher than that at any of the three military academies. Nevertheless, striving for excellence is not emphasized at the Friends schools. A relaxed attitude toward excellence goes deeper than a mere distaste for awards. At Mott, where four years of art are required, students are encouraged to try lots of different media rather than acquire expertise in one. The baseball coach at Dyer, deeply frustrated, said, "The kids just don't care about sports. . . . The whole Dyer attitude is that winning isn't important as long as you're having fun." When a group of juniors were asked how they thought they had changed since they'd come to Mott, they all agreed that they'd become less competitive. One girl confessed, "I think I did get more lax. I mean, academically. I notice I can get away with a lot of things here." Perhaps that would have happened eventually at her old school, too, she said, but there she had cared about grades: "If I'd gotten a D in my public school I would have cried, but now I say, 'Oh well.'. . . And I say, 'Good for you,' if someone else gets an A." She wondered aloud, her friends nodding in agreement, whether the lack of competition at Mott was good for students: "I think it has to do with being a Quaker school and I think that's good; it's supposed to be that type of school. But it's also supposed to be a prep school: is it really preparing us?" Asked if Mott taught any vices as well as virtues, a key staff member said ruefully, "I'm going to sound old," and then echoed the juniors' concern: that Mott didn't "place a high enough premium on competence among the students":

I don't think we demand enough of them, so that they will be able to achieve at the level that they are capable of. We as a faculty are lax in enforcing our requirements on kids, from minor things to major things. We don't *demand* that they do homework here [or] that they do some of the things that we all agreed they should do—wear shoes in the hall, dress a particular way, and things like that.

He worried that students would leave Mott with the idea "that it's relatively easy to slide by" instead of taking away "a need for competence." He found it particularly puzzling that adults whose personal commitment to the school showed that they valued their own and their colleagues' competence and hard work did not communicate these values to students.

Selflessness

In the professional military, selfless service is owed to one's country, superiors, subordinates, and comrades. Ultimately, selflessness means willingness to die in battle. The military school's closest equivalent to this virtue is service to the school in a leadership position even at the cost of one's independence. First sergeants like Lamont Sandler at Sherman or Gail Callot at Jackson devote an enormous amount of their time to the students in their dorms. Gail had twenty girls to discipline, drill, and counsel; as she put it, "I'm a sixteen-year-old Mom"—and that to several girls whose real parents had refused to have them home. Student leaders sacrifice more than just time and fun. Chapter One quoted a leader among the Pershing girls who felt that because of her position she could never relax. Similarly, the highest-ranking girl at Sherman said, "I feel like I can't be myself here. . . . The person I'm supposed to be is perfect. I should be overbearing and domineering and on top of things all the time, but I'm not really like that. I like to compromise, but here I can't." This is a selflessness that entails a genuine sacrifice of a coherent identity. One of the Pershing BAs (short for both *bad attitude* and, more admiringly, *bad ass*), a senior with the rank of private and a reputation for hitting younger cadets, said, "Most people around here have two totally different sides. They try to be perfect around grown-ups, because so much is at stake. I'm probably one of the few people that doesn't try to act different to make the grown-ups happy—and I have no rank!"

Promotion of selflessness as a virtue at military school can lead to glorification of suffering. At Pershing, for example, where only boys are cadets, the military system is closely linked both to pride in suffering and to a sense of manhood. This was clearly demonstrated in the 1970s, when girls were first admitted. Then, as now, the cadets' graduation from the academy involved a ceremonial passing of a sword from the headmaster to the battalion commander and then on from senior to senior. A woman teacher who was involved in Pershing's transition to coeducation remembered that when it came time to plan the first graduation for both sexes, the cadets were adamant that

the girls should not be given the sword . . . because they hadn't suffered . . . the way the boys had. There was a great suffering theme there that intrigued me, and I think it's still there. In other words, "We have to get up early and stand out in the cold, and we have to march, and that's all part of suffering, and we love it" sort of thing, you know. A sort of a stoicism.[13]

Even without a plebe system and military discipline, however, Pershing girls feel that they, too, suffer. One senior mentioned a talk given by an early graduate of the girls' school who had compared Pershing to Vietnam. The senior laughed over the extremeness of the comparison but nevertheless saw truth in it: "Of course it's not anywhere near that drastic, but when you graduate you have a kind of bond, because you've been through the same thing, you've been through leaving home and the rules and regulations." For the girls at Sherman and Jackson, who are cadets, stoicism is a central lesson. A Sherman sophomore said the school had taught her "how to be able to take things. . . . A lot of times I'm exhausted and fed up, but I'm not going to give in."

The bond created by the shared suffering experienced in military school produces another kind of selflessness as well: the cadet's identity as a member of the group becomes prominent, while his or her

sense of individuality recedes. As a plebe, recalled one Pershing senior, you are called "pond scum and low life and dirt." At the same
time that you are being denigrated, however, you are being encouraged to seek the support of the other new cadets:

I realized that while other people were out doing things they wanted to do,
we were washing the floors and getting ready for GI [general inspection], and
it was really a time to be together, and all the new cadets became a tight unit.
. . . Some of those guys I still hang around with after four years.

Not all the selflessness experienced by the cadets is tied up with
matters of military discipline; some of it also has to do with the
tremendous pressure they are under from their parents, teachers,
counselors, and coaches to perform well as scholars, athletes, and
leaders. One Pershing counselor worried a great deal about the stress
the cadets in his unit endure. In the name of "standards," he said, "we
bring them in here, beat the hell out of them, and ship them out. . . .
These kids have seen more stress! I tell you one thing, they leave here
so battle-ready, it's frightening. If anyone is ready for a tough position
in life, where there are tough choices and no clear-cut answers, it is
our kids." They do not have the time to work equally hard at everything, yet "each one of those coaches or teachers is going to say, 'Do
my thing.'" This counselor feels that although Pershing has "a bunch
of average to above-average kids who really work pretty hard," it is not
a school that attracts or produces top-level scholars. Many parents,
unfortunately, don't recognize this:

The parents are trying to make their kid into an academic stud, and it's not
going to happen. The kid is just never going to be number one in his class; he
can't. . . . As for my role, I sit there a lot of times and say, "You're right, you
did the best you could; feel good about it. And even though I'm asking you to
do this awfully early in life, be mature enough to understand that people can
make unreasonable demands of you."

Students at Quaker schools also suffer stress: they have tests, term
papers, soccer and field hockey games, play rehearsals, and other
commitments that sometimes tear them apart. But none of them
shows the kind of selfless devotion to duty exhibited by some of the
cadets. In addition, not one adult or teenager at Mott, Fox, or Dyer
suggested that suffering is productive for students. They are taught
that it is important for them to learn about others' suffering, and this

apparently makes an impression on a number of them. Charlie Mc-Dowell, head of Mott's religion department, said, "It seems like John Woolman [an eighteenth-century American Quaker who opposed slavery] is consistently the one who really grabs students and makes them think, because he is so willing to take suffering upon himself, as his personal way of avoiding contributing to evil." And a sophomore girl thought one of the benefits of going to Mott was that "the things you study make people liberal. I don't mean exactly open-minded, but aware of the point of view of those who are suffering. . . . In English class, for example, we read *Black Boy, To Kill a Mockingbird, I Know Why the Caged Bird Sings*: books that make you sensitive to others' needs." But selfless sacrifice and suffering were not expected of the students themselves. In fact, they were encouraged to feel that the school was a very safe place. Said one Mott teacher, "I tend to view the students here—with quite a few exceptions, but if I can oversimplify—as somewhat spoiled, somewhat coddled by us. The world is colder and crueler than we let our kids know."

Integrity

At Jackson, a teacher has a quote on her wall: "Confidence, once lost or betrayed, can never be restored again to the same measure." The importance of being honest is enshrined at Jackson—and at the other two military academies—in the form of a cadet honor code by which all students promise to abide: "I will not lie, cheat, or steal." If a cadet is caught breaking this code, he or she goes before a student honor council, which tries the accused cadet and, if he or she is found guilty, recommends an appropriate punishment to the commandant. At Pershing I saw the honor council try two cadets. One was a new sophomore accused of stealing several books and a hat insignia from friends. He sat in front of the council and, in a voice that could barely be heard, tried to defend himself, saying that he had merely borrowed the books and pin. The officers who were trying him did not believe him and berated him for the theft. "There is nothing this school hates more than a thief. Thieves are the lowest people on the totem pole. You destroy the sense of unity so the cadets can't pull together," said one. "You've got a hard row to walk now," another told the boy. "Everyone in the unit looks at you as a thief and a liar. When you walk into the shower, that's what they see. What are you going to do about that? You have to take responsibility for your actions."

The second cadet to come before the court was a four-year senior who was supposed to have taken $10.00 from a friend in his unit and then, when challenged, to have lied about how he had acquired the money. Discussions among the honor representatives before the accused cadet entered the room indicated that they were not only convinced he had committed this theft but also believed he was responsible for past thefts in his unit that totaled hundreds of dollars. They recommended his expulsion. From what the honor reps said, it was clear that stealing from members of one's unit was considered not only a crime but a terrible betrayal of trust. They could scarcely contain their anger against the accused senior; "I want to nail him; I want to punch him," railed one boy.

A more abstract form of integrity than the injunction not to lie, cheat, or steal is preached and practiced at the military schools. This involves a view of life as an honest exchange, where good behavior is rewarded and bad behavior punished. "If you break the rules, you pay for it" is a disciplinary theme heard frequently at all three schools, and from no one said more clearly than the retired general who headed Jackson. "The military system . . . impresses upon the young the idea that if they don't obey the rules and regulations, they pay a price," he explained, prior to listing the different types of punishments practiced at the school. As a result of this philosophy, the academies teach that one of the most virtuous actions a student can take is to own up—in other words, to play fair in the system of honest exchange and take his or her due punishment. Lieutenant Duncan Graham, the idealistic commandant of cadets at Pershing, felt strongly about the importance of confession. He worried that the military code he believed in was "not translating very well" into the school environment, since it was such a "demanding set of values by which to run your life." And yet he took hope from "the fact that people are saying, 'Yes, I did it and I'll take my lumps.' And telling the truth. . . . That's what this is really all about."

Many of the students like this emphasis on fairness, because it means that they know where they stand. It makes sense that if you break the rules (or, some would say, get caught breaking the rules), you pay a forfeit. As a girl at Pershing said, "It's up to you [to do your homework and clean your room], and if you don't do it, you pay the consequences, not anybody else. You learn that here." One of the most popular cadets at Jackson said something similar when asked how he had changed as a result of being at the school: "I've learned to discipline myself, and to accept what I do as my own. Like, if I get in trouble, it's not a matter of 'Well, it was his fault because he made me do it.' I've learned that if I do something, it was my actions that brought it about."

Although Quaker schools have no honor code, lying, cheating, and stealing are—not surprisingly—serious offenses there as well. Yet there is much less emphasis on the "honest exchange" view of life. Most adults do not seem to expect students to confess to wrongdoing and take their punishment; dorm heads hope students will tell their problems to the prefects and do not ask prefects to betray these confidences. Students, too, do not place the same value on the importance of paying the price for one's actions. At Dyer, when the students responsible for stealing a school video recorder were finally discovered, the dean refused to reveal the culprits' names to anyone, teacher or student. Teachers were angry, but a number of students agreed with the dean's decision, such as the girl who said that she didn't want to know who the thieves were, because it would destroy the unity of the school. Said another girl, "Until I know what happened, I can't judge. . . . [If they were known,] the thieves wouldn't be ostracized. They should have been punished, but they're probably not bad people, or at least no worse than anyone else."

Pride

Military pride is the outcome of practicing the other four military virtues, and it should show in a soldier's bearing, enthusiasm, and esprit de corps. One way the professional military instills this pride and sense of unity is by putting its new members through rituals of shared suffering that make them feel toughened and transformed. The military academies attempt something similar with their plebe systems. Cadets carry away from this rite of initiation a pride in themselves for having endured it and a sense of comradeship with their fellow sufferers. When asked how he had changed, a junior at Pershing answered, "I have a new respect for myself; it's a pretty big thing to go through a plebe system, being put through the torment and saying, 'I survived this and here's what I have to show for it.'" But simple endurance is not all the students are proud of. Many of them—especially the high-ranking cadets but also some of the less successful ones—are proud of their units and of their school and its traditions. A tough Sherman captain who was planning to join the marines upon graduation articulated this pride very clearly:

There's a feeling that you get . . . after Sunday parade when you're standing there waiting to see who won the parade. And all of a sudden they say your name. . . . There's just this feeling inside of you: " . . . *Yes*, my company did it! We won, we were good, we were the best out there today." And it's really a good feeling when your parents are out there . . . watching you. There's no other feeling like it in the world.

Lamont Sandler, the top-notch Sherman first sergeant, is proud, too, and his pride in the school, his company, and his ability to command is bolstered by his pride in his family and his Native American heritage. He plans on a military career because it is a tradition in his father's family, and he feels "it's the least I can do to live up to my name." On his mother's side he is an Indian:

People here think Indians weave baskets or something and live okay, but lots of Indians are living worse than in Harlem or the South Bronx. . . . But still . . . [they] stand tall, everything they do they are very proud of. Pride! I have a picture in my room of Sitting Bull, and the expression on his face and in his eyes—you can just look at him and see all that strength and pride and power and loyalty to his people and himself. He was great.

Both of these Sherman cadets have high rank, which could explain their pride, but even students without prominent leadership positions feel proud of their accomplishments. Explained one Jackson girl, "I say, 'Yes ma'am, no ma'am'; I feel proper now. . . . When I go back home I see how much better I am than a lot of the kids I used to hang out with. I'm not a low-life scum anymore."

In Quaker-school admissions catalogues and among teachers, there is a great deal of talk about bolstering students' self-esteem or bringing out their Inner Light, but little mention of pride. Pride is not a Christian virtue; Quakers are more concerned with the practice of humility. Mott's Charlie McDowell tried to explain the value of humility to his Quakerism class. "The kids in Quakerism were asking the other day, 'Why do all these people like John Woolman and George Fox think humility is important? Why is being rich an impediment and being poor supposed to be good?' Those are really important issues." Mott prefect and athlete Mike Dugan felt Mott had taught him to be more humble. "I have this incredible pride and cockiness. Not incredible, it's getting better." People have told him that his ego is a problem, and "that's blatantly obvious, even to myself." Mike says the challenge is trying to figure out "when I'm going overboard and looking for attention and when I'm just happy about where I am." He thinks "there is a pressure here to be over-humble, but I don't know if it's Quakerism or Mott." Yet he praises the school's efforts to tame his ego. For example, not being allowed to join a varsity team as a freshman, despite his skills as a player, taught him "that I needed to be a bit more humble than I was."

The Military Story:
Shouldering Responsibility

A *Struggle for Success*

At Quaker schools, the goal of bringing out the Inner Light applies to adults as well as adolescents, both of whom reject the idea of self-transformation in favor of nurturing what is believed to be already within. In contrast, the military-school project applies exclusively to the adolescents and emphasizes change. By learning to be loyal, competent, selfless, honest, and proud, a cadet becomes a leader and a bearer of responsibility. The focus is on acquiring something external to the individual: manners, rank, a code of behavior. A cadet is transformed through what he or she learns to do: stand straight, follow and give orders, keep a clean room, polish brass and shoes, be punctual, be courteous, obey the honor code. As one long-time Pershing teacher explained, "I've always felt Pershing . . . took an average kid, and turned him into an exciting person. . . . I've seen kids here do things . . . better than adults could do them: make good decisions, command, persevere . . . and I can only attribute it to the system." The key lesson the system teaches is responsibility, as both students and adults said again and again. The Pershing counselor who called the military system "a tremendous motivator" felt that it had "nothing to do with right face and left face and the manual of arms"; rather, it was a matter of "some kids being responsible for other kids." He called it "a kind of civic-mindedness" that one seldom found in the world outside the school. "In fact, very often the kids come here with values that are diametrically opposed to ours. But our values are spelled out explicitly in the Code of Conduct, and if we reinforce . . . [them] with all the goodies that we have to offer, the kids can change."

For those who care about it—and the majority of the students do—the goal of learning to shoulder responsibility means becoming a person others look up to, who gives orders and has power. At the very least it means becoming a different kind of person. A new Sherman sophomore, a huge, tough-talking boy who intimidated almost everyone, had been "marching tours" (marching back and forth in the yard as a punishment) every weekend since his arrival at the school because, as he said more sadly than proudly, "I'm bad. . . . I can't control my temper. . . . I talk garbage to everybody—I have a street mind." Yet he felt he was improving:

I've learned to listen to people and do what they say. . . . This school will make me make something of myself. . . . I don't really like not having friends—I try to please everybody. . . . I cried the first day I was here, but . . . I know it's good to be away from the trouble in the street. . . . What's going to enable me to stick it out is if I get rank. I'm making over 80s in all my classes. My father told me he was proud of me!

Another Sherman sophomore said, "Being here—it's like a prison without bars. . . . It will straighten me out."

While Quaker-school students emphasize being able to be themselves, cadets' statements show that they want to transform themselves. During her years at Jackson, first sergeant Gail Callot had given up her punk appearance and attitude, because "I've understood that you can't be rebellious all your life, especially in a military school! You've got to kind of conform. . . . I've blended in." When asked, "Do you feel like you've changed on the inside?" she answered, "I have changed. . . . I learned to accept the fact that I have to go along with society. Before, I used to say, 'Well, if people don't like the way I am, that's just too bad.'" Then she said something that few Quaker-school students would ever say: "My values haven't changed much. I've just accepted that I can't just be me."

Adults at the three academies echo these themes of transformation and self-control. Jackson's Henry Sedgefield, a retired army major, has seen a number of students through bad times and helped them change. One of them is Chip Lang. "When Chip came here I thought, 'Boy, here's trouble.' But he got himself turned around. He comes from . . . a real problem family. I've helped him arrange to go to college on the National Guard GI Bill, and he's going to a good college. Now he thinks he wants to be a career officer. . . . It makes me feel good." According to Chip, "Who's helped me the most while I've been here is Major Sedgefield. . . . He has a lot of patience and he always wants to help, but he won't take any crap." Although Major Sedgefield didn't know it, he had even provided Chip with a long-term goal:

It sounds kind of dumb, but I want to go into the army for twenty years and then come back and teach here, because I want to take over Major Sedgefield's job. Because he's helping kids like me, who have really no sense of what they are going to do in their lives at all, and turning them around to where they have something to shoot for.

Adults and adolescents at military academies use words and phrases like *respect, duty, the system, the chain of command, having a positive attitude, setting an example,* and *keeping up standards,* all of which reflect the desire to live by a code of behavior. Pershing's headmaster talks about "reaching for a star"; the head of Jackson, about "accountability." Said one Pershing senior, "They teach you to keep the right attitude and live by the right standards; basically, they program you to be a success. When you leave here, you have so much confidence and maturity. You can recognize a Pershing person anywhere, because they have such an air of assurance about them—people notice it."

Because striving to be a success is so important, one of the worst offenses in military school is to have a bad attitude—to be a BA. A person with a bad attitude doesn't even try to live up to what is expected of him or her. "A BA," explained a cadet, "is somebody who just doesn't do anything. You can be cocky and still have a military attitude—it's how you approach things. But a BA just keeps his attitude all the time." A freshman felt the BAs were bad for the morale in his unit. "The people who have bad attitudes I'd like to see get punished, to better them. Like, if your room's not clean or your shoes aren't shined, you should march tours. . . . If the military system's here, you should at least take it seriously."

Flaws and Failures

The military emphasis on an external standard of morality also has its negative aspects, even in the eyes of many of its supporters. One possible danger is an overemphasis on appearances. A long-time teacher at Pershing worried that "what some people think of as important—how shiny your shoes and brass can be—could cause us to lose sight of our academic priorities." A Sherman teacher felt the cadets had learned their lesson about appearances too well. "If you look at our kids, you'll see that they are very good at making you think one thing when something else is true," he said. "They are good actors, very good at presenting an image."

Another problem with teaching a strict set of standards is that sometimes the official code is too simplistic for the kinds of problems it has to address. A Pershing faculty member criticized the way leadership classes were taught, because the lessons seemed "canned," with all the teachers going through the same set of readings in the same way to reach the same conclusions, instead of "having confidence in the process of thinking itself." What emerged from the leadership readings was, in a nutshell, that "the Pershing Code of Conduct is the way we've got to behave." Such pat conclusions alienated students, particularly when the moral message was "the Boy Scout Oath writ large. They fight that: 'Well, I don't want to end up there.' . . . And I think they tend to view it as mickey mouse. 'That's what you want us to believe?—well, everyone knows that anyway.' . . . That you ought to be honest, that you ought to not steal, that you ought to not lie. 'Well, of course not.'"

Still another problem is that sometimes the system upholding the standards becomes a crutch rather than a base of support. An administrator at Sherman, a decorated Vietnam veteran, hoped that cadets who passed through the school became "more independent [and] politely assertive" but feared that "because the school is so structured, many of them become institutionalized and then they can only work in this kind of system."

Perhaps the most dangerous aspect to this emphasis on structure and continuity is the possibility that abuses will become self-perpetuating because they are part of the system, and abusers will be protected because they symbolize order. A cadet at Jackson and I discussed how another boy's arm had come to be broken a few nights before. The injury turned out to be the result of hazing, which the cadet felt had "stopped being a constructive thing" three or four years earlier, when the current officers were themselves new cadets. Since they "just got beat up for any stupid little thing, now when a new student comes and does stupid things, they give him a real hard time for it." I asked if anyone was going to lose rank for breaking the new boy's arm. My informant said he didn't know who'd done it, but he added that if it had been the BC, probably nothing would happen to him, but if it had been another boy who was a notorious troublemaker, "they'd probably bust him and try to kick him out." "Is that fair?" I asked. "I don't think so," he answered. "In a small way it could be, considering that the BC is supposed to have better judgment, so if he did it, he probably had a good reason. But I think they watch out more for their better students—better academically—because they make the school look good. So they try to keep them out of trouble."

The Military Story at Its Best

These statements show that the military-school emphasis on structure and standards can become simplistic, oppressive, and hypocritical rather than inspiring. At Pershing, however, I saw a military ceremony that showed how much the system can teach: pride, enthusiasm, hard work, team spirit, determination, poise. This ceremony is "BCI" (Biennial Corps Inspection), the official formal inspection of the school's JROTC program by a group of military professionals, who determine whether the school will get an honor rating from the army. The inspection itself takes only part of a day, but preparation takes weeks. It is a project that the unit counselors are told to "let the kids handle."

In the two weeks before BCI, drills, parades, and inspections of uniforms and barracks were conducted with even greater rigor than before, and faults were analyzed with an eye to timely correction. By Friday night, with the inspection only a weekend away, Pershing crackled with excitement. Few cadets were hanging out in the snack bar or whispering on the mess-hall steps with their girlfriends; most were in the barracks, straightening their rooms, checking their uniforms, and telling new cadets horror stories about the strictness of the inspection team. Rumors spread of a marine drill sergeant showing up to inspect the ranks, of army officers who would run white-gloved hands across surfaces to reveal dirt in the rooms. By Sunday the mood was euphoric. Walking around late on Sunday afternoon, I saw cleaning going on everywhere. Boys swarmed over the dorms, wiping windows, mopping stairs, raking yards, carrying out trash. Music blared from countless sound-boxes and stereos, and adult supervisors lay low. Five boys sat on the steps of their dorm, laughing and talking and polishing their shoes and belt buckles. Cans of shoe polish and bottles of Brasso were everywhere, but saliva was also much in use. A boy spat carefully onto his shoe and rubbed that spot for at least a minute before spitting again. Through the open door of another dorm I saw water cascading down the stairs, and from within I could hear boys sliding gleefully on the wet hall floors.

Eight o'clock on Monday morning: the formal inspection begins. Battalion Commander Tom Hurd and his staff arrive early at the JROTC building, looking magnificent with colorful sashes and swords setting off their dress uniforms. They are surprisingly self-possessed, talking quietly among themselves and with members of the visiting team of military men. The retired colonel who heads the JROTC program is there, looking correct but relaxed—he and his staff have been through this countless times before, not only at Pershing but in the service. Shortly after eight the briefing begins: speeches and slide shows about Pershing from the BC and several cadet captains. Tom is calm, serious but not stiff, and beautifully organized; his fellow cadets' presentations are almost as smooth. Afterwards comes the inspection of the barracks, which smell overpoweringly of lemon-scented furniture polish. The rooms look immaculate, but cleanliness is not the only requirement: the military inspector immediately spots an unlocked rifle lock in one room. The mood is not punitive; the cadets conducting the inspector through the dorm are earnest but not scared, and this inspector is not the terrifying martinet that rumor has led the plebes to expect.

Finally it is time for the parade. Each unit marches out onto the field in turn, and all 390 cadets show their paces: attention, present arms, parade rest, and so on. Then the entire battalion marches past the reviewing stand. Not just the visitors but the headmaster, faculty members, and all of the counselors are on hand to see them pass. After the parade most of the kids are done for the day—they break ranks and run off, yelling and jumping with relief. All that are left are the precision marching, driving, and riding performances by the honor organizations of the infantry, artillery, and cavalry units. These are executed with pizazz; the kids have been practicing for months. The day is supposed to end with the BC and his staff receiving the inspection team's formal comments on the cadets' performance. This is, sadly, a total letdown; the military team leaves early, after just a few words with the head of the military department, so the cadets get no feedback. The colonel, the counselors, and the commandant are furious for the kids' sake at the inspectors' insensitivity, but it seems that nothing can dampen the cadets' spirits. By evening many of them are punch-drunk with excitement, relief, and lack of sleep. I hear them telling and retelling stories about the events of the day, creating legends that will have become traditions by the time the next BCI rolls around.

Here is a narrative in the military moral tradition that depends not on the adults, the official upholders of the virtues, but on the adolescents they have worked to transform into responsible leaders. Without the cadets' loyalty, competence, selflessness, integrity, and, above all, pride, the inspection would never have been such a success—nor would it have given the students so much pleasure.

Two Visions of Change

The idea that life in a moral community is part of an ongoing story implies that some sort of change must be taking place. Obviously, at both sets of schools adolescents grow and mature, and in the process they are influenced by the traditions that surround them. But that maturation process is envisioned differently in the two traditions— and the visions are to some extent illusions. An analysis shows that change is a moral imperative in both environments. But the kind of change that is acclaimed is not always that which occurs.

Quaker Schools: Changing the Community
to Meet Members' Needs

One of the goals of Quakerism is to change society to make it a better place for nurturing the Inner Light in all people. This is why Quaker virtues—equality, community, simplicity, and peace—describe an environment, not an individual. Education at Friends schools encourages a process of eternal searching. "Fish gotta swim; birds gotta fly. Man gotta sit and wonder why, why, why." Kurt Vonnegut's words, written on a blackboard as a thought for the day, sum up a tenet of Quaker education that members of the faculty take to heart. They are constantly questioning the givens of the school community. Why can't we involve students in a work camp in Nicaragua? Why don't we change the schedule to make classes longer? Why not start a drug-counseling program? The emphasis is on improving the school, not the students. A Dyer student rejected the idea of moral socialization completely. When asked what lessons she thought the school wanted her to learn, she snorted with contempt. "I don't think there are any lessons. They want you to leave [here] with yourself. I don't think they want to influence anything . . . they just want to let you develop in the way you are going to develop and show you how to take care of yourself."

The clearest expression of this ideal of questioning conventions and creating a community that nurtures the best in everyone came from the headmaster of Mott. When asked what decisions had been particularly difficult for him, he told about his support of a gay woman teacher, the first faculty member in the school's history to come out. She wanted her lover to be allowed to live with her in her on-campus apartment. Mott rules say that unmarried teachers cannot live together on campus; yet these two women, who have been together for years, cannot legally marry. The headmaster described his conflicting goals: to enforce school policy consistently, keep a good teacher at the school, protect Mott from criticism, be able to defend his decision to the board, and also ensure that everything was "done in a way that's constructive, so that everyone's learning from it." In the end, the teacher's partner moved officially into the school apartment. "It's a challenge and a difficult thing that we probably haven't seen the end of," concluded the headmaster. "But . . . why the hell take up all this time and money running a Friends school if you are not going to try to struggle with real issues?" He felt that he and the school as a whole had "an obligation to help teachers and students celebrate their lives and their skills." The other side of that obligation was

to help people struggle with the pain in their lives and do it in a way that . . . produces wholeness rather than more brokenness. Anybody in this society who's gay has got a little more struggle than someone who's not, and . . . anyone who has the courage to struggle publicly needs to be supported by the people who care about them. So then that's what the school is all about. Whether we do it well or not, that's what we're trying to do.

His story expresses well the official Quaker-school attitude toward growth and change. From a Friends perspective, growth consists of finding out who you are and learning to show your real self to the community. It is then the responsibility of the community to receive you lovingly and, if necessary, adapt to fit your needs.

Military Schools: Changing Students to Meet Community Standards

Members of the Quaker-school community see themselves as faithful to the Inner Light and critical of the school. The majority of the staff and students at military academies try to be faithful to the traditions of their school and are critical of those who do not live up to them. Military academies are not as concerned about process as they are about product: they want to produce an adolescent who is as loyal, hard-working, responsible, brave, honest, and proud as possible, and they use the military system as a framework for meeting that goal. Cadets did not talk about learning to question; over and over again, they described learning "respect": respect for their officers, their teachers, the rules and traditions of the school, and themselves. A Sherman teacher said, "Our main goal is to mold the students," and students at the three academies do see themselves as molded by their education. Many described with great pride the kind of person they had become during their years away from home: more studious, more responsible, less of a troublemaker, better-mannered, more mature. "I've got a different outlook on life," one of Jackson's cadet captains said confidently.

The corollary to changing oneself is accepting the school. A Pershing cadet explained this succinctly: "People here complain about each other, not about the school. Because the school's the school; it's not going to change, and you can't fight it, because you're not going to win. That's a lot of energy wasted. You might as well go along with it and see what you can learn." For some teachers the apparently unchanging nature of military schools is frustrating. "I'm a tinkerer," said one. "I like to try different things." But at Pershing, he found, the attitude was often "we've always done it this way, and this is the way we're going to do it." But many other faculty members see loyalty to the past as an attempt to maintain high standards in a world that has lost them. Change occurs at the military academies—in the past twenty years, all three have begun to admit girls, for example—but change must occur in the context of respecting the past. For Pershing's headmaster, this is a matter of preserving values: "You can't attack the core tradition."

The Two Visions Compared

These two different visions of change stem from the Quaker belief in an internal morality and the military belief in external standards. The Quaker schools focus on conscience, for which a nurturing environment must be created, while the military schools focus on character, which must be transformed to match institutional requirements. Another way to describe this difference is to say that Friends schools support the "real" self and military schools, the "role" self. According to the Quaker viewpoint, adults' and adolescents' first identity is as persons, whose unique qualities must be preserved, while, according to the military viewpoint, adults' and adolescents' first duty is to learn to fulfill a carefully defined role as teacher or cadet.[14]

 Although their goals are different, both sets of schools probably achieve similar results: they change the receptive students, teach another group to blend into the environment, and drive a third and smaller group to open rebellion. Ironically, however, in spite of their official aversion to transforming the characters of their students, Friends schools are probably more effective agents of change than are the military academies. No matter how strongly Friends insist that they wish to leave the individual intact, the kinds of demands their schools make on adults and students are bound to affect the inner self. In a place where the most valued learning devices are speaking out in Meeting about your innermost concerns, keeping a journal, participating in group counseling sessions, presenting your ideas in class, helping your peers with personal crises, arguing with teachers and fellow students about current events, and questioning the status quo, your "real" self is a constant target for analysis and, in spite of genuine attempts to respect differences, for judgment and criticism. A similar process in utopian communities is called "mortification," which involves "the exchanging of a former identity for one defined and formulated by the community."[15]

At military school, by contrast, although the staff say they wish to change the individual, the demands the system makes can be met largely by changing appearances and behavior. If cadets learn to wear their uniforms correctly, keep their rooms clean, salute, be on time, and demonstrate a positive attitude when asked to do something, then they are perceived to have changed—as indeed they have, but perhaps not in a way the school would approve of. Learning to look military is considered by some students to be, not a transformation, but a form of "beating the system." Sherman cadet Erik Bergstrom—a strong supporter of the military—explained that the kids who suffered most in the hands of NCOs and officers were the ones who hadn't mastered this lesson:

They didn't learn how to beat the system. . . . It's like this. If the first sergeant is complaining about your shoes and your brass and your uniform, well, make sure that next time your shoes are shined. Then he can complain about everything else, but he can't complain about your shoes. . . . The next time, have your brass *and* your shoes shined, and eventually, you get to the point where you do everything. Everything he complains about, it's done. Then one day, he's going to be in a bad mood and think, "Hey, let me pick on that . . . kid," and he walks into that kid's room and his room is perfect, everything is done. What's he going to yell at him about?

Of course, Erik went on to say, the sergeant could still try to "get" the kid for "military respect." But "all you have to do is stand up at attention, keep your mouth closed, and say 'Yes, Sergeant; no, Sergeant; no excuse, Sergeant.' And that's it. You just beat the system. It's as simple as that."

The practice of the moral traditions at the two sets of schools has been portrayed thus far as orderly and coherent: a story with a clear-cut plot and a moral message. The virtues structure school life: they define how to act, describe how relationships among individuals and groups should be conducted, and help determine how the business of teaching and learning should proceed. Under these conditions, it should be easy for the appropriate moral narratives to unfold smoothly at the schools. As Chapter Two has shown, however, there are inherent conflicts in the two traditions, conflicts in particular between individual and community, that seem to threaten the moral projects envisioned by their adherents. An analysis of the schools' visions of change has shown that harmonious coexistence can be the product of shared illusions as well as shared virtues. The following chapter shows that even shared virtues can be an illusion, since they mean quite different things to different people. To share the virtues is to debate them, and to debate them is, in the long run, to strengthen them. In the short run, however, controversy over the nature and practice of the virtues causes anger and pain. Chapter Four discusses the origins and consequences of conflict at the schools.

Chapter Four

Conflict as a Source of Strength

Commitment, Conflict, and Moral Rhetoric

The schools are communities that inspire commitment. Adults work long hours for little pay, teaching classes and coaching sports, presiding over meals and supervising dormitories. Adolescents, too, are deeply engaged in the schools. To understand this commitment, it is helpful to think of the boarding school as a utopian community.

The School as Haven and Mission

In reality, of course, the six schools are not utopias; to survive, they must be businesses, attracting new students each year by providing goods that parents want to purchase for their children.[1] Nevertheless, the schools' attraction for parents depends in part on educational programs built around what Rosabeth Kanter has identified as utopian ideals: perfectibility, purposefulness, a patterned existence, feelings of brotherhood, coherence as a group, and separation from the outside world.[2]

Kanter explained that "to develop maximum commitment in its members, a group must form a unity or a whole, coherent and sharply differentiated from its environment."[3] To experience this feeling of unity, members of the group must detach themselves cognitively, emotionally, and morally from their old lives and reinvest themselves in their new world. As committed members, their sense of accomplishment will come from tasks they perform within the group; their emotional attachments will be to group members, and their values will be those of the group. Something like this utopian reinvestment in a new life occurs when a young adolescent leaves family and friends to come to boarding school. Because the new school is now his or her dominant physical world, it becomes his or her mental world as well, the arena for all successes and failures. This utopian phenomenon is particularly visible in some of the cadets, for whom success as a student officer comes to seem of overriding importance. Utopian expectations are present to some degree in all the students, however, and in many of the teachers and administrators as well. Indeed, these expectations are sometimes stronger in the adults, since many of them remain at the same school for years; the students, no matter how involved they become, always know that their commitment is for a relatively short and clearly defined time period, which will end upon graduation.

Commitment to the school goes hand in hand with detachment from the world around the school. This is not simply a matter of restricting physical movement across boundaries, but of using moral language to build what Kanter, in discussing successful nineteenth-century utopias, called "psychic boundaries." These boundaries were "laid down in terminology that clearly distinguished the outside from the community, conceptualizing the community positively and the outside negatively." [4] Two common ways of differentiating "us" from "them" are by defining the community as a place of retreat, or as a place of service. [5] Boarding-school administrators use both kinds of moral rhetoric. On the one hand, boarding school is a haven, protecting students from the corrupt influences of the greater society; on the other hand, it is a place with a mission, setting an example of a better life and preparing students to challenge the world's corruption. The schools' headmasters are not naive or fanatical enough to believe that, with their small staff and few students, they can actually transform the world. Still, they see themselves as taking a stand against evil influences in the world by advocating and acting upon a different and better set of principles. [6]

This vision is most clearly articulated among the adults at Mott, because of that school's emphasis on questioning authority and presenting an alternative viewpoint. One teacher spoke for most of his colleagues when he said that he didn't want Mott's students to "go out there and conform to the real world. The pressures to conform are everywhere—it's better to raise the spirit of challenging in them." Charlie McDowell formulated the continual tension between a Quaker school and the outside world even more clearly. To him, a Friends school has a responsibility not to simply "rest on the laurels" of what Quakers have done in the past: "We have to be seeking truth, and working for peace and justice, and worshiping, and trying to put our faith into action, or we're not Friends." To abdicate this sense of mission is to settle for being "mostly white, well-heeled, well-intentioned Americans who are trying to be open-minded":

I think we're supposed to be something different from that. I think we're supposed to be people who are seeking God's will and trying to do it with our lives and trying to help society to do it, too. In all humility, I think that's what we should be doing.

Although the military academies do not place as high a premium on challenging the status quo, there, too, the idea prevails of former cadets as special actors in the world outside the school. A popular and respected Jackson senior said he believed the school was "trying to produce a person who can go out into society and make a positive input, whether on a large scale or a small scale, . . . people who know right and wrong and do right." Jackson's Major Sedgefield talked, only half jokingly, about students who were "going to go on and save the world."

Talking About the Virtues

This crusading impulse indicates that what Georg Simmel called "the positive and integrating role of antagonism" is an important source of communal spirit at the six schools, where to live according to the Quaker or the military virtues means to live in opposition to many of the values practiced by the outside world.[7] Of course, members of the two types of communities are antagonistic to different aspects of the world. Quakers, with their liberal ideals, oppose its strife and intolerance, whereas many former military professionals, as conservatives, decry its lack of discipline. Both, however, use moral rhetoric to emphasize the divisions between insiders and outsiders. This rhetoric "strengthens the resolve of the community and the clarity of its boundaries."[8]

Thus, it is important at both Quaker and military boarding schools not only to live by the virtues but to talk about them; indeed, it is by talking about them that one determines for oneself what they mean. Such talk is encouraged by the fact that moral rhetoric is invariably ambiguous. Words like *community* and *concern* or *loyalty* and *leadership* are powerful unifiers and boundary-creators precisely because they are so all-encompassing. Teachers and students know and use these words, and their frequent invocation serves a ritualistic purpose, separating the user from outsiders and drawing him or her closer to his or her fellow insiders. At the same time, the words inspire debate about their meaning and their application in a small community. This debate can be bitter and at times even seem to threaten the stability of the schools, but in most cases it is also stimulating. "Culture . . . thrives on adversity"; it not only offers models for how we should act but also gives us "things to worry about, to be anxious about, and thus also reasons for discourse, for efforts to interpret the meanings of the world and of [our] place in it."[9] For adults and adolescents at the schools, the moral traditions offer plenty to worry about.

It would be false to say that the traditions *cause* disagreements at the schools. Conflict is endemic to school life, and boarding schools in particular, despite their orderly appearance, are potentially explosive places. People living cheek-by-jowl, the adults poorly paid, the adolescents under constraint, are bound to clash. Arguments about faculty salaries, workloads, and housing, and about students' grades, recreational activities, and whereabouts are commonplace. A shared moral tradition can mitigate some of these conflicts, providing administrators, teachers, and students with a common purpose. When conflicts flare up, however, as they inevitably will, the traditions will fan the flames in a particular direction. For example, arguments over how strictly children should be punished arise at any school. But at a Quaker school these discussions become debates about the Inner Light, as teachers argue about how far they must carry their responsibility to nurture "that of God" in even the most recalcitrant student. Arguments about punishment at a military academy will address the importance of maintaining standards and setting an example. In both cases, because of the strength of the traditions, what would otherwise be a mere disagreement about policy easily becomes a moral dilemma.

The Four Types of Conflict

Chapter Two described the conflicts that are an inherent part of the two traditions. A study of the schools shows that conflict is not only part of the traditions, it is also a crucial part of what sustains them. Debates over goals and how to carry them out, clashes over priorities, differences in interpretation of the virtues: these keep the traditions alive in the minds of teachers and students. Key concepts like concern or leadership not only give the routines of everyday life a special meaning but also transform many of life's upsets, heightening their significance and their impact on the community. When disagreements over discipline, salaries, grading methods, and so on develop into moral conflicts, these seem to fall into four categories, each of which has deep roots within Quakerism and the military. The dividing lines between these categories are not always clear-cut, since all four have to do with differences in interpretation or application of the key virtues, and all four stem from the classic tension between individual and community. Nevertheless, many of the conflicts at the schools can be classified as one of these four types.

First, there are the debates and dilemmas that arise when the values of the materialistic outside world encroach upon the moral community. In this type of conflict, which I call "austerity versus privilege," voicing anger over worldliness reinforces the threatened virtues of simplicity and selflessness. Second, there are arguments over how to incorporate particular virtues into school policy in a fair and caring way. These I call "mission-versus-men" debates, in which members of the school community search for a way to carry out their moral mission without sacrificing individuals to principles. The third type of conflict, which I call "obedience versus initiative," involves reconciling personal desires with obedience to the community's de-mands. At times these demands are resisted because they restrict autonomous action; at other times, because they threaten subgroup intimacy. Fourth and finally, conflicts are generated by the overzeal-ous application of the moral traditions, when virtues are carried to perverse extremes and become vices. I call this type of conflict "mod-eration versus excess." All four types of conflict arise out of the attempts of students, teachers, and administrators to practice the virtues, and this shared purpose keeps the arguments from being purely divisive. Although they show the dark side of school life, these inner turmoils, acrimonious discussions, and angry confrontations also demonstrate the power of moral rhetoric and the strength of the virtues—in talk and in practice—to shape life at the schools.

Austerity Versus Privilege:
The Threat of Worldliness

Quaker-School Conflicts

Austerity is part of both moral traditions, stemming from the Quaker virtues of equality and simplicity and the military virtue of selflessness. An expensive private boarding school does not lend itself to the practice of an ascetic lifestyle, however, and this disturbs some adults, particularly at Quaker schools. At Mott, the wealth of most of their pupils causes teachers to worry that they may be perpetuating inequality rather than undermining it. As one young teacher said when asked if anything at the school disappointed her, "Something I haven't resolved yet is that I often feel that we're teaching the elite. Granted, we have a fair number of scholarships, but . . . there are a whole lot of underprivileged people in this country and in this world, and I don't know if teaching at Mott is enough." For people who worry both about doing enough for those in need and about communicating the importance of equality, teaching at a boarding school is a moral dilemma, since the school's exclusivity generates a rarified environment that, far from encouraging equality, convinces pupils of their superiority. The elite nature of prep-school education also worries Mott's headmaster. When asked if he thought the school taught students any vices, he answered, "The most damaging one we teach them is that we perpetuate a sense of privilege and of entitlement. . . . I think it's better here than at most private schools, but it's a problem. Kids who leave here don't know much about being poor and helpless."

Every teacher who recognizes this problem finds his or her own way to deal with it. The young teacher who thinks about the needs of the underprivileged feels that it is better for her, and for society, that she be productive at an elite school rather than ineffectual in the South Bronx. Others of her colleagues comfort themselves with the conviction that the upper-middle-class students they are teaching are more likely than poor students to become prominent members of society and will therefore be in a good position to apply Quaker values in the world. Charlie McDowell believes that Mott overcomes the disadvantage of riches—both its own institutional wealth and the wealth of its pupils—by "not just trying to educate people to go out and . . . make as much money as they can, but . . . educating them in the context of . . . Quaker testimonies: peace, simplicity, integrity, truth-telling, service." Another faculty member solves the problem by using the traditional Quaker response of setting a moral example. For herself and her husband, she says, "Being here [at the school] is a moral dilemma," because it constitutes upholding the status quo:

Here we are in this comfortable cozy place with not too many real moral dilemmas facing us, because we're not in touch with the poor, and sometimes we ask ourselves why we're here. I think one reason we're here is to present ourselves both among the students and the faculty, not as holier-than-thou at all—we don't feel that way—but as people who aren't going to buy a TV and spend thousands of dollars on our clothes and get every new gadget that comes along.

A life of simplicity is one response to the elite side of Mott, but it is hard to reconcile with the business of running a private school. Simplicity means forthrightness and dedication to the essentials; its advocates shun delicate compromises, concern for appearances, and the use of stratagems for raising money—all of which are necessary to the survival of a private school. As one Mott teacher put it, "I don't think the school can communicate simplicity when it is in many respects a business. . . . We have to be competitive in the marketplace and attract more customers, and simplicity is not something you can package and sell."

Nevertheless, many Quaker teachers, and even headmasters and school-board members, continue to try to resist the threat of worldliness. At Mott, for example, a retreat was held to allow board and faculty members to spend a day discussing several important policy decisions that had to be made. One was whether faculty chairs would be created for various academic fields, as a means of raising funds for improving teachers' salaries. Many were uncomfortable with the plan, because it would create a form of merit pay for the chair-holders, which was seen as damaging to the spirit of equality at Mott. In the course of the debate, one teacher called the idea of faculty chairs "a marketing gimmick that we feel is necessary for raising the money."

This led a board member to question the wisdom of the plan, saying to the assembly:

I'm concerned about this whole concept, because there are Friendly values and principles involved here. How can we reconcile the idea of these chairs with the Quaker value of simplicity? Why do we have to use a gimmick to raise these funds? I'm not comfortable with the idea of a gimmick.

At Fox, even more than at Mott and Dyer, a traditional tendency toward simplicity clashes with the realistic demands of the business of running a school. Fox has been a simple place for so long that having to worry about such worldly matters as attracting students and raising money is stressful for everyone. The year I visited the school was its first with a full-time director of development. According to the headmaster, twenty years ago the school didn't even have a director of admissions. The unspoken expectation in the past had been that God would provide. Over the years, however, the school has shrunk to half the size it had been in its heyday and has perforce become a more worldly place, which recruits students and seeks donations. Nevertheless, a serenity about money matters, even after ten years of operating in the red, continues to prevail among the administrative staff because of their deep trust in God. The apparent nonchalance of the headmaster in the face of possible economic disaster disturbed several teachers and led to bitter words. Yet he retained his optimism. He described how a key staff member, when she knew that money for paying school bills was short, would ask several other devout colleagues to pray with her and, "sure enough," the money would show up. "You hang around someone like that who, not in big flashy ways, but just in day-to-day simple things, depends a lot on prayer and her relationship with God to lead us through life, and you begin to see how that can be used in your own life."

The egalitarianism, single-mindedness, and focus on essentials—including religious faith—expressed by Friends at the three schools is their defense against the threat of worldliness. It also leads to conflict over the practical aspects of running a school. At Mott the person who represented worldliness was the business manager. No matter how hard he tried to be sympathetic to Quaker goals, he was perceived by many of the teachers as an enemy of the tradition, chiefly because of his preoccupation with money and efficiency. Like most enemies, real or imagined, he served to unite his fractious opponents among the faculty, sometimes causing them to take a more consciously Quakerly stance than they might have done without his presence.

Military-School Conflicts

The three military academies, with their greater emphasis on the importance of competition and achieving success in the world outside the school, do not pride themselves on their lack of worldliness to the same extent as their Quaker counterparts. Nevertheless, key military-school staff members take selflessness seriously, and traditional military selflessness, like traditional Quaker simplicity, does not fit easily into the prep-school pattern. Selflessness is the product of intense involvement with the group, of facing danger with buddies, of learning to discipline yourself and to put others first. These are the values that Pershing's commandant, Lieutenant Duncan Graham, wants to teach the cadets. Those values are not always compatible with the cadets' competitive instincts, however, or with the expectations of their parents, who are more eager to see their sons and daughters learn to be first themselves than help others achieve success. Selfless service does not seem to dovetail with self-development or with getting into a good college. Lieutenant Graham often worries that the messages he is trying to convey about the value of sacrifice do not get through the privileged environment of Pershing. At times, he said, he feels that cadet officers are accepting a lot of responsibility:

They do understand this idea of taking care of your men; I can see evidence of guys staying up all night with someone or looking out for them. Then, at the same time, they promptly go to the front of the chow line and go through ahead of the whole group and [are] very insensitive to what that says.

Selflessness is a lesson that war teaches by necessity; it is harder to communicate during peacetime, particularly at an elite school. One Pershing teacher has long observed Graham's struggle to communicate the values he learned in Vietnam. "It was there that the notion that the collective must take precedence over the individual became incarnate for him, because if you don't think that way, you don't survive." Graham once showed the teacher a famous photograph from the war and told him, "This is what it is all about." It is a picture of a group of badly wounded soldiers, being cared for by a very young man with a plastic spider on his helmet. "That picture is one of Duncan's totems, and it's a powerful totem." It represents the dedication to others that he wants cadets at Pershing to learn. Frequently, Duncan seems to be fighting a losing battle, but at least his struggle against the cadets' self-centeredness keeps the idea of sacrifice alive for them. "The youngsters . . . see that it is not talk with him," says Duncan's friend; "even if they can't follow it, they still respect it as something very real."

"Mission Versus Men": Reconciling Principles and Private Needs

Quaker-School Conflicts

No one at a Quaker school questions the merits of equality and peace; no one at a military school, the merits of competence and integrity. But too great a respect for principles can sometimes lead to a disrespect for persons, whereas too great a concern with individual needs can cause principles to be sacrificed. Trying to reconcile the two is the source of a great deal of private reflection and public debate at both sets of schools. At Dyer, more than at the other five schools, these tensions seem to polarize the entire faculty into two camps, who could be labeled "nurturers" and "hard-liners." For the nurturers, what is most important is that the school be a loving and tolerant community. For the hard-liners, community life demands that rules take precedence over individual freedom. It appeared to one hard-liner that "those who are in favor of individual expression without limits invoke 'community' against anyone who would require standards of whatever kind. But I don't think that's a very sound position. In fact, I think one could argue pretty strongly that successful communities are those that *do* have standards." The idea of being "a kind of community of tolerance" meant that students could be eccentric without being rejected by their fellows, and this he found praiseworthy. "But it isn't a philosophy that helps us to pull together."

One disagreement that arose between nurturers and hard-liners was over the application of the peace testimony. The goal of upholding peace as an ideal and promoting peaceful behavior in the school community clashed with the community's desire to show sympathy and understanding toward those who were violent. Dyer's chief bully, together with his little band of followers, goaded and tormented a number of students. Once, while working in the school kitchen, the bully got into an argument with another boy and taunted him until the latter, furious, picked up a kitchen knife, flew at his tormentor, and was apparently kept from stabbing him only by others in the kitchen who held him back. Several students independently described this incident, and none of them could understand why the knife-wielding student had not been dismissed from the school. Dyer preaches non-violence, but when one student tries to kill another, nothing happens—so the students complained. It turned out that the discipline committee, made up of students and staff, had considered expulsion but had relented because the boy had such a bad family situation that apparently no one would be willing to take him in if he were sent away from school. In this case nurturing clearly prevailed over the hard line, man over mission.

The peace testimony also gives rise to controversy at Mott. Although the division between hard-liners and nurturers is not as pronounced as at Dyer, there, too, peace lends itself to both styles of interpretation. On the one hand, many teachers believe that peace means taking a pacifist position on world affairs and working to encourage a politics of peace. This attitude is accompanied by a strong stance against violence, in the world at large and in day-to-day affairs. On the other hand, there are those who believe that peace is best furthered by caring deeply for that of God in each person, even in those who are violent, and by encouraging open-mindedness and independent thinking, which are the enemies of the kind of hatred that leads to wars. While in theory these two interpretations of peace are compatible, they clash in practice. There is, after all, a contradiction in trying with one breath to convince someone to adopt your own pacifist stance and with the next breath encouraging her to think for herself.

This dilemma surfaced for Charlie McDowell when he discovered during his first year at Mott that a military recruiter had been allowed on campus. This was not standard policy, but a student had expressed an interest in joining the army, and the recruiter was invited to come and talk to him and anyone else who was interested. McDowell felt that the recruiter's presence on campus was highly inappropriate. As he put it, "My feeling was and still is that one of the things that makes a Friends school distinctive is that there are principles for which we stand. . . . One of the ways we are different is the whole emphasis upon peace and the peace testimony." He thought the school's response should have been to tell the would-be soldier that, while he certainly had a right to pursue such a career, "we as a Friends school cannot conscientiously cooperate with you on that because we as Friends . . . would say you are mistaken, that this is not a good thing for you to do with your young life."

Charlie McDowell's principled response to the idea of an army recruiter on campus led to conflict. The headmaster and the academic dean got involved, and a meeting was held to discuss what should be done. The college counselors, who had originally invited the recruiter to Mott, felt hurt and offended that their judgment was being questioned. They, too, had taken a principled stand: they believed that responding to a student's needs and interests was important. But McDowell disagreed:

I thought about it over the summer, and I came back and talked to . . . the head of college counseling, and I said, "In the future, if there's a student seriously interested in joining the military, let me drive him to the recruiter and sit with him and hear what is said and talk with him on the way there and on the way back." And that's how it was resolved.

This is an example of a clash between principles and individual needs that lent itself to a clear and sensible solution. But not all such dilemmas are so easily resolved—or even recognized. Can one teach Quaker principles and open-mindedness at the same time? Should one try? One teacher, a Quaker since childhood, felt strongly that Mott's role was to stand up for Quaker beliefs, especially the need "to deal with conflict in a peaceful way." "We present the students with an alternative viewpoint," she said. "I'm always saying that we don't need to present two views, because the other view is constantly with us, in the general society." Although she admits that sometimes those who stand up for principles appear to others to be self-righteous, she points out that "many weighty Friends seem self-righteous—what's the difference between talking about the right values and being self-righteous?" A determination to honor all sides of an argument can sometimes confuse students:

Perhaps there are certain issues that we adults don't see as black and white, and as a result the students tend to be wishy-washy about them or not able to get a right answer about them from the adult community. Now that's a two-way thing, because you want them to think for themselves, but you don't want to give them double messages.

There are others at Mott who argue that teaching kids to think for themselves requires teaching respect for all values. Said one non-Quaker, "Our way of teaching values is not to tell kids what's right or wrong and good or bad, but to give them the situation and all sides of the issue, along with the decision-making model, so they can make their own decisions." She felt that she and her colleagues went out of their way "not to preach to kids."

Ellen Kahn was aware of Mott's mission-versus-men dilemma. She strongly believed in "the school's philosophy about nurturing what's good in every individual and really getting kids to find out who they are and think for themselves. But," she added:

I'm not entirely sure how well we do that. I believe in it, and I think we try, but . . . the school does have an agenda and we really want them to be a certain kind of person. And so there is inevitably a little bit of hypocrisy and insincerity built into the notion of getting people to really think for themselves and be who they are, because if they really did think for themselves, we might not like what they thought!

A senior, more conservative politically than many of his peers, was well aware of Mott's mixed messages about freedom of thought. "A lot of Quakers here take a really liberal stance," he said. "Their message is to have an open mind, but that's a hypocrisy, because they exclude other views." He described an incident in Meeting for Worship, when Charlie McDowell got up and talked about the bombing of Libya:[10]

He gave a dramatic soliloquy about what the people in Libya must think and feel about what happened. Well, I was really angry, and I got up and returned a dramatic soliloquy about how horrible terrorism is—I talked about that American discotheque in Berlin that got blown up—and about what I think of people like the Libyans who harbor terrorists.

"What happened?" I asked. "Well," he said, "I think Charlie appreciated it—that I was trying to show that there are many ways to look at things. In fact, I think people respected me for doing that. But if I hadn't stood up, that view wouldn't have been expressed."

Military-School Conflicts

At Dyer and Mott, upholding the peace testimony in teaching and everyday behavior is not a smooth process. Decisions about curriculum, classroom methods, and student discipline require more forethought and more discussion because of the difficulties of combining a principled stance with a belief in tolerance. The result is more talk about peace—in all of its different guises—than would otherwise be the case. At Pershing, a similar mission-versus-men debate occurred in the name of the military virtue of competence. Here, too, the faculty are divided into two camps, referred to by one teacher as the "absolutists" and the "relativists." The main problem centers on grading methods. On the one hand, the absolutists, said this teacher, "believe that they are preserving the integrity and reputation of the school by an adherence to what they would like to call standards, which is a set of preconceived notions that they carry with them: that . . . an A that they gave in 1954 or '64 is the same A that they give in 1984." The relativists, on the other hand, say, "Hey, times are changing. . . . If I'm teaching a hundred youngsters today, those who are at the top of the heap . . . are just as deserving of an A today as those who were at the top of the heap fifteen years ago."

The absolutists believe that it is their duty to maintain Pershing's reputation for academic excellence. In order to ensure that the quality of instruction remains as high as it was in the 1950s, when many of them started teaching, they grade students in comparison with their predecessors rather than their peers, often using tests they developed over thirty years earlier. As a result, an increasing number of Pershing seniors—even those with high SAT scores—graduate with poor grades. This reduces their chances of getting into top-quality colleges. To the absolutists, the fault lies with the school for lowering its admissions requirements and with the students for not working hard enough. Absolutist teachers resent that students who are doing poorly in their classes can go to a dean and request—and often get—a transfer to another class. They are infuriated by what they experience

as administrative and parental pressure to lower their grading standards, which represent to them their worth as a tough teacher. "Parents used to want their kids to take rigorous courses where they could
learn and get prepared for college," said one absolutist. "We have
parents now who want the kids in classes where they are going to get
the highest grades for the least amount of effort." He is convinced that
the problem lies with the admissions policy, that "to meet . . . costs"
the school will "take those with lower IQ scores, with lower everything!" This, he believes, destroys the reputation of the school. The
Pershing he envisions is one "with an image of having very tough
academic standards" so that it will attract students "who are interested
in a real education and not just in getting a grade." Let the school
admit two hundred fewer students if necessary, he concludes.

This teacher and his colleagues put principles first—the mission
comes before the men. But there are other staff members who say to
themselves, as one teacher said, "If we have 220 seniors and there are
only four people getting an A in senior English, something is wrong!"
To many of the counselors, who know the kind of pressure the students are under and who have to comfort them (and deal with their
parents) when report cards come out, the absolutists are "real crazy
old guys . . . who lack compassion and aren't even in the real world," as
one put it. "One teacher in the English department is famous for
writing, 'Great attitude, great effort, D,'" another said. "And there are
a couple like that in history and science. Those are the ones who tell
their classes on the first day, 'You will not get an A—I do not give As.
You will probably flunk.' And then they just toy with the kids all during
the grading period." Another teacher was notorious for having everyone "do something he called Project F, which was a huge research
paper. . . . He called it Project F because he knew everyone was going
to get an F on it." The counselor found it "very embarrassing and
painful" to have to try to respond to parents who ask, "Why are we
sending them to Pershing to get Cs?"

Divisive as it is, this controversy is healthy for the school. It would
not be so heated if it didn't have such a strong moral component. The
old guard angrily defending competence, the newer and younger
teachers trying to temper their colleagues' principles with common
sense and compassion: both groups want what they feel is best for the
students and the school. Hopefully, the outcome is not only a better

grading system for Pershing but a better understanding of one of the important virtues in the military moral tradition.

Obedience Versus Initiative: Community as Support and Constraint

The strain between freedom and belonging is a defining characteristic of American culture and, indeed, of modern life, which presents us with, as Hewitt put it, "an inherent and continuing contrast between community and society," or between small-group membership and independent action in a larger sphere. "The tension between individual and community" means being "caught between the attractions of autonomous social participation and exclusive identification with community."[11] At Quaker and at military boarding schools, administrators, teachers, and students are without a doubt part of a close-knit community. Although they value the security that comes with this attachment, many of them—primarily the adolescents but also at times the adults—chafe at the spoken and unspoken rules that are an inevitable part of group life. They object to these constraints on two grounds: on the one hand, because rules impede their freedom of action, and, on the other, because rules get in the way of closeness.

Quaker-School Conflicts

At Mott, Fox, and Dyer, many students and teachers have problems with the idea that they cannot simply be friends. Because the real self is more highly valued than the role self, accepting the requirements imposed by the relationship of pupil to instructor is hard. One girl at Mott complained that faculty members were not "playful" enough with students. She wanted "buddies," she said, not people whose approach made you feel that they were "smelling your clothes, checking your eyes, and stuff like that [to detect drug use]." Even with one of her favorite teachers, "there's authority getting in the way. A friend and I brought her coffee in her house on Saturday morning. We thought it would just be like three girls together, giggling, but there was this weird tension, . . . some kind of barrier." The other side of the coin is the faculty's dilemma of how to relate to students. A young teacher at Fox said she worried constantly about "just how close do I let myself get to the kids." Because she cared "very deeply about them," she wanted them to confide in her about their problems and was distressed when they turned away. One of her classes had just cheated on a test, and she was extremely upset, particularly because they wouldn't talk to her about the reasons for their behavior. "It was a betrayal of a trust that I had in them," she said, "and they know how important trust is to me. Especially the students I have a friendship with."

Resentment of the teacher and student roles getting in the way of friendship assumes an added complexity when being "buddies" turns into being lovers. At all three Quaker schools I heard stories, perhaps nine or ten in all, of love affairs or attempted seductions between male students and female teachers, female students and male teachers, and female students and female teachers. No doubt some of these claims were exaggerated, but others were true, and they gained credence from the flirtation and physical contact that I observed between adults and adolescents. Only one Quaker-school faculty member raised the topic of student-teacher sexuality as an ethical issue of concern to her. "Some of the relationships that faculty have with students are more intimate than they should be," she said. "I think this kind of thing is dangerous . . . and the level of tolerance for it in the community is unconscionable." But the majority of adults seemed not to believe that teacher-student closeness could become sexual exploitation or manipulation. An administrator worried that what appeared to be excessive familiarity between adults and adolescents could be "misinterpreted," but he did not seem willing to recognize that these interpretations were sometimes accurate. The year before he had "raised a question . . . about the responsibility of a teacher with a student of the opposite sex." He felt it necessary to "raise consciousness" about the power of appearances, because some teachers were behaving in a way that he found "not professional. . . . Sometimes you'll see a teacher sitting in a meeting and sort of snuggling with a student . . . or a teacher dancing with a student the whole night. And there were some faculty having kids up in their apartments at all hours of the night." But when he tried to make the faculty aware that "appearances do matter in the world," they were "furious":

I think they still haven't forgiven me for that. They saw me as taking the uptight, moralistic position. They felt I was raising something that I had no business to be raising. Sort of, "Who are you to be bringing this stuff up? Am I supposed to field questions every time I walk up to my apartment with a student?" So I had to learn to calm down a lot and change my attitude.

Many of the young teachers are angry because the rules and conventions threaten to get in the way of the closeness that they consider an important manifestation of the Quaker virtues of equality and community. If it is difficult for adults to see that many of the schools' rules are a prerequisite, rather than a hindrance, to community, it is even more difficult for the students to understand this apparent contradiction. The problem, as one Mott teacher put it, is to know "how to balance respect for the Inner Light and the person and his rights to privacy and to be himself, with the discipline process that's for the good of the whole." To many who have absorbed the Quaker emphasis on caring for the individual, the idea of obedience seems a betrayal. "There still are a lot of rules here at Mott, and . . . there are always teachers disciplining someone—telling them what to do or not to do," complained one boy. "They say this is a Quaker community, but then they have a disciplinary committee and all kinds of organizations to keep people in line." All of this he considered "un-Quakerly," especially the school's various anti-drug programs. "I thought Quakers weren't supposed to impose their values on other people," he said. "They're always saying, 'We don't convert people, they come to us.' But what they're doing with these rules is imposing their values."

A Mott administrator sympathized with the students' confusion and anger about discipline. "We continue as a Friends School to send mixed messages to kids, I think: 'We love you, we care about you, but don't do anything wrong 'cause we'll nail your ass.'" Although he believes both in nurturing and in drawing the line, he sometimes wonders whether the Friends-school style is "less honest" than that of other institutions "where they say right from the start, 'We don't do these things here. Whether you're experimenting, confused, emotionally upset, or whatever . . . we don't do these things here.' So right from the git-go, [students] know what the status is." At a Friends school, by contrast, "our style implies—even though our rules don't say this—that we accept the realities of being an adolescent. And that includes some experimentation with drugs and alcohol, some rites of passage, some playing the game and beating the system. And I think kids pick up on that."

Some of what the kids pick up on is not only the adults' own ambivalence about obedience but also what one teacher called "a high level of denial—people just don't want to deal with these things, so they put them out of their minds." Yet there is also a positive side to the mixed messages about rules that both adolescents and adults sense. They are being made aware of the inevitable tension between obedience and initiative that exists in any healthy community, where a simultaneous need for security and desire for autonomy are bound to lead to ambivalence and conflict. There is probably not a school in the world where students do not resent the rules and teachers do not disagree with each other about how to handle pupils' misbehavior. At Mott, Fox, and Dyer, however, these conflicts, couched in Quaker idiom, become moral dilemmas; they provide an opportunity to debate the purpose of a Friends education. When they are handled well, they bring the key Quaker virtues into prominence and test the tradition's strength and flexibility.

Military-School Conflicts

At the military academies, too, obedience to rules is perceived by cadets as getting in the way of both independence and intimacy. The virtues cadets seek to defend are, not equality and community, but leadership, selflessness, and loyalty. The official interpretation of these virtues links them to the military tradition of service. Students should do what is best for the school, set a good example, and never stop striving to do their best. Student leaders are expected to work especially hard for the welfare of their subordinates. As descriptions of dedicated student officers and NCOs like Lamont Sandler at Sherman, Gail Callot at Jackson, and Tom Hurd at Pershing have shown, a number of the cadet leaders do indeed serve the schools at a rather large cost to themselves. One Pershing senior, a high-ranking officer, an athlete, and an excellent student, said that the school's expectations were "like you're on a cliff, and they keep pushing you to the edge. You're never going to fall off, but they keep pushing you . . . a little bit farther and a little bit closer. It gets nerve-wracking sometimes."

One of the rewards for obedience and hard work is autonomy: adults give student leaders a certain amount of leeway in running their units. These cadets can enforce their own interpretations of the military virtues, which means, for example, that selflessness is sometimes transformed from an ethic of service into one of suffering. The professional military code recognizes the importance of courage and the nobility of suffering, which is one of the reasons adults at all three schools sanction the existence of the plebe period. Not surprisingly, however, adults' idea of how much suffering is appropriate is not the same as students'. For the most part, cadets see the inflicting and enduring of pain as an important part of the military tradition that it is their responsibility to reproduce for one another, because it teaches courage and respect. It is an article of faith among cadets that the people who are mistreated enjoy their suffering or at least look back on it fondly. Pershing's Kyle Bennett assured me that "even the ones who got hung out the window and had darts thrown at them . . . , they just loved it and wish they could do it again!"

Given the adults' own ambivalence about the meaning of selflessness and about the degree of cadet initiative that is compatible with obedience, it is not surprising that the definition of *hazing* is rather vague. A Pershing teacher described a junior who had been in tears over losing his rank because "he was accused of taking a group of plebes out at some ungodly hour in minus-14-degree weather and running them through some sort of training for two hours in the cold." The teacher, who heard the story from the cadet's mother, asked him if it was true. "Yes," he answered, "but did she tell you that I didn't leave them there? I stayed out there with them." By "staying out there" with the plebes, the cadet officer demonstrated his own capacity for selflessness even as he taught it to others. His response to being accused of hazing was, "Well, it's nothing that they didn't do to me." He saw himself as setting an example for his subordinates and following in the footsteps of his superiors, both qualities of leadership that are highly recommended at Pershing. He was genuinely puzzled at being accused of disobedience for doing what he thought was his duty; "I don't know why they stopped me," he insisted to his teacher.

Similar conflicts over student initiative in teaching toughness and obedience to their charges also occur at Sherman and Jackson, although it is sometimes hard to tell which fights between cadets have their origins in the enforcing of military discipline and which are just plain fights. Compared to the Pershing faculty, adults at the other two schools have more of a boys-will-be-boys attitude, and black eyes, bruises, and even broken jaws and arms are accepted with a certain philosophical calm.[12] One Sherman teacher, the alumnus of another military academy, criticized school authorities for overreacting:

You're going to find bullying in any situation where you have boys living together. . . . They're going to respond physically when they're mad or jealous. . . . In my day, schools were physical, and you didn't have an attorney running up every five minutes. . . . But we succumb to threats these days: fears of lawsuits, going to court, adverse publicity. We allow the parents too much latitude.

At all three schools, students disobey rules about hazing in order to demonstrate their initiative as leaders. In addition, at military schools as at Quaker schools, obedience to community rules is also perceived by students as a hindrance to intimacy. Like the teacher who resents parents' interference in the business of the school, the students resent teachers' interference in the rituals of peer loyalty. In the professional military, loyalty to the army as a whole can sometimes clash with loyalty to the squad or platoon; this same tension is present at the military academies. Adults expect loyalty to the school to take precedence over loyalty to peers. Among the students, not surprisingly, loyalty to friends is held to be the higher virtue.

No one in the military community likes a tattletale. Nevertheless, adults expect students—especially officers, but also the younger students—to keep them informed of what is going on in the units. In response, adolescents at all three military schools have developed strong "no-narcing" codes.[13] Kids suspected of narcing on their peers are ostracized or beaten up; in one case two Pershing girls (who were subsequently identified and expelled) poured urine all over a suspect's bed. Sometimes newcomers are beaten just to see whether they will tell. A Sherman senior told how, as a plebe, he was tied by his hands to a fourth-floor banister by two of his classmates, with his body leaning over the staircase. "They put one of those big straw coolie hats on my head and painted my eyes with eyeliner and then they started calling me a gook: 'You're a gook, you're a gook.' And they started whipping me with a belt. I just kept my mouth shut. The whole point is to see if they can trust you. It's a test to see if you're going to follow the unwritten law, which is, 'Don't narc.'" His classmate Erik Bergstrom, commenting on some boys who had their first sergeant busted for harassing and hitting them, sympathized with them but still shook his head over their narcing:

You can't say the kids are doing the right thing to turn their sergeant in. You've got to understand, these guys are narcing on their peers, and you've got to consider: What about when you're in business with someone, are you going to turn them in? What about your family—are you going to turn them in? These are the people you have to work with and live with.

Loyalty is owed to the unit above all. As a result, the no-narcing code doesn't frown on a cadet telling someone about an incident, so long as that someone is within the company. A new sophomore at Pershing saw one of his plebe brothers cheating on the student-administered test that plebes must pass in order to become privates. When the cadet officers and NCOs caught one cheater and wanted to know "if anyone had seen anybody else cheating," he told them. Asked if his behavior was perceived as narcing, he answered, "I don't think so. . . . The people who knew I'd told thought it was the right thing to do." A key point was that "nobody was turned in to Honor Council." In other words, the incident was taken care of within the unit and kept secret from the adult community. Even the adults assigned to the various units as counselors or tactical officers are expected by cadets to put loyalty to the unit before obedience to the rules. One counselor said that when there was a problem in his company, "the kids always want me to cover things up, or deal with it myself or, better yet, let them deal with it. Well, they don't deal with it. So they accused me early on of just being a right-hand man of the commandant and a narc."

In spite of the no-narcing code, some students do tattle to adults. At least, school authorities find out about a good many escapades (although by no means the majority), and it is usually assumed that "somebody narced." One of these accusations had dramatic consequences at Pershing. A plebe was suspected of having narced on his roommate, and several officers in the company persuaded a group of the boy's plebe brothers to punish him with a "blanket party," a form of attack common at military academies—and other boarding schools—which consists of several boys going into the victim's room in the middle of the night, throwing a blanket over him, pummelling him, and leaving before he can pull off the blanket and identify them. In this case the blanket-party attackers made the mistake, however, of marking the suspected narc's face, which led to questioning and, eventually, to their being caught.

This beating incident caused an uproar in the school; it was the only blanket party to come to light during that year and most people, including students, thought the beaters should be expelled. The faculty voted unanimously to dismiss them and never permit them to return to the school, but the headmaster decided otherwise. The boys were officially expelled, so that a dismissal showed on their records, and were then readmitted. In an all-school assembly (a rare occurrence at Pershing), the headmaster explained to the cadets and teachers that he was going against the faculty's recommendation of expulsion because he did not want to make martyrs of the beaters. To me later he described the situation as "a tough crisis," which he saw as "an opportunity to confront two codes of conduct that exist on this campus." One was the official set of school rules, and the other was the code of loyalty to peers and the unit. In the assembly, the headmaster accused students of undermining the lessons that Pershing wanted to communicate to new students. He told them, "It isn't enough for us to hand the new students the Pershing code and say, 'This is how we operate.' You have to operate that way. Because while the new students may read it, they know as well as I know that the values that are honored are the ones you live. They want to know what values we really honor here." [14]

The blanket party and its aftermath are dramatic examples of how conflict over community rules can lead to intense discussion of the virtues upon which the sense of community is based. At Jackson and Sherman, too, loyalty to the school and obedience to the adults' understanding of the military tradition clash with loyalty to the unit and obedience to the adolescents' understanding of military values. At all three schools, cadets' definition of the military system leads them to interpret and enforce selflessness in their own way, which results in many examples of what adults call hazing and students call lessons in discipline and respect.

The disagreement between adults and adolescents about the virtues of suffering is not easily discussed by the two parties; most of the "disciplining" goes on in the barracks when no teachers, counselors, or tactical officers are present, and adults find out about particular incidents only occasionally and then chiefly by accident. Cadet violence seems to be a taboo subject not only between adults and adolescents but also among adults. Yet an unspoken awareness of the presence of violence colors a great many faculty discussions—about leadership training, the plebe system, the responsibilities of officers, and adults' role in the barracks, for example. It forces staff at all three schools to examine critically the military tradition and to emphasize over and over again the service-related interpretation of selflessness and leadership, in order to counteract the cadets' attraction to their own version of these virtues. Cadets, too, pass judgment on their own and others' behavior. First Sergeant Lamont Sandler at Sherman was proud that he no longer "used his hands to discipline people" but had developed other methods of earning their respect and obedience. He defended his repudiation of violence not only to me but to one of his best friends, who tried to dissuade Lamont from always "going by the book." Both cadets mentioned this argument, which apparently ended with their agreeing to disagree. Such talks among friends over how to apply military values are a crucial part of what makes the tradition come alive for cadets.

Moderation Versus Excess: Racism and Sexism as Perversions of the Virtues

A distorted understanding of equality at Quaker schools can encourage sexual relationships between teachers and students, and a distorted understanding of selflessness leads cadets to put each other through humiliating and often painful tests. Perhaps the most disturbing perversion of the virtues is as a justification for ethnic intolerance at four of the schools and for sexism at the three military academies.[15] Thus far, conflicts over the virtues have been portrayed as strengthening the moral traditions, since recognition of the different ways that the virtues can be understood and applied ensures their adaptability to different situations that may arise in daily life. The tensions between races and ethnic groups and the contempt for girls and women that exist at some of the schools, however, do not serve to promote the health of the traditions. Perhaps this is because so few people are willing to acknowledge prejudice openly and discuss it honestly, not only as a problem that should be addressed within the context of the traditions, but—what is more painful—as a problem that can even be encouraged by certain interpretations of the virtues. The primary culprits are *community* at the Quaker schools and *pride* at the military academies.

Quaker-School Conflicts

Fox's student body in 1988 included six blacks, one boy and five girls, in a total student population of fifty. Four of the five African-American girls, plus a brown-skinned Asian-American girl, were inseparable companions and were usually joined at dinner by the black boy. During the meal, the six sat together laughing and having fun. Their apparent cliquishness was seen by some students and even more teachers as a rejection of the school's philosophy of togetherness, although the other easily identifiable student subgroups (brains, punks, and hippies) did not generate much comment. The real issue, clearly, was race. The warm sense of community the African-American students shared among themselves, which had its roots in their difference, seemed to threaten the larger, school-wide community based on sameness.

According to one of the black girls, people often complained that she and her friends were too loud at dinner or left their table in a mess. Three additional black students, also members of her group, had left the school earlier that year. "They were loud," she admitted; "I grant that, they were loud. But the faculty and students have to learn, that's the way they were; you can't change that. I guess it scared people." When asked if things had become more comfortable since the departure of the three "loud" kids, she was quick to answer, "No":

It's quieter now, but . . . they still can't trust us, they still believe we're going to hurt the white kids, hit them, or tell them something bad. That's basically what it comes down to. I guess our group hangs so together, they just can't believe it. . . . The black people in this school are the example, and we're supposed to be perfect. But we can't do that, I'm sorry, but we're not going to do that. And they just aren't going to break us up.

The oldest black girl, a student leader who was not a member of the younger girls' circle, was in the difficult position of seeing two sides to the issue. Asked if anything at the school had been a moral dilemma for her, she answered, "I guess the racism. I see some of the black kids being obnoxious, and I can see how people can be offended by them, and since most people don't feel that way against me I don't know what to do. But I understand why the black kids are upset, although I don't approve of how they are reacting." Sometimes, she added, she didn't know whom she should support, "so often I just don't say anything." Like the younger black girl, she too felt that being black at Fox meant having to "be better." It "may be ridiculous," she said, "but . . . I can't let them associate ignorance with being black, crying with being black, or stealing. Some of the black students were stealing, but some of the white students were too, and the first people blamed were black. And we feel like saying, 'How dare you blame all the blacks?'"

The whites at Fox would be hurt and angry to hear their resentment of the black students' togetherness labeled racism. They see themselves as wanting racial integration and are disturbed by what they perceive as the blacks' rejection of a Quaker definition of community. There is no doubt, though, that the black kids' style makes some of the whites at Fox uncomfortable, and this is an issue that the school does not seem able to address.

At Dyer, too, relations between black and white students are affected by the clash between the whites' desire for a single community based on sameness and the blacks' need for their own community based on difference. There, however, the greater anger seems to be on the part of white students, many of whom believe that two African-American faculty members, both strong and beloved Dyer authority figures, favor blacks. A couple of black students laughingly and somewhat apologetically mentioned this special bond, and one boy with light skin but African ancestry said he felt excluded because he was not black enough to be part of the black teachers' group. Even those white students who were able to see that the black faculty members had good reason to feel a special attachment and obligation to Dyer's black population were still hurt. "There's a definite segregation of the black students and black faculty from the other students," said a white girl. "The black students are treated by the black faculty as their children—they go out of their way to make them close friends." On Martin Luther King Day, for example, black students were invited to one of the teacher's homes to "celebrate their holiday. And it was very offensive to a lot of students and some faculty, too." The girl struggled to understand what it was that hurt her; she used the words *segregation* and *separation* and then said, "I don't know what it is. I guess it's common interests or whatever, but there is a favoritism there, and it's very apparent. . . . I love [the two teachers] very much, the two of them are very strong about being black, and they create a little tension about it, and it bothers me because it's how prejudice gets started."

For this white girl, acknowledging one's blackness, being "strong about it," is threatening to the sense of togetherness in the community; she would be more comfortable if the two black teachers would downplay the issue of race. In spite of the official emphasis on "being oneself" that exists at Dyer and in spite of the apparently very harmonious relations between the school's black and white students, self-conscious blackness is a form of difference that many students and teachers find difficult to understand. A thoughtful white senior tried to analyze why it was disruptive to the community, volunteering the information at the end of an interview. Asked if he had anything to add, he said that he considered one of the black teachers, who was also an administrator, to be "prejudiced." "I'm not a minority, so it's hard for me to say where the line is between being really conscious of racial issues and being prejudiced. But he's the one that's always stressing . . . how we should be a community, and yet he deals with black people differently." The student admitted that maybe he was the one being prejudiced, and he realized that "being black you relate better to black people," but nevertheless it seemed clear to him that the teacher "really wasn't as kind to me as he was to blacks in the class." The real problem, he felt, was that the teacher's special concern for black students wasn't compatible with his role as a Dyer administrator:

It's good for some people to be like that, because it makes everyone more conscious that blacks are separate, and they need to be recognized and they need that identity. But as an administrator who's stressing community, no matter what you really think, you can't let it come out. I know that's not being honest, but as an administrator you have to make sure that what you're doing is for the community. After all, part of community is losing personal ideals.

For many of the white students and teachers at Fox and Dyer, tolerance of difference in the name of community can extend only so far. When it comes to the blacks' pursuit of community through difference, tolerance is all but lost in bewilderment, discomfort, hostility, envy, and hurt. These are stressful matters, which are not talked about openly. Yet only when these tensions and their impact on the schools are discussed will the virtue of community be enriched to accommodate black solidarity. Perhaps when black students at Fox and black teachers at Dyer no longer have to feel defensive about their identification with their fellow African-Americans, they will be able to abandon some of the vigilant exclusivity that is so painful to many of the whites around them.

Military-School Conflicts

At the military academies, the virtue that becomes an excuse for prejudice is pride. School officials and cadet officers promote loyalty to and pride in the unit by encouraging fierce competition between companies—in sports, drills, parades, inspections of barracks, and so on. As a result, students often speak disparagingly of their peers in other units. Some of the rancor is assumed as part of a lively game of rivalry, but some of it is real. One unit, it was said, consisted of "total sucks," another of nothing but drug users, another of wimps, and so forth. The real problems arise when this rivalry is fed not only by competition but by sexism and racism.

At Jackson, for example, unit competition came to a head between two company commanders, a boy and a girl. According to the girl, the boy "didn't like that I was a girl, black, and had the same position as him. I'm the only girl he cannot tell what to do, and, besides, my company [which is all girls] was doing better than his. So he started trying to undermine my authority. He'd go around saying nigger this, nigger that, and then he got busted for fooling around with one of the girls, and that made it worse." The hostility escalated, and all the other cadets "started choosing sides." The boy did his best to sabotage her command. "He'd ask my friends, 'Why do you hang around with her?' . . . He'd say bad things about me in front of the whole battalion. . . . Finally, when he told one of the girls in my company not to listen to me, I had to go to [the head of the military department]. We're supposed to have company rivalry, but officers aren't supposed to go against each other like that."

On his part, the boy was convinced that the girl cadets had ganged up on him. One of them had flirted with him and then "framed" him. "Tina starts making her little faces at me," he explained, "and we start wrestling, and I hit her real lightly on her hip, because she's trying to push me in a mud puddle. . . . So she goes off still teasing me, and next day I'm called into the commandant's office." He found himself accused by Tina's first sergeant and captain (the black girl quoted above) of grabbing Tina's bottom and "throwing himself all over her." Although he told the commandant exactly what had happened, he was still by his own admission guilty of "physical contact," which is forbidden, so he was reduced one grade of rank, because of "conduct unbecoming to a cadet officer." He found the accusation particularly unfair and humiliating, because "I haven't done any of the stuff with girls that other guys around here have." It was after this painful incident, which he was convinced had been a plot cooked up by the female captain, that his campaign against her became particularly bitter.

Pride was at stake here, and pride at military school is a dangerous virtue. In the army's basic field manual, pride is described in terms of "bonding," "cohesion," and "esprit de corps." [16] What is not said about this bonding is that it is between men. Women in the armed forces can and do have dignity and a strong sense of honor, but these qualities do not add up to the kind of pride that their male counterparts can easily recognize, because pride as experienced by men in the armed forces—and by many men, whatever their occupation—is intricately tied up with their sense of masculinity. Anthropologist David Gilmore calls the idea of manhood a "prize." He points out that very different cultures around the world exhibit "a constantly recurring notion that real manhood is different from simple anatomical maleness, that it is not a natural condition that comes about spontaneously through biological maturation but rather is a precarious or artificial state that boys must win against powerful odds." [17] Male pride arises in part from "passing the test" together with other men and feeling a special sense of oneness with them.

The idea of pride as a male preserve exists at all three military academies, among male cadets and among many male adults, and it gives rise to conflicts over the presence of girls at the schools. Whether the girls are cadets with their own companies, as at Sherman and Jackson, or live in a separate organization with a different system of leadership and different customs, as at Pershing, they are resented. By their very presence they rob the boys of some special sense of integrity and togetherness that they associate with their manhood; by their difference they generate among the boys rumors of injustice and favoritism. As one Sherman cadet said, "I don't respect any of the girls. They cry about how they can do anything a guy can do, and I can deal with that. But when . . . they screw up, they do not get treated like guys." Comments like this were echoed by cadets at all three schools: the girls got special treatment. Another common theme was that the girls "get in the way." The battalion commander at Jackson said, "The girls are more trouble than they are worth. . . . We're here to complete a mission, to reach a goal, and they're just a hindrance."

At Jackson and Sherman, boys resented competing with girls for military honors; this was particularly true at Sherman, where the top-ranking cadet and third-in-command were both girls. At Pershing, where the girls had nothing to do with the military, they were resented because their presence supposedly lowered the standards of the school. One junior was convinced that the school would function better without girls, although he would never want to get rid of them, because they were fun companions and "made the classrooms look nicer." Another junior took an even stronger stand: "The girls' school is so different; I hate the girls' school. I mean, I like having girls around, I'm not gay or anything, but . . . their leadership is a joke, the girls are slobs, no one listens to them. If I could, I'd boot them."

This was essentially the opinion of many of the male teachers at Pershing as well. One department head called the girls an unfortunate economic necessity, and another teacher accused them of "pull[ing] down the flash and tradition and polish and dignity of the corps." An administrator felt the boys were too distracted by the presence of the girls to fulfill their leadership responsibilities properly; another lamented the deterioration of unit identity and the lack of sufficient competition among the different military companies, troops, and batteries at the school, blaming this erosion of unit spirit on the fact that the girls were organized by class and not by company.

What is most striking about the Pershing attitude to the presence of girls is that a great many of the boys and male teachers talk as though the girls' school were a small experiment or a recent innovation. In fact, girls were first admitted to Pershing in the early 1970s, and in 1988 over 40 percent of the student body was female. However, in the minds of many students and faculty members these years of coeducation still stand out as an aberration in the hundred-year history of the school. As one man on the staff ruefully commented, "I've never been at a place where there is more male chauvinism than Pershing. . . . It's an uphill battle, getting the girls onto some sort of a par with the boys. You have to remember that this school is steeped in tradition, and by those standards the girls are complete newcomers."

Military pride—the need to feel bonded with one's fellows as an upholder of manly standards—was also tied to some of the incidents of racial and ethnic prejudice at Sherman and Jackson.[18] Five Russian-born Jewish cadets at Sherman who lived in the same company filed a complaint against their first sergeant, who had given them extra demerits, kicked and hit them, and used anti-Semitic epithets. The issue came to a head when a swastika was painted on the door of the room two of the boys shared. Their parents came to the school to talk to the commandant, one boy was withdrawn, the others were divided into separate companies, and the first sergeant was busted to private. I found little sympathy for the Jewish boys. Almost every student (and two of the adults) I talked to about what had happened agreed that they had brought their troubles on themselves, chiefly by making their unit look bad. All but one of them, it was said, talked back, didn't clean their rooms, wore sloppy uniforms, and acted contemptuous of the military system. (One girl even thought they insulted the United States by speaking Russian at an American military school, which was "disrespectful.")

Interviews with two of the boys revealed that one hated Sherman and had hoped his parents would withdraw him. The other, Seth Nater, said he liked the military in general, "but only if it's run properly, which it isn't here." What he resented most was the way the school bored him. "I like to read, so I bring books from home. But during weekends, it's just murder. There's nothing to do but just walk around aimlessly; I'm even too bored to go to sleep." Here was someone who did not feel a need for the sports, drills, fights, elaborate pranks, and other tests of manhood that filled many of the cadets' time. Like the young black girl at Fox, Seth recognized that his and his friends' difference and their loyalty to one another threatened others. "I think what bothered Angelo [the first sergeant] so much about us was that we stuck together. He kept trying to break us up, like by making us move in with incompatible people. I know him pretty well, and he's kind of childish—he just can't take defeat. And Ben Stein [another member of the group] *is* very lazy—he won't do a thing if he can get out of it."

"I was hard on those kids," Angelo Rossi admitted. "I use my hands too much, I know, but there has to be fear if you're going to control people. . . . The Jewish kids didn't make their beds, they taunted me; Horowitz laughed at me in company meeting. . . . I kicked Horowitz, but I never touched Stein, just gave him demerits—you can't hit a 105-pound kid." What Angelo is trying to say is that he is not simply a bully; he has his pride and his standards, which the Jewish boys seemed to undermine. It is terribly important to him to make his mark on the school, which is his fourth in two years. "This school lets me be someone," he said. "I want people to be impressed, I want them to remember me. And I want to make this school something. . . . I lost my rank for something I believe in. If they gave me my rank back tomorrow, my methods wouldn't change."

Angelo is convinced that the Jewish cadets didn't understand the "underlying meaning" of his treatment of them. But Seth, at least, understands something about what motivates Angelo. "I don't hate Angelo," Seth said. "He beats up on everybody, although I guess us especially." Shaking his head with incredulity, he explained, "Angelo loves this school—why, I don't know." Seth senses Angelo's desperate need to prove himself at Sherman and make his experience there meaningful, to show that even though he is sometimes, in his own words, "a bully," he can also "lead by example." Angelo was willing to acknowledge his bullying, but not the anti-Semitism that colored his actions. Other students defied military discipline, but they were perceived as difficult individuals rather than as a rebellious group. Other students, too, were kicked and taunted, but not with such systematic intent. Anti-Semitism singled out the Jews for special persecution; a misplaced sense of military pride justified the attack.

Black students were also held to special standards in the name of school pride. Those who worked within the military system were accepted into the corps. In fact, at both Sherman and Jackson a black cadet was the most liked and respected student on the campus. But blacks who resented military orders and discipline and had trouble accepting the authority of their fellow students were despised. The fact that a percentage of the white students also resented the military system and showed "bad attitudes" was irrelevant: the rebellious blacks were "niggers."[19] This resentment was particularly strong at Jackson, where a top-ranking cadet described the majority of the black cadets as "hang[ing] around together for protection, because they aren't really accepted. But they bring it on themselves, the way they act." According to him, they "cause a lot of trouble, get into fights, and make the companies look bad." Military pride, again, is threatened, and so, it turns out, is male sexual pride. "There're no fights between the blacks and whites, but trouble's brewing up. . . . Some of the scummy, low-life [white] girls are going out with the blacks; that's making a lot of people mad."

One sign of the complex relationship between racial and ethnic prejudice and military pride is the attitude of most students toward Hispanic cadets. Although the word *spic* is not uncommon and jokes are made about Spanish accents, the many Central and South Americans and U.S.-born Latinos at Pershing, Jackson, and Sherman seem quite well accepted by Anglo students. Not one of the Hispanics mentioned experiencing discrimination, and several Anglo students made a point of praising the Spanish-speaking cadets' commitment to the military system. At Pershing the units with the most Hispanics were the models of the corps. Although they sat separately at meals, usually spoke Spanish with each other, and sponsored separate parties with Latino music, they were not perceived as outsiders, because they liked the military system and strove to make it work. In military parlance, they had "good attitudes." By upholding the reputations of their units and the school, they were for the most part spared the dark side of pride.

The Power of Ambiguity

These illustrations of the four main types of moral conflict at the schools show the value of arguing about virtue. The things that are argued about—budgets, salaries, student discipline, grading systems, and so on—are subjects of periodic conflict at most schools. But when these topics are invested with moral significance, even apparently mundane disagreements give people the chance to articulate their values to themselves and others. Conflicts that pit austerity against privilege, principles against compassion, and obedience against independence or intimacy generate a great deal of anger at the schools. Yet the moral traditions are enriched by their capacity to encompass these arguments, to offer solutions to problems, and, when necessary, to change in response to them.

There are other, less positive, ways to view a moral community's capacity to generate and absorb conflict. Sherryl Kleinman, for example, in *Equals Before God*, a book based on fieldwork at a Protestant seminary, paints a different picture of moral socialization, one that portrays the humanistic rhetoric of the seminary as deceptive and confusing for ministry students. Seminary language has much in common with Quaker language: words like *equality* and *diversity* are prominent, as is talk about finding and being one's "real self." The centerpiece of the professional school's moral rhetoric is the concept of *community*, which "becomes a high-level abstraction which may mean all things to all people—faculty and administrators use it ambiguously and variously." [20] For Kleinman, the bond between teachers and students that arises out of the widespread and sometimes contradictory use of *community* at the seminary is manipulative, a ploy on the part of the "socializers . . . [to] create identification between themselves and recruits by using ambiguous words that recruits already value." [21] Teachers use this rhetoric to build a "false consensus. . . . [T]hey led students to believe that they shared an understanding of the language, even when they did not." [22] When students discover, as many eventually do, that the "community" they value is a cover for differences and disagreements, they grow disillusioned. Those most committed to the ideals expressed by the rhetoric are the most likely to respond with anger and to use the same rhetoric to challenge the faculty.

At Quaker and military boarding schools, as at the seminary studied by Kleinman, teachers, administrators, and older students use moral rhetoric to obscure differences among members of the community and to promote identification with the school. At the boarding schools, as at the seminary, the same rhetoric is also used to question, resist, and challenge, and to justify rebellion. But Kleinman divides her moral world into the powerful and the powerless, the consciously manipulative socializers and the deceived recruits. Because the word *community* means so much to so many people, it becomes meaningless except as a tool to "get students to do things they might otherwise have resisted." [23] In this climate of deception, conflict is positive only because it indicates that recruits have penetrated the falseness of the socializers' stand and are able to "turn . . . what they have learned from their teachers against their teachers." [24] This conflict over the meaning and uses of moral rhetoric is not presented as either thought-provoking for the future ministers and the faculty or healthy for the seminary and the profession as a whole.

An equally negative interpretation of the use of moral language at the six schools would not do justice to the complexity of the relationship between students and staff. To divide them into powerless and powerful, recruits and socializers, manipulated and manipulators is too simplistic. Obviously, socialization is taking place: most ninth graders arrive knowing nothing about Quaker or military values, and many leave four years later with a high-school education that has been deeply colored by the language and beliefs of the tradition of their school. But the learning and growing, the questioning and challenging, are not simply on the part of the students. Many of the adults are trying as hard as—and sometimes harder than—the adolescents to learn and apply the virtues; some are as idealistic and capable of disillusionment as any teenager. Those whose disillusion is greatest leave the schools; most of those who stay continue to use the language of the virtues and to teach it to their students. This sharing of an ambiguous and powerful moral rhetoric is not necessarily a sign of false consensus imposed on the unsuspecting; it can also be a vehicle through which deliberation and debate about the meaning of virtue are made possible. Without a shared vocabulary discussion cannot occur, and without discussion there can be no constructive change. Rather than think of words like *community* and *loyalty* as the tools of mystification, it is productive to think of them as *magnet words*, examples of moral rhetoric that, despite all their power to attract and link together, also have the power—as magnets do when turned around—to drive apart. Although the ambiguity of moral rhetoric, with its power both to attract and to repel, can be used to deceive, it can also be a "marvelous invention" that keeps one group's interpretation of the good from dominating another's and permits people to develop their moral capacities through reflection and debate.[25]

At the schools, the ambiguous magnet words cause conflict that is often angry and sometimes destructive. But when students, teachers, and administrators are able to question thoughtfully their own and their colleagues' ethical judgments and express differences of opinion to one another in conversations and group discussions, disagreements become tools for maintaining the consciously moral nature of the communities. Such conflicts keep the moral traditions from being taken for granted. As MacIntyre has pointed out, "When a tradition is in good order it is always partially constituted by an argument about the goods the pursuit of which gives to that tradition its particular point and purpose."[26] Many arguments about the virtues at the schools are indeed proof that the traditions are in good order.

But not much that is healthy for the moral traditions can be found in the distortions of the virtues that emerge at some of the schools and contribute to violence and prejudice. Perhaps the best one can hope for is that a few strong and perceptive adults and adolescents, who are honest with themselves about some of the vices the moral traditions can produce, will work within their respective schools to eliminate these excesses. If the dark side of the virtues can be clearly identified, perhaps even they can serve to strengthen the traditions, by causing the communities to reflect upon how easily a virtue can be perverted.

Chapter Five

Making, Breaking, and Enforcing the Rules

Authority Relations and the Influence of Concern and Leadership

At both sets of schools the headmaster is answerable to a board, made up primarily of alumni and parents (and, at the Quaker schools, members of the Yearly Meeting). Teachers do not have tenure. They report to the headmaster and the academic dean, with department heads serving as liaisons. Parents, particularly those who are generous contributors to the school, can affect decisions. Students, too, have some influence over school policy, although they rarely exercise it. Given their similarity in organization, and making allowances for their differences in size, one might expect the six schools to be administered similarly. But in this realm, too, the moral traditions exert their power over routines and relationships, turning decision-making procedures at the schools into illustrations of the influence of the virtues on everyday life.

Chapter Two identified a key difference between the two moralities: the contrast between internal and external. This is a shorthand reference to the difference between the Quaker belief that morality exists primarily as a Light within the individual, to be discovered, developed, and expressed, and the military belief that morality exists primarily as a set of standards outside the individual, to be internalized and obeyed. This difference between Quakers and members of the military contributes to their opposing attitudes toward violence, cere-mony, and authority; it is the third axis of difference, authority, that this chapter addresses.

Concern and leadership are key to understanding the Quaker and military models of authority relations. Among Quakers, decisions are traditionally made by consensus, which for Friends means not a pas-sive acquiescence but a uniting of strong convictions. Action on any important matter should be inspired by concern, which is God-sent and heartfelt. The job of the clerk in a Quaker Meeting for Business is to make sure that all who are concerned have a chance to speak and time for silence, so that a "sense of the Meeting" can eventually be achieved. The clerk who feels that the Meeting's members are harmo-niously united behind a particular course of action expresses what he perceives to be the will of the group—and of God—in a "minute" or short proposal. If it is accepted, consensus has been reached; if it is challenged, the process continues until the sense of the Meeting coalesces into authority. These moments of deeply felt unity are hard to achieve among the most devout Friends; they are even more of a rarity in a Quaker-school faculty meeting.

Among members of the military profession, obedience to authority is of utmost importance. Orders must be followed; the mission must be accomplished. A military professional must be a loyal subordinate capable of accepting orders and an inspiring commander who sees that they are carried out. But leadership, in theory at least, is a more complicated process. Assuming there is time for reflection, the good leader does not issue an order without consulting his subordinates, and, as he expects honest advice from his staff, so he owes honest advice to his superiors. Although it is his duty to obey orders, it is also his more difficult duty to take responsibility for their outcome, even in cases where this means standing up for what he thinks is right or even defying an order. Such heroic behavior is not commonplace in the professional military; at military school, where lives are not at stake and jobs are sometimes precarious, being a leader is not a teacher's main ambition.

Different visions of concern and leadership shape the ways that adults and adolescents decide their stance toward authority and bal-ance their commitment to the school community with the desire for self-determination—or the wish simply to be left alone. Their choices of whether to become involved in the business of running the schools—and if so, how—illuminate the impact of the moral traditions on school life.

Teacher Involvement in Self-Government

At all six schools, teachers are expected to enforce rules among students and live by these rules themselves; to encourage students' sense of belonging to the community; and to inspire young people to contribute to the school, in class and also through participation in dormitory life, extracurricular activities, and student government. But to what extent are these adults involved in making the rules they enforce and determining the philosophies of the schools for which they work? The answer to this question varies from individual to individual and school to school; for some teachers this kind of participation is of no interest whatsoever, but for others it is a burning issue. The answer also varies depending on whether the school in question is Quaker or military, since at Quaker schools many decisions—in theory at least—are made through the joint consensus of the entire faculty, following a version of the Quaker Business process.

Quaker Schools: Attempts
at Consensus and Concern

The Pros and Cons of Consensus   Full faculty meetings are common at the three Quaker schools. During the 1987–88 school year at Mott and Dyer, these meetings were clerked by a teacher, with the headmaster usually present to contribute items to the agenda. At Fox the headmaster ran faculty meetings and, while he encouraged teachers' comments, did not appear to seek a sense of the Meeting on any topic. Of the three schools, Mott seemed to include the teachers in decision making most often. Yet even the most dedicated advocates of consensus agreed that at a place the size of Mott, with 100 faculty members, not every decision could or should be made consensually.

I asked the business manager, a non-Quaker struggling to understand and follow Friends' ways of doing business, how he decided which decisions to make on his own and which to bring before the faculty. He sighed and said, "That's hard. You make mistakes, and you learn." When asked to give an example of such a mistake, he told the story of damming the school's creek. Housing developments with artesian wells, built near the campus, were causing Mott's pond to disappear. The business manager thought something should be done. "I consulted one faculty member who had experience in water management. We put together a proposal to the appropriate [state] authorities to build a small dam on the creek and a pipe to connect the dam to the pond." It took them six months to get permission to build the dam. Then,

just about when we were ready to put it up, I began to be aware . . . that several members of the community felt Quaker process had been violated, that we were damaging the ecology—even though we'd spent a lot of time demonstrating to the authorities that we were ecologically responsible. The main argument was that it's "unnatural" to divert water this way.

Much of the opposition came from the science department, which used the creek to teach ecology. The business manager learned that the main theme of the general science program was water, and a central science project was a mock hearing about the building of a dam. Students were taught that "basically it's the bad guys who build dams versus the good guys who let nature take its course. I really walked into that one, unaware of all this." In response to the controversy, a pond committee was established, and open faculty meetings were held. Eventually it was decided that the dam would be built with a large pipe underneath it, "so under no circumstances would water ever stop flowing down the stream."

One major lesson the business manager had learned from this experience, he said, was that "to make good decisions, you have to know a lot of school history, a lot about personalities and relationships." The dam crisis at Mott was fueled by personality conflicts, but at heart it was a moral dilemma. It did not simply represent a difference of opinion over whether to dam the stream. Instead, it became a test of the validity of principles: what was taught in the classroom should be practiced at the school. More important, the Quaker decision-making process had to be respected. Those with concerns for the environment had to be given an opportunity to express their feelings to the community; consensus had to be sought on the proposal. As a teacher who had objected to the dam said, "I don't want to make enemies on campus. But I couldn't go into the classroom and talk about dams and then ignore that one was being built here. . . . I couldn't tell the students to protect the environment and not do it myself here at school."

Most teachers at Mott essentially approve of consensus as a decision-making method, although they admit it can be wearying. One man called it a mixed blessing. "I've had to sit through hundreds of hours of talk on subjects that don't interest me much. On the other hand, no petty bureaucrat has ever called the shots around here. . . . But it has cost me a lot of time to pay for that privilege." Said another teacher:

Discussing what is going to happen at this school and . . . what our duties will consist of is a rare opportunity. It's also what we have instead of money. Because you can go to public school where you can earn more and have someone tell you what to do and have two faculty meetings per year for announcements.

Of course, not everything can be decided in a meeting. A department head said that the headmaster "would run me out of town if every little thing that gets decided at my desk had the whole department in on it. . . . The trick is to know the right call!" The headmaster himself spoke positively about the consensus process as a way of uniting faculty behind a decision. He described how, at any administrative, departmental, or school-wide faculty meeting,

absolutely anybody can stand up and say, "I really oppose this, it's crazy." And a lot of people waste a lot of people's time standing up and saying they disagree with things. It's an incredibly inefficient way to run an institution. But one of the nice by-products is a great deal of unity on most issues and a great deal of pride that students and teachers feel about the school.

Not all Mott's teachers want to be involved in decision making; some find the numerous faculty and committee meetings a waste of time. One person, a non-Quaker, couldn't understand why so many of her fellow teachers felt the need "to know dumb details" and "to be involved in everything":

I just pick the things that are important to me, and I roll up my sleeves and get bodily into it. The rest I leave to the people whose job it is. But Quakers need to be involved in the most minute administrative decisions: Shall we start the day at 8:50 or 8:55? . . . I think that there's an efficiency to saying occasionally, "This is the way it's going to be."

The majority of the faculty, however, worry that in spite of an attempt to follow Quaker process, too many decisions are forced. In a true Quaker Meeting for Business, one person said, no issue "that's really potentially harmful to one or two of the members of the Meeting [is] resolved until they feel good about it." At Mott, because of the size of the staff and the urgency of many of the decisions, "you just can't wait two years for somebody to come around before you do something, so you have to railroad some things." Another Quaker teacher, who had been at Mott for many years, felt that the school was increasingly run by the administrators rather than by the professional staff as a whole. "I see that from the administration's standpoint it's simpler now," he said; "you make experts out of the decision makers, and it's quicker, but it's not Quakerly. That's not what's meant by consensus." Of course, he admitted, the administration did keep bringing issues to the faculty for discussion. "But the process has become decision-by-wearing-down! Either the administration says, 'The faculty couldn't make up their minds so we had to do this,' or they say, 'Everyone has spoken up and we think they must mean this.'" Such tactics do not represent Quaker process, he felt, where concerns are expressed and a true sense of the Meeting is reached.

Learning the Language of Concern   In a community where discussion is so important, language takes on a special significance, and some power is bound to rest with the rhetorically gifted. Historically, however, Quakers have frowned on eloquent rhetoric, because it suggests that the speaker is voicing his or her own "creaturely" thoughts, perhaps even in a prepared speech, rather than speaking as the Inner Light directs. Even in a faculty meeting at Mott, Fox, or Dyer, where only a minority of the teachers are devout Friends, a few words that seem to come from the heart are more valued than a speech. More important than obvious rhetorical skill is command of the Quaker idiom. A non-Quaker teacher at Dyer spoke bitterly about the divisions in faculty meeting caused by the moral weight of Quakerliness. Many people quickly learn to use the right language, she said; they talk of "'sensing this,' 'feeling comfortable with that,' 'having clarity' about something," and so on. "One plays along. There is more . . . space given to those who 'really know.'" When she first came to work at the school, she put a lot of effort into just watching and listening and figuring out who was a Friend and who was not:

My first year here, we were discussing a really difficult issue, and one teacher . . . finally got exasperated and said, "Why don't we just vote?" And the room fell silent. . . . Even I . . . knew that that was just an absolute no-no, and that he had just shown everyone that he was not in step. And one of the Quaker teachers finally said [mimicking a soft, supercilious voice], "Friends don't vote."

At Fox, almost all the adults are comfortable with a Quaker vocabulary, but they use it in different ways. Some give such words as *concern* and *leading* a religious meaning, while others use them figuratively. The headmaster explained that this division is recent; it did not exist when the entire staff "were all members of the Yearly Meeting . . . [and] weighty Friends." Today, "our younger staff tend to be Quaker-oriented, but they [have] . . . theological and political differences" with the older teachers and members of the Meeting. Many of the young teachers are attracted to the school because of Quakerism's liberal political stance, and some come to Fox "at best without an interest in the spiritual elements of it and at worst with a chip on their shoulder about it." They forget that "the roots of the school are quite Christian." The headmaster shook his head as he recalled the year before, when "a teacher stood up [in Meeting for Worship] and said, 'I don't believe in God.' There was a furor about that that I thought would never die down. . . . It got all through the whole Yearly Meeting, and people wanted to know why I didn't fire the guy."

Several young Fox faculty members are uncomfortable with spiritual language of any kind in faculty meetings. "When spiritual arguments are used to support . . . faculty policy," one of them said, "it strikes me as a tactical move—a way of assuming the moral high ground. . . . Those are the sorts of arguments that are very hard to respond to. . . . I'm very cynical, because I can see how manipulative these statements are. If you say, 'I've thought about this a lot, and I am led to this position,' as if by the Light, well, it's very hard for someone else to respond on a rational, logical level." Another person at Fox, a non-Quaker, had started out thinking that the Friends' way of making decisions was "marvelous," but the longer she observed, the more strongly she felt that "it was fairly unworkable at a school, where you have to decide things quickly. . . . It amounted to an excuse for doing nothing."

For both of these people, *concern* means neither a strong expression of conscience nor a statement of religious conviction, but, rather, a tactic for discouraging dissent. The non-Quaker described faculty meetings in which

> if anyone raised a strong concern against doing something, even without any valid reason—just "I have a feeling that this isn't right"—then, bang, everything stopped, and nothing would be done. . . . It made me realize how powerful one person could be if they wanted to manipulate the system. . . . I remember one man in particular who did it a lot, a well-thought-of Quaker. It seemed like whenever anything important came up, he would get this "feeling."[1]

Clearly, the expression of a concern, when not tempered with strong convictions held by other members of the group, can be a tool for individual control rather than a means of reconciling conscience and community. Sometimes a concern is used to push forward an unwanted change; sometimes it serves as an excuse for stagnation. Even sincerely felt concerns can raise instant opposition, instead of eliciting sympathy, when they are couched in certain vocabularies. The use of a political vocabulary at Mott, a Christian vocabulary at Fox, or a psychotherapeutic vocabulary at Dyer is likely to cause tension, because each represents a particular, and at times controversial, attitude toward the purpose of the school. The content of the concern is often lost because of the language in which it is spoken, and the Quaker decision-making process is reduced to wrangling between the different camps.

When Consensus Fails Faculty meetings at Fox and Dyer were tense.[2] Teachers' faces and body postures often expressed anger, frustration, or exasperation. Several ostentatiously read magazines during the meetings or moved restlessly around the room. At both schools, agendas seemed to be set by the headmasters. Discussion about a new drug-counseling program at Fox and about whether Saturday classes should be offered at Dyer were heated, but no resolution was reached, nor was any minute offered to sum up a sense of the Meeting about these issues. At Fox the new drug-counseling program, a sort of in-school version of Narcotics Anonymous, was presented by the headmaster and a faculty member as a fait accompli; although the headmaster asked for questions from the assembled teachers, there was no sense that their contributions would affect the program. Serious questions raised by dorm staff, such as how to coordinate the new policy of helping drug users with the old policy of busting them, were left unanswered. At Dyer, it was clear that most of the teaching staff had strong reservations about holding Saturday classes. Yet even as the plan was under discussion in faculty meetings, the brand-new admissions catalogue arrived from the printer with Saturday classes included as Dyer policy. At the end of an especially stressful Dyer meeting, one teacher, a non-Quaker, shocked the group by articulating what many were clearly feeling:

Teacher: I feel that we have no power; I don't know if what we've said here will be taken into account. . . . It's okay to have a few special classes on Saturday, but that's opening the back door to the possibility of having a six-day school. I feel like the school is a caravan, and the horses are pulling in different directions.

Faculty clerk: [upset] You need to have trust in the process! Why are you assuming that a decision will be taken without hearing these voices?

Teacher: I'm frightened. I'm not sure our voices are heard.

Teachers had already talked at length in earlier faculty meetings about these disputed topics, so it seems unlikely that being heard is a problem at either Dyer or Fox. The final decision-making process, however, is not as visible as it would be in a true Friends Meeting for Business. The connections between what is said in faculty meetings, what (if anything) is resolved by the group as a whole, and what is presented as policy by administrators are not made clear. Even faculty discussions about difficult students at both these schools are a chance to air concerns rather than to find solutions. In Mott's special meetings to discuss problem students, the presentation of each student's case ends with a concrete proposal for action approved by all present. At the other two schools, in faculty meetings teachers express genuine concern about individual students, but frequently the problems they raise—poor grades, rudeness, class cuts, possible drug use, and so on—are not met with practical responses. Information is exchanged, but decisions are not reached. The result is a terrible frustration among the faculty and a sense of betrayal, particularly at Dyer.

Many of the aspects of their decision making that bother Quaker-school faculty members—the time-consuming meetings, for example, the need for "substantial agreement on values, goals, and processes," and the "emotional intensity" of interpersonal relationships—are typ-

ical of what Joyce Rothschild-Whitt calls "collectivist-democratic" organizations.[3] Worry about conflict and how to handle it is also typical.
Rothschild-Whitt points out that a difficulty in absorbing conflict is
endemic to collectivist organizations, first, because their decision-
making process requires unanimous agreement, which leaves no legitimate, institutionalized role for dissenters (such as the role of the loyal
opposition in party politics), and, second, because the process demands face-to-face discussion of issues. This "personalizes the ideas
that people espouse and thereby makes the rejection of those ideas
harder to bear."[4]

While there is much that Rothschild-Whitt would recognize as
typically "collectivist-democratic" in a Quaker faculty meeting, a great
many of the tensions that are felt and expressed there have their roots
specifically in the Quaker moral tradition. Whether to speak or be
silent is, as Chapter Two described, a typical Quaker dilemma; how a
message is spoken is also traditionally problematic for Friends.[5] Does
a particular leading come from God or not? Should one advocate
action or waiting? Should one express a concern in the face of opposition from others, or should one go along with the opinion of weightier
Friends? These and other dilemmas have a long history in Quakerism,
and they are complicated today by the fact that so many people
become Friends for political reasons, and so have trouble understanding that concern is a religious concept.

Conflict over the meaning of virtues and the way they should be
practiced invariably occurs in running a Quaker school. Silent soul-
searching, dialogue with colleagues, strong words at faculty meetings,
and even anger are inevitable. To work, the Quaker decision-making
process requires strength and sensitivity on the part of the clerk and
empathy and respect on the part of the decision makers. At Dyer and
Fox, the teachers' frustration and sense of powerlessness and the
administrators' despair over the inefficiency of the meetings reflect a
failure of Quaker process. The environment of the meetings is not
conducive to expressions of concern in the true Quaker sense. Quakerly concern demands not only passion but also serenity, which shows
itself in sympathy for one's colleagues, openness to their concerns, a
willingness to see one's own concerns questioned and tested, and,
above all, faith in the process of consensus. Without these, the moral
voice in Quaker decision-making can easily be lost in a storm of

arguments and self-important pronouncements or be drowned in resentful silence.

When Consensus Succeeds: Quaker Concern over Nicaragua The debate over Mott's role in Nicaragua is an example of the Quaker decision-making process when it is fired by concern and tempered by sympathy with others' viewpoints. In the fall of 1987, board members, administrators, teachers, and some parents and students were caught up in a conflict over a proposed student work camp in Managua; the debate culminated in a half-day meeting to resolve the issue. The project had been initiated over two years earlier: several members of the staff, including the headmaster and the academic dean, had been in touch with the faculty of a Managua public school; the Nicaraguan principal had visited Mott; and a group of Mott teachers had been to Managua. To these teachers, the logical next step was to take students with them to Managua, to help with repairs on the dilapidated schoolhouse. These kinds of projects have a long history among Quakers, through such organizations as the American Friends Service Committee. It was no coincidence that the chosen site of the new program was Nicaragua, at a time when the United States government was still supporting the Contras' war against the Sandinista government. The Managua work camp was important to many members of the Mott community because of their distress over U.S. policy in Nicaragua. As one teacher explained, the project was part of "a long tradition of Friends being reconcilers . . . who want to try to find a stand between hostile camps, find common ground, find ways of keeping dialogue open in the midst of hostilities." It was important that students should spend time in "a country that according to current policy is considered 'the enemy,'" so that they could see that "the people aren't the enemy, obviously."

The more activist members of the faculty, the ones who interpreted the school's Quaker heritage as a political responsibility (among these were the headmaster and the academic dean), supported the Managua work camp. Other teachers, many—but by no means all—non-Quaker, were less enthusiastic about the project. Some offered it their qualified support only because of their great affection and respect for the academic dean, the proposal's main champion. Others actively disapproved, either because they felt the school shouldn't, as one teacher put it, "proselytize," or because they honestly felt the trip might not be safe for students. "From the news, it sounds scary and dumb to send kids down there," one teacher said. "Yet the people [on the faculty] who have been there say it's not like that inside, that the media is blowing it out of proportion. . . . So I have decided not to get involved, because I'm really torn. I think safety first for the kids." In addition, she worried about the school being sued if anything should happen to a student.

Some supporters of the Managua trip felt that their colleagues' expressions of concern for students' safety and the school's reputation were attempts to disguise aversion to the trip for political reasons. Debate about the work camp spread from the faculty to members of the school board (almost all of whom were Friends) and from the board to parents and alumni. The board, finding that its subcommittee for student affairs could not reach consensus on a proposal for the full committee, brought up the trip for discussion in one of its regular meetings. When prolonged debate left the issue still unresolved, an all-day retreat was organized to allow concerned board members and teachers to continue the discussion and attempt to reach consensus about the Managua work camp.

The retreat was clerked by the head of the board or "school committee." The approximately fifty people who attended (about half teachers and half committee members, plus one or two students) made a masterful attempt to balance their strong personal convictions with affection and respect for one another, on the one hand, and with self-discipline in the interests of school unity, on the other. The meeting on Nicaragua lasted all afternoon, and the history of Mott's work camp program and of the relationship with the Managua school was discussed in detail, as were such practical matters as liability insurance coverage and the U.S. State Department advisory report on Nicaragua. Dialogue culled from my field notes illustrates how the teachers and committee members struggled to balance the demands of conscience with the requirements of community, in order to come to a right and Quakerly decision.

At one point a school committee member asked, "Why don't we just approve the program under a non-Mott banner, so the Mott image isn't involved?" Somewhere in the room, someone murmured, "That's wimping out," and another school committee member said firmly, "If we are going to do this, we have to stand up and be counted." This generated many murmurs of agreement. Later, a teacher proposed a compromise: "Suppose we plan to go ahead with the trip if talks begin between the Sandinistas and the Contras. . . . We'll go if things get better." The academic dean, a non-Quaker, responded to this suggestion by explaining the roots of his long-time association with Friends:

It was very moving to me to hear about how Friends reached out across hatred to Indians and slaves. . . . The history of Friends is one of having courage in spite of dangers . . . during World War II, after World War I. They have always acted with considerable costs. What we are proposing [in Managua] is in the best tradition of Friends.

In response to worries that the trip would be dangerous, he emphasized the dangers of not going to Managua:

At a time when people in our country are taught hatred, isn't it appropriate to teach kids to feel humanity? To fail do that—that is what is dangerous. To put the kinds of concerns that have been raised today before Friends' history is . . . [he paused, upset]. We are deciding not to do what is the right moral thing to do, and that is a bad message to give to faculty and students.

Another non-Quaker faculty member said that she, too, had come to Mott ten years earlier for the reasons the dean had given. Added an administrator, "If we are going to make our stand as a Friends institution, we have to take risks. That's part of our heritage—Quakers do take risks." "But should we put our children at risk?" someone asked. This was exactly what a school committee member said he had been wrestling with. "I must separate out what I would do myself from what I would do as a board member. Am I as a trustee comfortable with the responsibility of deciding that Mott should send a group of students to Managua in 1988? The answer is no."

The discussion went on. "Three or four weeks ago I was leaning toward being against this work camp," said a committee member, "but I'm convinced today that it's appropriate." But still he felt the time was not right. Another committee member, a weighty Friend, was not convinced at all:

I find it hard to adopt a rigid position, saying Managua cannot go forward because I am against it. But in conscience I would have to put myself with those who feel that the overall welfare of the school . . . would be unnecessarily placed at risk by our insisting that a pure Quaker conscience demands that we go to Managua.

As it became clear that the meeting would find it impossible to unite behind the idea of a student work camp in Managua, a number of those present turned to the faculty members who were most committed to the project, offering sympathy and promising general support. One of the board members who most strongly opposed the work camp assured the academic dean of his great respect for him. The clerk asked if "the faculty who have put so much energy into Nicaragua can . . . compromise and put their energy in other directions?" Charlie McDowell, the head of the religion department, answered that "as Friends historically, we act out of . . . the concerns we have within us." Compromise, given such strong convictions, is not easy. In addition, he reminded the school committee, Mott already had a relationship with the Managua school. "I feel personally very disappointed that after they have received us so hospitably and been so warm, we have to tell them we can't come."

"What can we move forward on?" asked the clerk of the school committee. He turned to the headmaster, who answered:

I had lunch with someone recently who was headmistress of a Quaker school in Germany in the mid-thirties. She had to make three important political decisions. Should she allow pictures of Hitler to be put on the walls? The answer was no. Should the students and teachers use "Heil Hitler"? The answer was no. Would the school expel a Jewish student? The answer was no. She had to flee Germany because her life was in jeopardy. I'm not suggesting a close analogy, but sometimes decisions that don't seem clear at the time they are being made are very clear thirty or so years later. By deciding against the work camp, we're making a decision that allows Mott to survive. But it is dangerous. The people in Nicaragua are broken people, and they are broken people because of American policies. We need to be doing something about that. Perhaps it is the responsible decision not to go—but it troubles my soul.

"My Light says we should go," responded a committee member. "Mine, too," said another. And so the discussion went on, as the group searched for a proposal they could unite behind. All afternoon the clerk had periodically proposed minutes that were rejected. Finally a minute was agreed upon; it stated that the *adults* in the Mott community would pursue "continuing and expanding contact with the Managua school." As is often the case in Quaker consensus, there were many in the group who were not in complete agreement with the minute—some because they found it too activist, and others because they found it too weak—but for the first time in the long debate these dissenters tacitly agreed to "stand aside" and accept this interpretation of the sense of the Meeting.

This retreat was a power struggle between activist faculty members and more cautious committee members, and, in the end, caution won. However, although supporters of the work camp might not see it that way, the meeting was also a victory for the Quaker moral tradition and for the reconciling possibilities of concern. Teachers' and committee members' sincere expressions of concern about the Managua work camp brought Quaker values to the fore. The antagonists were angry with one another, but they were also forced by Quaker process and the disciplined setting to listen to one another and to experience their shared attachment to the school. In this context, decision making became a highly personal responsibility, even a moral duty, rather than merely a task to be accomplished. The outcome demonstrated the kind of moral stability that can be achieved through conflict, when it is conducted with mutual respect.

Military Schools: Ambivalence
About Leadership

Military decision-making is not usually thought of as involving much debate. Theoretically, however, an officer consults his staff before issuing an order, and staff members, whatever their rank, respond with suggestions and criticisms. Once an order has been given, they obey it, unless they believe it is illegal. Written procedures also play an important role in the military decision-making process, because of the emphasis on consistency and fairness. In practice, a great deal of military "decision making" means accepting an order from a superior, deciding how it should be accomplished, and seeing that it is carried out correctly. But it can also mean objecting to an order or deciding to disobey it, as Chapter Two showed. All this is part of the responsibility of leadership.

Teachers Who Are Denied Leadership Roles Leadership is the primary lesson that adolescents are taught at military academies, which makes its practice among the adults particularly interesting to observe. It starts at the top, with the headmaster. During the 1987–88 school year, both Pershing and Jackson had strong headmasters; at Sherman, the headmaster was too busy trying to placate the school board and resolve squabbles among his administrative staff to put much effort into running the school. He admitted that he was tired of his job. "I'm not as hard as I should be," he said. "I could do a much better job. . . . I spend too much time at this desk, but . . . I have to do a lot of paperwork. . . . I could be a lot more involved with the kids, I could go down at night to the barracks. . . . But I need time for myself." He felt that real change in the school was almost impossible, because of a "very uncooperative board" and "the factions" among his employees:

The tacs hate the teachers; the teachers hate the tacs; this one hates that one. They've all hated each other for twenty years. I can't come in like a big guy and make them all love each other, because they . . . won't, and they don't like me. . . . Whenever you inject change, they don't like it. . . . Some of the key people on the staff are dead wood; the faculty has a lot of dead wood, too.

Such weak leadership from above does not encourage involvement from below or commitment to improving the school. Teachers' meetings at Sherman occur only once or twice a year and are intended to allow the academic dean to impart information, not to engage teachers in decision making. Informal contact and consultation between administrators and teachers is also minimal. One teacher said I was the first person to observe his class in seven years, since "no one here cares about what happens in the classroom." No one, he said, thought of evaluating teachers' performances and setting standards for improvement if there were problems. Indeed, recently a teacher of four years' service had been summarily fired without ever having been warned that anything was amiss, while another learned that his contract was not going to be renewed only when he met his already-hired replacement at a conference. The administration was content to ignore problems in the classroom "so long as no one outside the school complains and there are no repercussions," because "it's easier to just maintain the status quo." As soon as someone, especially a powerful parent, raised a stink, however, a teacher was in danger of being fired. Why this pattern of neglect and punishment? "I don't know if it's callousness or cowardice," answered the teacher. "I think it's cowardice, a reluctance to deal openly and honestly with problems."

If supportive relations between teachers and administrators are rare at Sherman, so are friendships among teachers. Teacher after teacher echoed the man who said, "When I first came here, someone gave me a good piece of advice, which was, 'Don't get involved with the other people here.' And I've stuck to that." Even the cadets are kept at a distance by the adults, most of whom see their students only in the classroom. A man who had taught at Sherman for over twenty years and lived on campus said he had no idea what values the cadets were learning, because he had little contact with them.

The only regular administrative meetings are those the headmaster holds with his staff, and the formal talk there goes on against a background of whispers. In the meeting I attended, the various heads of departments—academic dean, commandant of cadets, admissions director, business manager, and so on—reported on upcoming events and their probable costs and responded to the headmaster's questions. The academic dean also informed the group about new admissions, suspensions, and expulsions of cadets. It was clear that the purpose of the meeting was to keep the headmaster informed, not to share problems with colleagues and solicit their advice or come to any decisions. In interviews, teachers, tactical officers, and even some members of the administrative staff indicated that they didn't know how decisions were made and for the most part didn't care, unless the decision affected them personally. At Sherman, it seems, the trappings of military leadership are present—many faculty members wear uniforms and call themselves captain or major—but an interest in sharing the burdens of running the school is absent.

At Jackson, faculty feel a stronger attachment to the school, thanks largely to several dedicated administrators. One of these is Major Sedgefield, who makes an effort to communicate informally with teachers and keep them abreast of changes in policy that may affect them. Any sense of autonomy, however, is impossible, even for the members of the administrative staff. Although Jackson's headmaster is as dominant as Sherman's is weak, their impact on leadership opportunities among faculty is surprisingly similar. Jackson's head insists on being completely in control of all aspects of school business and refuses to delegate even mundane administrative matters. He allows his staff to make only minor decisions, and teachers at Jackson, like those at Sherman, have no say whatsoever in policy-making.

I attended one of Jackson's weekly administrative meetings. The headmaster, or "the general," as he is called, entered the room without greeting any of his assembled staff, sat down, and ordered, "Report." Each person spoke at length and in extremely respectful tones about the week's occurrences. Possible changes in the following year's calendar were discussed, and the staff offered tentative timetables for Parents' Day, the post-Christmas intersession, and vacations. The general's responses to these suggestions were vague. A long discussion about the need to "crack down" allowed him to express anger about "poor military standards" and resulted in the only clear directive to come out of the meeting—that the commandant's office bring all the cadet officers together and ask for their recommendations on improving discipline. After the meeting, one person remarked that my presence had spared them the general's "weekly tirade." Although all but one of the people present at the meeting had had experience in the professional military, there was no sense of collegiality or joint leadership responsibility, nor did the general issue orders in a traditional military manner. Someone took me aside after the hour-long meeting and asked if I had any idea what follow-up the headmaster expected of his staff. When I said that, except for the cadet officers' meeting, there were no clear orders, he looked both amused and relieved. "I'm glad it's not just me," he said. "I never get any clear signals in there."

Teachers Who Reject Leadership Roles   Only at Pershing are the faculty, thanks to the current headmaster, involved in decision making. The system of faculty governance, as it is called, is only a few years old. Elected faculty representatives meet twice a month with the academic dean, who presents the agenda and chairs the meeting. Items on the agenda that require investigation are delegated to one of eight committees responsible for different aspects of school life: academic affairs, student affairs, discipline, and so on. Committee members report back to the executive committee. Most final decisions are made by the executive committee or the head of the school. Full faculty meetings at Pershing are rare; one long-term teacher said he could not even remember when the last one had been held. Nevertheless, proposals on school policy are sometimes put to the vote of the entire faculty and white-collar staff.

I attended a meeting of the executive committee of the faculty. The tone of this meeting was serious but not stiff: the eleven representatives sat in straight-backed chairs around a large, polished table and followed *Robert's Rules of Order*. Discussion was brisk and, under the firm hand of the academic dean, who positioned the debates and summed up points, resolutions were reached. A casual observer would have awarded the participants high marks for articulateness and efficiency; the teachers and counselors who composed the committee seemed at ease with one another and willing to air their views. What called into question the strength of the system were the two main topics under discussion: first, whether the faculty committee on financial aid and admissions should be dissolved, and, second, whether nonteaching staff (housemothers, development officers, admissions counselors, grounds supervisors, and so on) should be permitted to vote on matters relating to curriculum, the academic calendar, and other faculty concerns. Debate about the admissions committee revealed that the members of this committee were unable or unwilling to define a useful role for themselves in the face of the admissions director's hostility to their overtures; discussion of the second topic indicated a growing tension between the teaching and nonteaching members of the community.

After the meeting, one of the participants talked about some of the problems with the decision-making process. The main one, he said, is that faculty at Pershing simply aren't used to being asked for their opinions: "It goes against the grain of what has traditionally characterized this school." Teachers and even administrators are accustomed to orders being issued by an "omnipresent and omnipotent" headmaster and then passed down the chain of command. The new faculty governance process "lumbers," he said, because "the initiative does not proceed from the ground level as it should." The debate about the admissions committee was an example of faculty reluctance to take charge. "If there is any facet of this school that faculty seem to be concerned about and to express themselves about, it's admissions, and here is a group that clearly has within their mandate the opportunity to initiate activities in the admissions area. Yet they want someone from on high to tell them what to do, so they can then complain about it! It's a very frustrating situation."

He went on to say that, whereas a few people are disappointed that the new system of governance hasn't led to more discussion and New

England town meeting–style democracy, most of the faculty "would go crazy if they had to assemble to vote on all the things that . . . have been delegated to administrators. I think there is a great desire that all manner of things should be discussed, but then, when there are meetings for that purpose, they pride themselves on the speed with which the meeting can be transacted." Even the teachers who are renowned for their disagreement with administrative decisions, "who like to sit around and sip their coffee and bemoan it all," would rather complain than act: "They certainly don't want to get together in a formal meeting and demonstrate dissent." After a century of "chain of command, orders from on high," and the headmaster acting as a kind of "post commander," this teacher felt it was difficult for faculty members to take responsibility for decision making.

A senior Pershing teacher who doesn't like the faculty government system—"The irreverent cliché, God so loved the world that he didn't send a committee, says it all"—said he knew why teachers were reluctant to "demonstrate dissent" in public:

We know . . . that if the head of the school starts shaking his finger at you, what you better do is shut your face. . . . The reason people feel that way is because the headmaster has the power to fire you on the spot and has, not once, but several times. Not this man. But anybody who's been here any length of time remembers. . . . [He is referring to a former headmaster who "was like a scene out of *The Godfather*" and fired a number of people, including teachers with many years of service.]

The current headmaster, he added, "has a very difficult time under-standing that," because he believes that in a meeting everyone should be able to "disagree and yell at one another" but after the meeting is over still be friends. But "it doesn't work that way." The fact is that "no one is willing to . . . gamble" on the headmaster's goodwill, and that "put[s] a damper on any open discussion when people get to feeling strongly one way or another about a subject."

Fear of being fired is one reason teachers do not participate actively in the faculty governance system. Another is that some of them see the system as a ploy to gather faculty endorsement for administrative policies. One teacher said that she and several of her colleagues felt disillusioned, because what they had thought was "democracy in ac-tion" seemed no more than a matter of using committees to validate decisions that had been predetermined. "It's a matter of manipulation," she concluded. Yet another objection to the system is that it puts the decision-making process in the hands of the whole professional community, instead of just the teachers. In the executive committee meeting I had attended, it was decided that nonacademic staff would not be banned from voting, because it was important to preserve community feeling even at the expense of efficiency of governance. At the same time, all present agreed that nonteaching staff would be encouraged not to vote on issues that were "not their concern." Even with this restriction, the decision met with disapproval from some members of the academic faculty, one of whom said he felt it was wrong that safety officers, maintenance supervisors, and other white-collar school employees "who never see the kids" were allowed to vote on "strictly educational" matters.

Some faculty had been enthusiastic about the decision-making system when it was first introduced and had participated eagerly, serving on the executive committee of the faculty or on one of the many subcommittees in charge of gathering information and proposing solutions to particular problems. Their disillusionment began when they received no response to their reports or when their solutions were rejected without explanation by the executive committee. Someone who had served his term in the government system and refused to run again said that many of the committee members "work very hard, they study, they investigate, they spend a lot of time preparing a document or some kind of recommendation." Sometimes the proposal they submit is "shot down"; sometimes it is passed on to the headmaster to be implemented or rejected. In any case, "it might be months, or it might be never, that we see or hear what has happened to it."

The most common reason for teachers to object to the faculty governance system, however, is not that they are afraid to speak their minds, or that they feel manipulated, or object to nonteaching staff involvement, or resent the lack of feedback about subcommittee reports. Rather, it is that most Pershing faculty and staff think that, not they, but the head of the school should make the decisions. As one teacher said, "There comes a time when you just have to Ayatollah a decision through . . . and then it's our duty as faculty members to say, 'Yes, sir, that's the way it is and that's the way it's going to be.'" Another put it even more bluntly:

The committees are just a pain. Decisions should be made from the top, with no waiting for committee recommendations. . . . I don't believe in too much input. . . . I could care less about a lot of this stuff they talk about in committee—who cares? My job is to teach, the headmaster's job is to run the school. He shouldn't need all these committees to do that.

The attitude of the majority of the Pershing faculty toward self-government is not very different from that of many committed public-school teachers, who want to teach their classes, help students, be involved in extracurricular activities, and then go home and grade papers. As far as they are concerned, administration is the job of administrators, not teachers. Many adults at Pershing consider themselves sufficiently overworked and underpaid not to wish to add self-government to their duties. In their eyes, they are called upon, not to be leaders themselves, except in the classroom, but, rather, to accept the decisions of the head of the school, whom most see as a competent, intelligent, and personable headmaster, a leader they can be proud of. The irony of the faculty's attitude toward decision making is that Pershing tries to teach a different understanding of leadership to its cadets, in which service to community and military unit, an assumption of personal responsibility for your actions no matter what your rank, and close involvement in the running of your company are paramount. These lessons encourage not only obedience to authority, which the Pershing faculty embraces, but also a desire to assume authority oneself. Cadets compete with one another for increasing amounts of responsibility in supervising the corps, and adults encourage these ambitions. The faculty's dislike of the responsibilities of school governance, however, indicates that they reject this side of leadership for themselves.

Faculty Decision-Making and Visions of Change

This overview of faculty involvement in the decision-making process at the six schools shows that teachers are given the opportunity not only to teach concern or leadership as the moral approach to the demands of daily life but also to exercise it themselves. At the three Friends schools, most teachers are eager to be part of decisions made on campus and willing to express their concerns about the running of the school, even when their opinions are not solicited (as the story of the Mott dam shows). Unfortunately, distrust of the consensus process has transformed many teachers' concerns into anger, cynicism, or pettiness. Nevertheless, attempts to reach consensus continue, because teachers feel so strongly about their right to have a say. Only at Mott, however, does there seem to be a supportive environment for the expression of concerns that encourages faculty members to assume personal responsibility for difficult decisions, as the story of the Nicaraguan work camp shows.

At the three military academies, the majority of teachers, counselors, tactical officers, and other staff are not active in the decision-making process. At Sherman and Jackson, this option is simply not available. At the former school, strong adult leadership is lacking; at the latter, autocracy masquerades as military leadership. At Pershing, the majority of teachers not only feel that the faculty governance system is not working but also seem to resent being asked to help run the school. This is well illustrated by the faculty admissions committee's inability to define a function for itself. For the most part, teachers do not see a moral role for themselves except in their relationship with students. The lesson that above all others they wish to convey to adolescents—the importance of assuming responsibility—is one that many of them reject for themselves once they are outside the classroom.

One reason for these different attitudes among the two sets of teachers is the contrasting visions of change that are part of the Quaker and military traditions. As Chapter Three explained, Friends feel a moral responsibility to improve society for the sake of the individual, while the military focuses on preserving society and improving the individual. Teachers at Friends schools have no trouble seeing school governance as part of their job, since making a better school is one of the most important ways they can serve students. In addition, Quaker-school adults place little emphasis on formal roles: the inner self of each teacher or administrator is more important than his or her official duties. At military school, where roles are a key source of identity, a teacher defines his or her job as imparting knowledge to students and sees no reason to assume the role of administrator as well. Running a Friends school is perceived by the staff as a moral project—the building of a loving, egalitarian community. For military-school faculty, running the school is the more mundane task of daily maintenance, which provides a secure backdrop against which the real business of moral education can occur. At Quaker school, teachers practice the virtues by making decisions; at military school, the virtues are applied through the proper enforcement of decisions.

Student Involvement in Self-Government

The Quaker moral project emphasizes helping adolescents to bring out their Inner Light and become deeply aware of and able to express their concerns. The military moral project encourages adolescents to shoulder responsibility and be good leaders of their fellow students. Beneath these divergent narratives, however, run a number of common themes. Adults at both sets of schools want their charges to be self-confident. They want them to be self-disciplined. Above all, perhaps, they want them to be committed: to the school, to a set of values, to a future. The adults, judging the adolescents' decisions in terms of the goals set for them, are often disappointed. As a result, adults and adolescents clash over students' choices, particularly the choices they make—or fail to make—in response to school rules.

Students are permitted some involvement in the running of the six schools. At the three Quaker schools they may sit in on faculty meetings, and Mott has student representatives on several faculty committees. At the military academies, the top cadet officers can use the military chain of command to pass on student opinions and requests for changes in the rules. In general, however, neither Quaker- nor military-school students are deeply involved in the business of school governance. Yet many of them are deeply involved in governing themselves. At the Quaker schools (and Pershing's girls' school), prefects supervise dormitories, and students serve on the committees that recommend disciplinary action. At the military academies, cadets have a great deal of control over their subordinates, and those who break the honor code are tried by their peers. At both sets of schools, then, students have the potential to exercise authority and affect adult actions. Under the influence of two different traditions, the adolescents handle that potential differently.

Quaker Schools: Apathy or Independence?

Concern as It Is Defined by the Adults   Mott's Ellen Kahn likes her
pupils, her colleagues, and the school. Beneath her affection for the
adolescents in her classes, however, lies a puzzled distress at what she
sees as their complacency. She worries that perhaps in some way she
and her fellow teachers are to blame, that they've not "been very good
at . . . getting kids to take responsibility for themselves." She finds
Mott students "very passive in a lot of ways." Not, she explains, that
they are silent in class; on the contrary, "they're very willing and eager
to jump in, and volunteer, and discuss, and all of those things that
make teaching here wonderful." But they are rarely willing "to
challenge things that I say in class, which is a little disconcerting.
They'd much rather just write it down." In addition, she has "a sense
that students really don't take a lot of initiative and show leadership for
their own way of life here."

Take the students' involvement with the school newspaper. Kahn
remembers that when she edited her high-school newspaper, she and
her friends "were really challenging and pushing every moment." But
when she sponsored the Mott student paper, she found the kids
"unimaginative in the kinds of things they wanted to write about,"
unwilling to do "a lot of real hard work to investigate anything," and
wary of "writing anything controversial. . . . They'd rather complain
than follow through."

This view of the students as apathetic is shared by a number of the
more activist Mott faculty members. One reminisced about how much
excited exchange there used to be on the school opinion board, adding, "No one's got any good opinions any more." Another lamented
"the decline of challenging." And a third expressed his disappointment
over the students' egotism and lack of sensitivity but admitted, "That's
the nature of teenagehood!" One of the sponsors of a student peer-
counseling group called Students Helping Students, or SHS, commented on the group's members, some of the brightest and most
involved students in the school:

They don't know what to do to change a rule: how you find out where the rule
is written down and who wrote it and propose an alternative. I'm always
trying to tell them how to raise hell, but they don't seem to know how to

challenge authority, and they don't appreciate that Mott is challenging authority.

According to another faculty member, "I think the dominant theme in their thinking is, 'Am I treated justly or am I not treated justly? . . .' They see themselves as victims and as operated on, rather than as operators."

A speaker in one of Mott's all-school assemblies, a civil-liberties lawyer who knew that the school had a policy permitting students' rooms to be searched for drugs, talked passionately about their privacy rights. "I went out of the assembly thinking, 'I can't wait to hear the discussion at lunch,'" a teacher said. "But only the faculty were talking about it, not the students." Another said afterwards that he sat in the assembly thinking, "This is great; there are going to be some kids . . . up in arms, and there are going to be opinions, and they are going to start petitioning and making demands." But the result, as far as he could see, was "Nothing, nothing! . . . Nobody complained, there was no underground." Was it apathy? he wondered. "It would be interesting to quash some of their rights and oppress them a little, or have a war for them to get upset about. . . . But there's nothing that upsets them."

These adults are lamenting a lack of concern, in the Quaker sense of the word. To them, the students do not appear to feel moved by any strong personal conviction to act: to plan and put together the controversial newspaper than Ellen Kahn would like to see, to "raise hell" by challenging the rules for the sake of the students who come after them, as the SHS advisor urges them to do. These activist adults see the adolescents as rejecting a chance to try to change the school and, perhaps, later the world. A teacher at Dyer, who shares his Mott colleagues' worry about students' apparent apathy, feels that many of the teenagers are unaware that the ability to take a moral stand, to put forward a concern, depends upon knowledge:

They feel that changing the world is simply a matter of changing themselves. . . . There's a real fuzzy-headedness and a lack of ability to engage other people concretely about issues. Here the emphasis is: what you feel is right. Well, feelings may lead to good positions, but that will not equip you to argue for your positions in the outside world and to effect real change. You've got to be prepared intellectually to address the world.

Concern as It Is Defined by the Adolescents What this teacher forgets is that for an adolescent, especially one who has spent four years listening to talk about the Inner Light and deeply felt concerns, understanding one's feelings *is* more important than changing the world—or, rather, the two are inextricably mixed. One Mott senior said, "Right now I'm struggling with what I should do, and Mott has a very important impact on that. . . . It encourages me to struggle, tries to make me face the world. . . . But a lot of my struggle is within myself." Mike Dugan described a similar conflict. He listed what he thought were the "major moral dilemmas" of his time: apartheid in South Africa, world hunger, U.S. involvement in Nicaragua and Afghanistan. But the biggest moral dilemma facing him, he said, "is how much should I do for the world . . . and how much should I concentrate on myself. . . . I don't feel comfortable about . . . posing moral ideas to other people, until I've got it all worked out myself." How could he tell other people to stop hating each other when he still felt hate and prejudice? How could he protest war "when I still have a war going on in myself"? There had to be "a balance between how much you work on yourself and how much you work on other people. . . . I guess maybe a lot of the people in the community who pose these [political] ideals are older and have found that balance for themselves." But Mike is still looking for it.[6]

When Mike refers to "working on other people," he isn't just talking about Contras and Sandinistas. He is one of the fourteen members of Students Helping Students, the student-run peer-counseling service. The SHS center, furnished with beat-up, comfortable couches, is a haven for students who are high on drugs, drunk, depressed, lonely, or worried about families, roommates, girlfriends, or boyfriends. Not everyone is willing to turn to SHS members with problems, but many do. For Mike, SHS means "people constantly coming to me in need with emotional traumas, and me trying as best I can to help them cope and be a wall for them to bounce ideas off." In the past two years he has handled one attempted suicide and at least one severely depressed girl. "I took the knife out of one girl's hands after she'd already slit her wrists. The other one, earlier, hadn't gotten quite that far; [she was] walking train tracks." He is grateful that "SHS has a wonderful referral program, so one of the first things you learn is that you are not a psychologist and you are not God, and you can't handle all the situations."

Mike was one of several teenagers at Mott who described responding to a friend's talk of or attempt at suicide. At Fox, too, students' supposed apathy vanishes in the face of such emergencies. A few weeks before my visit, most of them had staged a sit-in in the headmaster's office protesting the decision to send home a sophomore who had made two suicide attempts. They argued that life with her, by all reports, disastrous family would make her worse and insisted she be kept at the school. The sit-in moved to the assembly room and turned into a long, heated, impromptu meeting between students and staff, in which the headmaster and dean tried to explain that what was best for the girl was not necessarily best for the school. After the meeting, a teacher started making inquiries and was able to find a psychiatric clinic that would take the girl until she was well enough to return to school. The sit-in participants were triumphant over the success of their intervention.

At Dyer, the most organized example of student activism in the 1987–88 school year was on the part of a student who was about to be expelled—after many previous run-ins with the staff—for coming late to a nonacademic event. The offense was minor, but for most of the faculty it was the last straw. Students, however, were incensed that anyone should be expelled for tardiness, and at community meeting many of them stood up in his defense. The exchange between adults and students was bitter, and several students lost their tempers and yelled insults at the teachers they felt were out to get their schoolmate. In the end, the boy's student supporters won the battle, and he remained at school.

These examples show that students at the three Quaker schools are not necessarily apathetic; they just aren't concerned about the issues adults want them to be concerned about. They don't want to work through the proper channels—the student government, the school newspaper, petitions, and committees—to change school rules. They aren't committed to the school as an institution in the same way that the teachers are: the teachers live at the school, whereas the students are only passing through on the way to the rest of their lives. They are surprisingly well informed about national and international politics, but those issues are too distant to engage most of them. What they are committed to is one another, not as a student body to be governed or persuaded but as individuals to be protected from hurt and injustice at the hands of adults. School policies, particularly those relating to discipline, are more worthy of defiance than discussion. As one boy asked rhetorically, "Are we supposed to respect their rules more than our friends?"

Many of the adolescents thoughtfully examine the limits imposed upon them and acquiesce to being controlled, sometimes because they perceive the rules' utility to the community and sometimes because they fear punishment. But when they disagree with a rule, they rarely work with school administrators to have it changed, as the adults would like them to do—they simply (and usually discreetly) disobey it.[7] The adults perceive students' lack of interest in school politics as apathy and the disobedience as immaturity, but for the students this behavior represents independence. Mott senior Leah Brodsky, who regarded herself as "being torn between what society wants me to think and what I definitely do think," said, "Basically I stick to the rules that . . . I think are right for me to do. Rules like signing out of the dorm to go the library I just don't even think twice about, because they're so dumb. Whereas signing out to go to town is important—in case someone gets kidnapped or hurt or something—so I always do that." She thinks that students having to leave their dorm-room doors open during the mandatory evening study period is "just ridiculous," since "a person should be able to have their privacy sometime during the day." But "the rest of the rules are pretty reasonable."

Occasionally there are times when adults are the first to acknowledge that the ability to put school rules into their proper perspective is a sign of maturity, as an incident at Mott had proved. A group of about twenty students sneaked off campus one winter day for a little alcoholic celebration in the snow. One girl, who had recently been seriously ill, suddenly passed out. Most of the kids panicked and ran back to school, but a few carried her to the road and hitchhiked a ride to the hospital, where it turned out that their prompt action may have saved her life. A boy who was there said:

I was wondering if I should save my own butt and just leave . . . or stay . . . and make sure that she got to the hospital. That was a dilemma. I ended up staying and helping to carry her to the road. . . . And it was really shocking to me that I had considered just leaving, and it was even more shocking how many people did just leave.

The teenagers who went to the hospital were punished for drinking and being off campus; the rest got off scot-free. Yet "the kids who stayed bore their demerits with pride, and they got nothing but respect from the faculty," a teacher commented.

Looking at the students' and teachers' different ways of demonstrating concern, one can see that, in a sense, the Quaker-school adults reap what they sow. Although the majority of them are greatly attached to their school and committed to it as a community, they preach "listening to your inner voice," "being true to yourself," "finding your own values," and other anti-conformist, and also anti-communal, slogans. It should not surprise these adults, then, that a student like Leah would obey only the rules she thinks are right for her. The adults, particularly at Mott, share social, religious, and political concerns that take them outside themselves. The students, however, taught to look inward, are concerned chiefly about themselves and one another. This self-awareness and sensitivity, more than anything else, is what "being Quakerly" means to them. As one Mott girl said, "The Quaker religion seems to breed nice people. They may not really change anything or make a difference, but they really care and they are more aware than a lot of other people. I really respect that."

Military Schools: Disobedience or Resourcefulness?

Leadership as It Is Defined by the Adults   If the adults at Quaker schools give mixed messages about the meaning of concern, messages about leadership at the military academies are not much clearer. For all their talk of teaching responsibility, adults are not sure how much real power to grant students and how much to hold them responsible for the behavior of their fellows. The emphasis on leadership means that cadets, much more than Quaker-school students, are asked to govern themselves, and officers are assumed to be in charge of their subordinates. But those in charge are also expected to lead the way in obedience, setting an example by meticulously following school rules. Student leaders may tell others what to do, but when their orders are ignored, their only official recourse is ignominiously to turn the offender over to an adult.[8]

The adults expect student leadership to be based on trust and dialogue, on a sharing of responsibility and information between faculty members and cadet officers. This ideal scenario presumes that the two groups share a vision of what should be accomplished and merely need to negotiate, in courteous and efficient military fashion, how these duties should be performed. The reality is different. Over the past few years at Pershing, counselors and cadet leaders have been battling for control of the companies. At present, the counselors are ascendant. "It was a little more volatile place when I first came," a counselor said. Student officers "did what they wanted to, and they felt comfortable . . . telling us, 'Listen, you're out of line, pal.'" He told about a colleague who "went through hell" getting his unit to "toe the line." At the beginning, "he'd have meetings where he'd say, 'This is what we're going to do,' and some kids would say to his face, 'No, fuck you, we're not doing that,' in front of forty other kids."

The ideal of shared authority based on trust and dialogue is problematic in part because adolescents and adults at military school have trouble talking together. A counselor in Pershing's girls' school worried about how little she really knew about the students assigned to her care, whom she sometimes saw for only "a minute a day." A girl who smiles in the hall and says hello could have "just had a horrible thing happen, and I wouldn't know." As a counselor, she feels she knows the girls a little better than most of the teachers, but that doesn't mean they necessarily want to confide in her. "I think they feel that I can use information against them, and I guess I could, whether consciously or not. So they are vulnerable, especially in a situation where they don't have much freedom, and I might be in a position to take even more of their freedom away."

Not all adults are as sensitive to the young people's needs as this woman is. One girl, a prefect whose poise led me to imagine that she was on close terms with her teachers, said, "I don't really confide in any adults here. There is a definite faculty/student relations problem on this campus. They are faculty, we are students, and that's as far as it goes." When asked which adult at the school was most important to her, she laughed and described a faculty member whom she valued because he had taught her "how not to deal with people—one of those 'learn by observing' things. He's the most impersonal individual I've ever met. You go in his office, and his attitude is, 'I will do anything to get you out of here.' . . . It's actually just that he doesn't care." One of the most damning statements came from a junior whose remark shows that he couldn't even imagine turning to a faculty member for guidance:

I have to rely on myself to get things done, I don't have a parent right there saying, "Okay, you need to do this; now you need to do that." It makes it hard, growing up as a teenager without your parents . . . because every now and then you're just stumbling along, and you want somebody to lean on, but all you've got is basically yourself and your friends. So you learn to rely on your peers more.

Some kids do find adults at school to talk to: the chaplain, their coach, a tac, or a counselor. But many of them, like this junior, rely solely on their peers for support. This makes it especially hard for them, when they become leaders, to defend school rules to their friends and to turn their fellow students over to the adults for punishment.

Another reason student leaders do not want to alert adults to problems in their companies is that, under the military system, they are personally responsible for what their subordinates do. Theoretically, in fact, if a lieutenant mistreats a plebe his captain is as much to blame as he is. In practice, student officers are not blamed for all the trouble the members of their companies get into; adults recognize that one seventeen-year-old captain cannot keep track of what thirty or forty teenagers are up to day and night. Nevertheless, student officers know that drugs, drinking, vandalism, and violence in their part of the barracks—not to mention poor performance in military formations, general inspections, or parades—will be held against them. Problems in their companies make them look bad and stand in the way of promotion.

Most cadets dream of becoming battalion commander. The best way to achieve this goal is to be perceived as a good leader by both cadets and faculty. This isn't easy. Battalion Commander Tom Hurd thought that maintaining this balance had been the on-going moral dilemma of his school career. "One of the big problems I've always had since I've had rank," he said, "is, how far do you support the students in their disagreement with the school, and how far do you support the school in what they have entrusted you with the rank to do?" To be the only one to uphold school policy among a group of students can sometimes cost a cadet officer respect and authority; it "hurts your ability to deal with them" later on. "So it's a real tight line to walk a lot of times." Disciplining his own classmates is particularly hard: "A senior doesn't always want to hear from another senior about what's wrong."

Leadership as It Is Defined by the Adolescents   The student officers feel themselves to be in a terrible bind—they are held responsible for the behavior of their subordinates, yet they are given permission to punish them only by turning them over to the adults, which causes the officers to lose credibility as leaders in the eyes of their fellow students and, consequently, to lose authority. What they want is to be able to do their own disciplining of subordinates, to show their independence from the counselors and the commandant and demonstrate their toughness and resourcefulness. Yet if they do punish other students, they run the risk of being accused of hazing. Tom Hurd, a very successful BC, seems somehow to have managed to do a good deal of his own punishing and still maintain good relations with the adults. "I can't think of any time that I've ever turned anyone in for any offense," he said. "I always handle it on my own." He went on to say what so many other boys and girls at Pershing, Sherman, and Jackson had also said: that he thought student leaders were almost unanimous in wanting to deal with the problems in their units themselves, because it was "a lot more effective" than using the proper disciplinary channels. Tom tried to think of a case where he would willingly seek faculty help. "If someone was having a real problem with drugs . . . and I couldn't handle it," he decided, "I'd turn them in. Or in a situation where an 'old guy' [upperclassman] tries to push [drugs] on a freshman, then—no, I'd be tempted to handle something like that on my own, violently! That I won't tolerate, and I think a lot of people feel the same way."

Handling things on their own, "keeping it in the company," taking care of problems efficiently: cadets use these phrases to dismiss adult interference in the companies. One favorite code phrasing is to wish that the school were "more military." To the cadets, what makes their leadership "military" is independent action and a willingness to use force to promote company loyalty and keep things under control. Being "military" means something different to the adults who have been in the armed forces, like the Pershing commandant, Lieutenant Duncan Graham. A counselor described bringing a particularly gung-ho cadet officer to Graham for hazing plebes; it was a second offense, and Graham had already talked to the boy at length, after the first hazing incident, about the proper way to treat new cadets. This time the commandant stripped him of his rank, saying, "This is how it's got to be, and if you want to see what's really military—following orders is really military, and I gave you an order and you disobeyed me, so here's what the military is all about."

To the adults, leadership means having the moral courage to stand up for what is right—which in adult eyes means allying oneself with the rules and the adult community even if that involves facing the scorn of one's peers. To the adolescents, leadership means having the wit and physical courage to enforce the rules by oneself, without having to fall back on adult assistance. The adults expect leaders to uphold the honor of the school by setting an example—by which they mean an example of obedient service. The cadets, however, feel they can best uphold the honor of their school by fighting for the independence of its cadet officers, disciplining its plebes, and maintaining unit pride and loyalty. Ironically, therefore, because of the different meanings the two groups assign to the words, the more the adults preach initiative, discipline, and commitment to the school, the more they encourage the kind of "military" excesses that many of them deplore.

Joe Novak at Jackson is a typical cadet captain, not one of the school's superstars but well liked by seniors and underclassmen and, as his high rank shows, respected by the adults. It is hard to imagine him as a bully, nor has he that reputation among his colleagues. He is responsible for twenty-five cadets. "Being a company commander, if you don't care about your people, then you might as well hang it up," he said. He is proud of the way he handles problems in his company. For example, at the beginning of the year he had four young cadets who sniffed glue:

I would talk to them and try to convince them not to do it again, and then they'd do it. Finally I got real mad, so I sat down and talked to them individually. I took my rank [insignia] off my collar and said, "Listen, you talk to me today the way you want to, and I'm going to talk to you the way I want to." So we got things worked out. And now two of them are two of my best cadets.

Joe thinks that giving demerits, Jackson's chief official method of punishment, simply does not work. In theory, people get demerits and then work them off on "D-squad" at the rate of one half-hour per demerit, by spending their afternoons cleaning the school or running around the playing field. In fact, D-squad members—some of them with hundreds of demerits—do not seem to mind their plight and often pass their punishment time sitting around talking to one another instead of working or running. Joe scoffed that it seemed to have become "an honor to be on D-squad, because you don't do anything." So now, he said, when he catches cadets breaking the rules, he offers them a choice. Either Joe will turn them in and they'll get demerits, or he'll put them to work himself. "I caught someone smoking. . . . So I gave him a choice of twenty demerits [ten hours on D-squad] or thirty minutes of PT [physical training] with me. The guy's a smoker, so his lungs aren't exactly great, but he chose PT." Joe had him do push-ups under the shower for half an hour, and "I haven't caught him since." But Joe's methods of discipline do not meet with adult approval. "I've been out there, busting my butt for half the cadets, yet I'm always being nailed by the commandant. I even got burnt [given demerits] for walking around during CQ [closed quarters, or mandatory evening study hall]. I was doing my job, checking on CQ, and I got burnt because I wasn't in my room!"

Joe is frustrated because it seems to him that he is being punished for trying to be exactly what the school says it wants him to be, a leader. His statements (and other students' reports of him) make it clear that he upholds school rules, cares about his subordinates, and approves of the military system. School discipline is lax, he feels, and this makes his job harder, as well as making the school look bad. Yet when he takes matters into his own hands, he gets in trouble. Joe's complaints are typical; they are similar to those of Angelo at Sherman, Kyle at Pershing, and many other student officers and NCOs who talked with me.

At military academies, as at Quaker schools, adults seem to reap what they sow—and with a vengeance. Attempting to use the military system to promote self-confidence, academic striving, involvement in school activities, and obedience, most of the adults see rank as a reward for good behavior and leadership as a mandate to "set an example." Adult rhetoric, however, extols military leadership as a way for cadets to "face up to challenges," "be a take-charge kind of person," and "make their mark." Why, then, are they so taken aback when students like Joe try to take charge?

Chapter Six

The Adolescent Moral
Worldview

Different Backgrounds and
Common Influences

Clearly, it is almost impossible for any adult or adolescent at one of the Quaker or military schools not to be affected by that tradition's ways of speaking, making decisions, handling conflict, and viewing the world. Whether a student dresses neatly or sloppily, competes eagerly with others for good grades or barely scrapes by, participates in student government or finds it boring; whether a teacher lectures or encourages student presentations, is strict or lenient, is eager to influence administrative decisions or content to accept directives: at the six schools these personal preferences are also moral statements, and they have different meanings within the two different traditions. Over time, adults and adolescents who are part of these moral communities come to see their own and others' behavior in the light of its Quaker or military significance. They learn to use Quaker or military language, interpret actions in relation to Quaker or military virtues, discuss problems within a Quaker or military frame of reference, and make or break the rules for Quaker or military reasons. Even though most of them will never become members of the Religious Society of Friends or the U.S. Armed Forces, they are socialized by their colleagues—adult and adolescent—into practicing the moral traditions.

There are people who remain at the schools and yet remain aloof from the traditions: some teachers at the academies who have nothing to do with the military program manage this quite successfully, for example. In general, however, the socialization process is surprisingly effective, considering the variety of backgrounds and expectations people bring with them to the schools. One girl attends Dyer because her parents are Friends and alumni; she has heard the language of Quakerism since she was born. Another girl from an inner-city public school has won a full scholarship to Dyer without ever having seen it; she arrives with only the vaguest idea of what being a Quaker means. One Jackson teacher is a retired army officer with a long and successful military career behind him; another is a former public high-school teacher who lives nearby and came to Jackson hoping its cadets would be easier to manage in the classroom than her former pupils were. There are students at Mott whose parents have sent them there from across the country *because* of the Quakers' liberal political philosophy, and there are students from the neighborhood whose parents have sent them to Mott *in spite* of Quaker liberalism, because of the school's good academic record. At least two students I spoke with had attended both Quaker and military schools during their high-school careers, and one administrator had worked at both types of schools. Interviews showed that members of the Quaker-school communities were more likely to come from liberal backgrounds—to vote Democrat or have parents who did—while those at the military academies were more likely to be conservatives—to vote Republican or have parents who did. But there were many exceptions to that generalization and many factors besides politics in the personal baggage that people brought with them to the schools and that influenced how they responded to the moral traditions.

Administrators, teachers, and students all learn to practice and pass on the traditions; the socialization process affects them all. But it is the students—the paying members of the community—around whom school life centers. Who are the thirteen- to nineteen-year-olds who come—willingly or unwillingly—to spend some or all of their high-school years at Mott, Fox, or Dyer; Pershing, Jackson, or Sherman? They come from all parts of the United States and from foreign countries, from various family backgrounds, races, and religions. The main factor they have in common is that they are among the tiny minority—about 3 percent—of American high-school students who attend boarding school.[1] Although there are scholarship students at all six schools, most families pay at least $8,000 a year in tuition. So something else these teenagers have in common is a relatively wealthy background. At Dyer and Pershing, both of which cost approximately $12,000 in 1987–88, the majority of the students interviewed reported parents who were doctors, dentists, lawyers, bankers, corporate executives, small business owners, salesmen, engineers, contractors, and educators.

There were also differences between the two groups of parents. Dyer mothers were more likely to be professionals, Pershing mothers to work at home (although housewives, nurses, teachers, professors, and businesswomen could be found in both groups). Dyer fathers included artists, Pershing fathers included farmers and military men. A boy at Dyer grew up on a commune; a girl at Pershing, on army bases. Despite these contrasts, the majority of students at both schools placed themselves firmly in the middle to upper-middle class.

I asked every student I interviewed why he or she was at boarding school. The most common answer was unhappiness with the student's former school, which was perceived either as dangerous—a place where, as one boy said, "even the girls carried switchblades!"—or as academically weak. These critiques of the former school sometimes turned into confessions of bad grades, which were blamed on boredom, "fooling around too much," and "getting into trouble." But students rarely gave only one reason for being at boarding school. Here is a sample of the type of answer that a Pershing cadet might offer:

Well, my father and uncle came to the summer camp; I always heard how great it was here, with the horses and everything. I started having some trouble in junior high, and my parents thought it would be a good thing to send me here. I didn't want to go at first, but then things really started getting tense between my dad and me. So I visited this place, and I got into the military stuff. And the sports are just fantastic.

Here, "trouble" in junior high is coupled with family connections to the school, tension between father and son, interest in the military, and enthusiasm for the sporting facilities, which together lead to attendance at Pershing. And this relatively superficial answer may only begin to explain the boy's presence at the school.

At both sets of schools, some students say they were sent against their will, and others say they bullied their parents into sending them; some followed in parents' or siblings' footsteps, and others came from abroad to learn English. There are those who talk about wanting to get away from a stepparent or messy divorce, those who admit to previous alcohol or drug problems, and those who say they came after a year of reform school. Some have parents in the same town; some have parents in Saudi Arabia; some are orphans. The stereotype is that problem children are sent to military school, but in fact only 15 percent of the thirty-four students interviewed at Pershing mentioned school or family problems or feeling "sent away," as opposed to 62 percent of the thirty-four Dyer students interviewed. Of course, Dyer has a reputation among Quaker schools as a "last-chance" school. A comparison of Sherman and Mott yields a more conventional picture: 32 percent of the Sherman cadets interviewed mentioned personal or family problems, as opposed to 16 percent of the Mott students.

The important word here is *mentioned*: the number of students who mention problems in an interview is not the same as the number who have problems. Teenagers' comments about their backgrounds must be treated with caution. Some of the reasons they give for their attendance at a particular school—a Quaker or military history, a long family association with the school, learning disabilities, the death of a parent, expulsion from their last school, and so on—can be verified from their files, but these facts may tell only part of the story. Some youngsters dramatize their family situation; others keep their secrets to themselves. A girl who says her stepmother treats her terribly may be going through some fairly normal adolescent conflicts, while another who says she came to boarding school for the horseback riding may in fact be fleeing incest. As an interviewer, one settles for knowing that one does not know the whole story.

Apart from their presence in boarding school and their relative wealth, the main thing these students have in common is their adolescence. Being a teenager—or at least an affluent American teenager in the late twentieth century—has its own moral mandates. Indeed, their common adolescence permits a few cautious generalizations about them. What do psychologists, sociologists, and educators—and adolescents themselves—think is important to teenagers? How do these priorities influence the way students receive and respond to the Quaker or military moral tradition?

The Experience of Adolescence

Consistency and Sincerity

Erik Erikson considered the main developmental goal of adolescence to be what he called fidelity: the search for something and someone to be true to. "In all youth's seeming shiftiness," he wrote, "a seeking after some durability in change can be detected," and he used such words as *accuracy, sincerity,* and *reliability* to describe this adolescent concern.[2] Writing about adolescent girls, Lyn Mikel Brown portrayed the concern with fidelity in terms of the "coherence" and "integrity" that young women seek through sustained relationships.[3] The search for fidelity leads to an obsession with consistency and a hatred of anything that even hints at hypocrisy, lying, back-stabbing, or faking. Among the teenagers at the six boarding schools, this insistence on sincerity is almost ubiquitous. Peers are judged according to this standard, and so are adults. At Fox, two girls said they liked their teacher Andrew Henley because "there are quite a few teachers who try too hard to fit in. They want to be popular with the popular crowd, so they even start talking with students about other students behind their backs—gossiping to be accepted. Whereas Andrew is who he is: people respect that." A freshman at Pershing compared two seniors, one his unit captain, and the other a private and BA. He said he had "a little bit more respect" for the BA, because he was "consistent in being bad all the time." The captain, on the other hand, was "bad while he's telling other people to be good." Another Pershing cadet said of a fellow student, "I respect him . . . because he's so constant in his decisions . . . [and] shows no favoritism to anyone."

Some students also apply strict sincerity tests to their own behavior, as well as to that of peers and adults. A Pershing senior, for example, was invited by a bunch of friends to join them in "a blanket party, because one lieutenant was going crazy. He was so military that it was just outrageous. I said, 'No, that's stupid. I would just be as bad as him almost if I went and did that.'" What bothered this boy wasn't the idea of beating up the lieutenant per se, but the hypocrisy of using violence to teach someone not to be violent.

This obsession with consistency means that most adolescents, even when they break rules, need some sort of assurance that the rules are being enforced. Spansky, one of the "lads" in Paul Willis's study of rebellious working-class British youths, is caught smoking and is caned by the deputy head of his school; he tells his mates, "Well, he couldn't do a thing, he had to give me three [blows]. I like that bloke, I think he does his job well. . . . You know he couldn't let me off."[4] Similarly, a Pershing senior who was caught using drugs as a freshman and has been receiving regular urinalysis ever since says he approves of this school policy, even though it results in his being taken out of class or roused from his bed at unexpected times for tests. "If they're going to have a rule, then they should enforce it," complained a sophomore girl at Fox; herself a smoker, she resented the inconsistency with which the school enforced its anti-smoking policy.

This complaint illustrates another adolescent obsession that stems from their need for consistency: their hatred of favoritism. In their work on high schools, both Nancy Lesko and Robert B. Everhart described students' anger over apparently preferential treatment of their peers, often ascribed to parents' wealth or influence.[5] James Macpherson has cited seven studies by different scholars indicating that students expect equity in punishment.[6] Chapter Four showed how deeply a number of white students at Dyer resent the favoritism they believe two popular black teachers show to black students; at Pershing several students commented on the favoritism they thought was shown to the school's top athletes, and one cadet told about a boy with three honor offenses who supposedly was saved from expulsion only because his father had made a donation to the school.

Consistency is important to adolescents because they are in the process of building a sense of their own identity, searching for continuity and sameness both in their experiences of the world and within themselves. As part of this process of consolidating an identity, they must establish increasing independence from their parents and, by extension, from adults acting in a parental capacity. Anna Freud wrote about adolescents' "feelings of oppression by the[ir] parents . . . [and] impotent rages or active hates directed against the adult world"; she also described their ambivalence about independence, demonstrated in a tendency to reject their parents one minute and cling to them in the next.[7] Sharon Rich has found that adolescent girls want their mothers to "be there for them" and at the same time to "recognize their ability to care for themselves."[8]

This ambivalence colors high-school students' relationships with their teachers. On the one hand, they go out of their way to defy teachers; on the other hand, they want their approval and affection. Perhaps it is teenagers' distress at this complicated mixture of fury and yearning within themselves that makes them judge so harshly what they consider sycophantic attitudes toward adults, which they usually call "brown-nosing." The kind of teacher-pleasing behavior that gets labeled as sycophantic varies from person to person and circumstance to circumstance, making it difficult for adolescents to strike a balance between rebellion and obedience that will gain them acceptance from both peers and adults. As one Pershing cadet said, "If you are a plebe and you're a hard-on [very serious about the military system], your [student] officers will see that as possible leadership characteristics. . . . But the people above you who are the BAs, they'll call it sucking for rank and brown-nosing and all that, which sometimes it is, and sometimes not." While competition for rank makes teenagers more alert to brown-nosing at the military academies, a sensitivity to goody-goody behavior exists at all three Quaker schools, too. After a Mott teacher offered extra points to anyone in his class who would attend a special conference during the coming weekend, I overheard a withering exchange between two students: "Since when is bribery part of Quaker education?" "Not bribery, brown-nosing—an essential part of Quaker education."

Several recent studies of high schools have found this hatred of hypocrisy and "brown-nosing" among working-class students in particular. Penelope Eckert's "Burnouts" pride themselves on their consistency and honesty and accuse the college-bound "Jocks" of phoniness.[9] A "white-trash kicker" in small-town Texas considers the conformity of the "rich bitches" and "all-American boys" to be a giant cover-up that enables them to manipulate their parents and teachers and misbehave at will; she and her friends, with nothing to lose, are open about their sexual behavior, drug use, and drinking.[10] The "burn-out" girls in a Catholic high school call the "rich and populars" hypocritical.[11] At the six boarding schools, there are no middle-class and working-class crowds. But there is still one group of students who are deeply involved in school activities and sports, assume leadership roles, earn good grades, and are often physically attractive and popular with the opposite sex, and another group of students who receive bad grades and are discipline problems. A plebe's comment about the honesty of a BA, compared to the phoniness of a captain, has already been quoted. In general, however, it seems that the demand for sincerity from peers and teachers prevails at all levels of the student hierarchy, and one does not have to be a member of another clique to be accused of phoniness.[12]

Acceptance by Peers

Friends need to be true and consistent, because their actions and reactions serve as a touchstone. Searching to answer the question "What am I like?" an adolescent looks to peers for a response. Ideally, he or she has a special group of peers to turn to. "Through groups, that is, through association with people similar to oneself and those who are different, personal and social identities are wrestled with and visualized."[13] At the same time, the adolescent experiences self-doubt; he or she looks to peers for approval. In James Coleman's words:

[The teenager] must see himself through the eyes of a world he did not make, the adolescent world of his community, into which the accident of residence has thrust him. If, in its eyes, he has done well, then he can be at peace with himself; if he is not accepted, recognized, looked up to, nor given status of any sort, he finds it hard to escape into another place in society where he can find recognition and respect. Instead he turns inward; he must question his very self, asking whether it would not be better if he were someone quite different.[14]

It is extremely important to students at both Quaker and military boarding schools that their peers think well of them. The senior who said he approved of the "piss-test" for drugs that he had been undergoing since his freshman year still worried about his "image" with the other students as a result of being "the veteran of the group [getting urinalysis]." At Sherman, girls were afraid of getting a "bad rep" (sexual reputation), particularly in the eyes of other girls. At Mott, where students pride themselves on their kindness to each other and their lack of cliquishness, three senior boys nevertheless worried about their friends' approval of their girlfriends:

Tim: Here's a dilemma for me—having to choose a girlfriend and worrying what people will say about her. When you live so close together, everyone knows absolutely everything that's going on. So your relationship will get talked about: Who's together? How do they act? Are they right for each other?

Steven: You feel like you have to choose someone that everyone else will like. . . . Usually there are these terrible rumors about everyone. "She's screwed up." "She's weird." And awful examples of things she's supposed to have done.

Paul: And girls won't even consider a guy if her friends say something about him. I mean, girls can be evil! You can get a hex [they are all laughing], so you might as well leave town. Out of commission. Out of business.

Steven: [now serious] Yesterday at soccer practice, a guy made a comment about this girl I'm seeing—he didn't know I was seeing her—and everyone looked at me. And it made me think again. I really like her, but his comment made me think again. One little thing from someone else makes you feel terrible. We're so influenced by other people. No one escapes it.

The boys' discussion shows that the usual adolescent problems with peers are exacerbated by being at boarding school, where, as Tim says, "everyone knows absolutely everything." At public school, the teenager who feels he or she is not accepted by "the crowd" at least has the escape of home and family, but at boarding school there is no refuge—not even in bed at night, since almost everyone has a roommate. Relationships with other people are intense. It is the constancy of interaction, as much as academic and extracurricular pressures, that makes boarding schools into "crucibles, from which some students emerge . . . as tempered steel and others . . . simply burnt to a crisp." [15]

No matter how intrusive they are, however, friends are crucial at boarding school. As one plebe at Pershing said, "Once you have friends, you can always survive." Most adolescents eventually manage to win acceptance, although it isn't easy. A senior in his second year at Mott said, "After a year and a third I've come to feel that I'm a part of the school. . . . Last year I didn't have anybody I could talk to, except when I called home." For some, the process of proving oneself can be like running a gauntlet. At Pershing it took an entire year before a boy with a lisp was accepted by his company. "Everybody would imitate him," his captain said; "he went through a lot. . . . But now everyone knows that he's a really nice guy, so . . . no one laughs any more." A girl at Dyer planned to leave after her first year: "When I came here, I really lost a sense of who I was. . . . These people really seem to have an aversion to me. . . . I'm not certain if it's me being paranoid or what, but I get that feeling. And it's sort of like, well, am I a bad person, or are they just not seeing me for who I am, or what's the deal?" That same morning she had told some dormmates that she wasn't coming back the next year, and one of them had assured her that "the people here who know you really love you and want you to stay." This made her feel "totally uncertain," not knowing "whether to believe this person or not."

Given the crucial importance of friends for one's self-esteem, learning to make and handle friendships and, as students said over and over, "to deal with people" is a central part of education at boarding school. These lessons are particularly important at the military academies, where teenagers spend so much time with the members of their unit. "Because they are constantly responsible for each other and responsible to each other, it's very much like a huge family," said a Pershing counselor about his unit. "The squabbles that break out can be incredibly intense and they can be over trivial things, just as in a family. But at the same time, if you ask them, 'What are you going to remember from Pershing?' they would all say, 'The friendships!'" He considers some of the boy-girl relationships to be "closer than marriages," because the couples spend so much time together and are so dependent on one another. This was true at Jackson, where a first sergeant, a powerfully built seventeen-year-old, portrayed his girlfriend as his salvation:

Being a leader you have a lot of pressure. . . . I started dating Karen and that helped me a lot. I had somebody to talk to, to share my problems with. Somebody to look after and care about me, I guess. . . . Before we got together, I used to keep my problems to myself. . . . Before, I just wanted to kill everybody, and now it's different.

For some at boarding school, the loneliness and the feelings of rejection by first parents and then peers never go away. This is true not only for the obvious outsiders but even for some teenagers who appear to have found their place in their school. An attractive Pershing senior, who was involved in extracurricular activities, made excellent grades, and went out with a popular girl, said that boarding school and especially being a captain had taught him "that I don't like people. . . . I place a high value on trust, and it takes me a long time to trust

people, because I've seen [my trust] betrayed many times. . . . Sometimes it really gets depressing."

By the time they are seniors, most kids who have been at boarding
school for three or more years feel at home there. They are involved in
classes and activities, have made some close friends, are proud of their
independence. But most of them will also admit to some very hard
times. Leaving one's family at thirteen or fourteen is not a normal part
of the American child-rearing pattern. In some cases, where the child
truly is not wanted at home or where a parent is ill, drug- or alcohol-
addicted, abusive, or disturbed, the child is probably better off at
school. In other cases, however, being away from home can inhibit the
process of normal adolescent development. Lightfoot quoted a counselor at Milton Academy who says, "Sending kids to boarding school
circumvents the *natural* process of breaking away from family. . . .
[S]tudents come to boarding school with unfinished family issues.
They do not have the opportunity to do the daily work of separating
and integrating with family." [16] This makes their relationships with
teachers and peers, as surrogate parents and siblings, all the more
tumultuous.

Adolescent Moral Judgments

Searching for continuity and something to be faithful to, striving to
create new, more independent relationships with adults and to gain
peer acceptance, working to handle the loneliness and strains of
boarding-school life: it is under these conditions that adolescents pass
moral judgments on themselves and one another and face moral
dilemmas. The stereotypical moral issues identified by many adults
when they talk about adolescent behavior—drugs, alcohol, and sex—
do not fall into the same category of judgment for most of the teenagers interviewed. Moral judgments are passed, not on those who take
drugs, drink, or have sex, but on those who, for example, bust others
for taking drugs when they themselves are users, drink in the same
room as a roommate who already has one alcohol offense and can be
expelled for "condoning," or betray their sexual partner. The moral
transgressions, in other words, have to do with behavior that breaks
adolescent codes of consistency and fidelity.

Sex

When students talk about their or their friends' sexual relationships in moral terms, the exact nature of the involvement—"How far do they go?"—seems unimportant, perhaps because it is assumed that most of them are having intercourse.[17] What is important to them is the possibility of hurt. Several students at Fox, male and female, were critical of a popular senior for treating his girlfriend cruelly. At Mott, a boy talked about his problems with his girlfriend, who held grudges: "If you've done something to piss her off, you'll know about it a week later. . . . And you feel like, AIIIIEEE! Why didn't you tell me about this a week ago?'" Finally he decided that his "frustration and anger . . . [was] just not worth the love . . . in this relationship," but he had trouble knowing what to do. "You just can't blow somebody off in this community, because you see them every day." The relief he felt when he finally discussed the whole thing with the girl and "got a friend back" was enormous, because "a problem like that . . . is right there and you're always thinking about it, and it's always putting a damper on your day." At Sherman, a freshman girl whose comments about the school had been childish spoke with surprising wisdom when asked to describe a moral dilemma:

Right now there's this person I've been seeing, Jim. We still like each other, but even his best friends think he's just using me. . . . This other guy Chris likes me, and people say I should chop Jim and go with Chris. I think Chris can give me stability and Jim can't. Jim and I just don't seem to have time for each other. I still like him, but I don't feel very attached to him. I'm worried about hurting Jim—I don't want to ditch him. But I think I can have a normal relationship with Chris: he and I have a lot more in common.

These and other conversations showed that most adolescents want what most adults want: a "normal," loving, nonexploitative relationship. This is extremely hard to achieve in the boarding-school environment. It is particularly unlikely at Sherman and Jackson, where girls are in such a minority. Even at the Friends schools, because of their small size and emotional intensity, student involvements are full of tension. A senior girl at Dyer said, "We're so few people that everyone has the same boyfriends eventually or the same girlfriends. So you have these incestuous [situations]—it's very bizarre." There were lots of "two-week relationships," too: "I have friends here, guys, who their first year here were with like thirty people. It's the atmosphere here: you kind of compromise yourself a bit." She described the lack of privacy, the gossip, and the resentment, and then added:

I don't know of any healthy relationships here, not the kind people deserve to have. A lot of these long relationships, most of the time one of the two people is very controlling and overbearing: they want to have their cake and eat it, too. And the other person in the couple would do anything for them. A lot of the short relationships are just sex. Or else people wanting more and not finding it.

Drugs

The Dyer admissions catalogue states baldly that sexual intercourse between students is prohibited, but clearly sexuality is one realm where students apply their own standards. Drug use is another. Estimates of drug use at each school varied a great deal from student to student, with non-users guessing a low percentage of regular users, and users, a high percentage. At all six schools there seems to be quite a lot of marijuana, some LSD, a small amount of cocaine, and, very occasionally, such drugs as PCP, crack, and heroin.

At the academies, cadet officers like Joe Novak and Tom Hurd try to handle drug problems in the barracks without going to the adults. Preventing younger students from heavy drug involvement seems to be important, even to officers who themselves sometimes use drugs. At the Quaker schools, students who don't take drugs or drink heavily rarely condemn those who do, but they often worry about them. The dilemma is how to respond. A group of junior girls at Mott discussed this. One of them, Debbie, said she was starting to worry about a friend who was doing drugs, but she felt uncomfortable about lecturing her (especially since the friend never put any pressure on Debbie to take drugs) and even more uncomfortable about telling a teacher, since "you don't want your friends to be kicked out of school." She called it "a big dilemma":

Debbie: How can I say to them, "You shouldn't be doing that," if they don't say to me, "You should be doing this." And then I guess I have to draw the line someplace and say, "Well, maybe I'm a little more clear-headed, and they really shouldn't be doing it."

Clare: But it's hard. Because when I'm in a similar situation with friends who have [substance abuse] problems or . . . [are] suicidal . . . I wouldn't want to make it worse by possibly getting them kicked out of school, [because] . . . that would be the limit and they would probably go overboard and go off the end. But by the same token I'd feel like I had to do something.

Helen: You don't know if you are close enough to them because . . . I mean, you don't know how good a friend you are. Of course you're friends, but you've only known these people for three years at the most, and you don't know how much right you have interfering in their lives, because after the last year, unless you make an effort, you are probably never going to see them again.

Clare: Not only that, but . . . I think there are people here that I'm close enough to that I could say something, but I'm so worried, I don't know what I'm going to say. I don't know if it's going to have a worse effect or a better effect.

For these girls, the most important question is clearly, "What is best for my friend?" Will saying something to the friend about his or her drug use help the situation or worsen it? Will saying something to an adult—betraying the friend—really do some good, or will he or she just be expelled and perhaps forced "off the end"? Worries about consistency also surface—if my friend doesn't pressure me, what gives me the right to pressure my friend? There are also doubts about one's own worth and the worth of relationships—am I really a good enough friend to interfere? Will I be able to say the right things?

The girls' discussion combines concerns about reciprocity and justice with concerns about responsibility and the need to care, both aspects of fidelity. This mixture of concerns emerges frequently in the interviews with adolescent girls that Carol Gilligan and her colleagues conducted at a New England boarding school; they found that relationships with others were central to the way the girls defined and explained moral problems.[18] My interviews showed that many boys, too, define moral dilemmas in relation to their friends. A cadet at Jackson worried about another who was "living like a death wish"; a boy at Sherman (himself no model cadet) talked about his friend who had been "seriously into cocaine":

That scared me very much, because I saw what drugs did to people [at my last school], and I seriously thought about turning him in for his own good. But then I thought, "Would that be narcing?" . . . So instead, I got on his case. I said, "Hey, you want to do drugs, fine, do as much as you want, but just don't do it around me." And every time he did, I hit him. . . . Eventually he stopped doing drugs around me. My next step was, I spent so much time with him that there was no time for him to do drugs. And after a month . . . he was drug-free!

Teenagers who use drugs regularly have their own, often clearly-thought-out criteria for moral judgment. A girl at Fox, when asked if anything at school was a moral dilemma for her, answered, "Drugs, I guess. I don't know. I came here against doing most things, but I changed through boredom and wanting a new experience, plus feeling that it's really not that bad. . . . I don't get into experimenting with these heavy potent chemicals, but just smoking pot." Lately she'd been smoking a lot less, partly because she "got tired of walking around in a daze all the time and not remembering things" and partly because of pressure from her boyfriend, who "doesn't get into that." The moral dilemma was "learning whether it was right for me or not, and how much of it is right and how much of it is wrong":

I guess I've learned that it's not bad unless you overdo it. So I'm not saying that it's wrong to smoke pot at all, because sometimes I like it, but it's wrong to do it as a party thing, and it's wrong to go out into the woods and just smoke and smoke and smoke until you puke all over the place, and it's wrong to base your life around it.

A boy at Fox who was the senior member of the druggy group said he would "never, ever start anybody on anything":

If they've never smoked dope, I'll never give it to them. If they've never had a drink, I'll never give it to them. . . . Because I remember how I was influenced through peer pressure, and now that I think about it, I wish I would have never started. Because I'd be a pretty fine athlete right now, and I might have scholarships to places, but I messed that up.

The Importance of Self-Presentation

Many of these statements by boarding-school students show that, while an adolescent frequently passes moral judgment on others, the person he or she is most conscientiously observing and judging is himself or herself. This is part of the process of forming an identity. Erikson wrote that "the conscious feeling of having a personal identity is based on two simultaneous observations: the perception of the selfsameness and continuity of one's existence in time and space and the perception of the fact that others recognize one's sameness and continuity." [19] Even as they look for consistency in others, they test their own "true" consistency by consciously assuming a variety of personae. They ask themselves, "Even if I do this (use cocaine, act devoutly religious, sleep with three different boys in a month or with someone of the same sex, become a fanatic vegetarian, and so on), am I still me?" Further, they ask, "If I do these things, how will other people treat me? Will they still recognize me as me?" Adolescence becomes a process of testing different roles and of simultaneously testing those around one, the audience, to see how they respond to these roles.

Many roles are meant to be seen through—teenagers want to believe that people around them can't be fooled, that their "real" identity is strong enough to shine through. For example, a girl who was leaving Dyer said she disliked it because "I think I came here before I was really ready, and I gave myself an image that was meant for other people to overlook. And the part that I don't like about Dyer is that they stuck to that image." A lonely young black girl at Pershing took refuge by assuming a tough, unapproachable persona, all the while wishing that people would approach her. She said:

I'm very obnoxious and I'm very outspoken, that's just a part of my personality. I wear my sunglasses 90 percent of the time. I intimidate others, and I love it. My sunglasses keep me out of trouble, because most of the time I'm rolling my eyes at people or giving them ferocious looks. . . . Sometimes I would just like, once, for someone to stand up to me.

In his book about Little League baseball and preadolescent male culture, Gary Alan Fine showed that boys' main concern is self-presentation. Within baseball culture, it is important to learn to display appropriate emotions, control fear and aggression, show a desire to win, and maintain peer unity. The boys play different roles at different times, and "the popular and socially integrated preadolescent is not the one who behaves consistently but the one who has mastered techniques of impression management." [20] Douglas Foley, in his study of high-school students in a small Texas town, talked about teenagers as skillful managers of their image both among friends and in the classroom. The popular males, in particular, were "impression management experts," who knew how to "play the game," appearing "straight" to adults, attentive to their girlfriends, and "cool" to their peers.[21]

The teenagers at the six boarding schools were no strangers to impression management, especially when it came to being what many of them called "discreet" around teachers. One has only to think of a group of seniors at Fox telling sophomores that "being subtle" about sex and drugs is part of "the game" that everyone plays, or of an infamous Pershing BA calling himself "one of the few people that doesn't try to act different to make the grown-ups happy." Nevertheless, many of the roles the students play, particularly with one another but also with adults, are not merely manipulative. They are also experimental. Self-presentation is also self-construction. Teenagers do not always behave consistently, but they are nevertheless striving to achieve some sort of internal consistency, an identity that is clearly recognizable to themselves and others.

The Quaker and military moral traditions that shape life at the six schools are incorporated by the adolescents into their identity-formation process. When one looks at the traditions' impact on the adolescent moral worldview, one must ask not only, "How do the students interpret the key virtues?" or "What kinds of decisions do the students make?" but also "What kinds of identities do the students want to project?" It would be wrong to suggest that Quaker or military influences cause teenagers to assume certain identities. Quaker-school students, with their more liberal backgrounds, were already different from students at military academies before they ever arrived on campus. If both groups never went to boarding school but instead ended up together at the same public school, many would still project contrasting images, because—to use Ann Swidler's useful metaphor—they draw upon different cultural "tool-kits" to construct strategies for dealing with life.[22] What the two traditions do is help to stock the tool-kits during a crucial period of development, providing some of the structure, vocabulary, goals, and ideals for which the adolescents are searching during the process of identity formation. But adolescents don't simply build an identity; they tinker. For many of the students, the traditions are "part of a fluid process of everyday negotiation" that helps them make sense of themselves and the world.[23] The traditions encourage one set of typical adolescent concerns to come to the fore at Friends schools and another, different set of typical concerns to be emphasized at military schools. Among adolescents at

Quaker schools, the focus is on truth; among those at military schools, on survival.

The Quaker Adolescent Image: The True Self

All adolescents are searching for a sense of their own reality and consistency, but the Quaker tradition, with its emphasis on the Inner Light, openness, and speaking from the heart, makes this quest for the true self particularly prominent among adolescents at Friends schools. In publications by different Monthly and Yearly Meetings of the Religious Society of Friends, the phrase "the Inner Light" refers to that of God within each person; for adolescents at Quaker schools, "the Inner Light" is a special quality within themselves that they must find and express. Quaker-school teachers feel responsible for bringing out their students' special qualities, but this goal is certainly not unique to Quaker education; it is common at liberal high schools and colleges. At Kleinman's Midwest Seminary, for example, students are taught that they must minister to others with their "real" selves, not merely in the "role" of minister, and part of their education focuses on helping them "achieve a higher level of 'personhood.'" [24] Swidler has described how students at Group High were rewarded for "being uniquely themselves. . . . Group High teachers cherished students as they were but also sought to change them—to make them *more* themselves." Like their Quaker-school counterparts, Group High students were listened to, praised, and encouraged to express themselves and to "assume that what they thought or felt was of interest to others around them." [25] In an environment where everyone is expected to express his or her feelings and expose vulnerabilities, kindness becomes an important element in group relations. Again, Quaker schools share this emphasis on caring with other liberal schools, such as Group High. There, as at Mott, Fox, and Dyer, students "were inhibited from practicing the extremes of clique formation and cruel exclusion so characteristic of traditional adolescent society." Instead, it was expected that "at least during school hours all students treat one another in an intimate, friendly way—considering, including, listening to others because they were part of the school." [26]

What, then, differentiates Quaker schools from humanistic or alternative schools like Midwest Seminary or Group High? One difference is that the true self as defined by many of the administrators and teachers at Friends schools is actually a certain type of self that conforms to each school's version of Quaker ideals. Both staff and students articulate the injunction to "be yourself," but what students actually feel is a confused mixture of their own desire to explore different identities in order to find the "true" one and the school's desire to mold them into something Quakerly. A senior said, "I think Mott has a challenge: can you conform? . . . There's a certain image or stereotype that Quakers put forth and say this is how every person should be. And I think having that drilled in me—it's never said directly, but . . . in my own experience, the Quaker influence has been there." Shortly afterwards, however, he echoed the standard student comment about Mott: "There's a real sense of be who you want to be, do what you want to do." This boy contradicts himself with good reason: the messages he receives are contradictory.

Students' search for their true self takes on a special urgency because many of them sense from teachers and peers that there is a special type of true self they are supposed to find. In spite of the code of acceptance, adolescents know that they are being watched and judged according to this special "trueness" standard. Mike Dugan was proud that "Mott kids just have this incredible knack of seeing who's really being true to themselves and who isn't, . . . who is struggling to find out who they are and be their own person and who is just—not." Yet Mike did not identify "being one's own person" with fidelity to one's background. "There's such a diversity of kids here that the only common ground is for everyone to find out who they are, because if everyone followed the social doctrines that they are brought up with in their own societies . . . then nobody would get along with anybody." Finding out who you are, then, involves rejecting your past and looking within yourself to find something that makes you unique and, at the same time, more like everyone else at Mott. The more true you are, the more you will "get along" and be accepted. Yet, as Mott's Leah Brodsky pointed out, being "unique" and true to yourself only works "if you have that inner confidence inside of you. If you don't, and you deviate from the norm . . . people will just see you as someone trying to be different—and very unsuccessfully." Such people, those with an aura of what Leah called "falseness" about them, generate "repulsion," and they are the ones who are ostracized at Mott: "Many of them have left the school."

Students can feel burdened by the demand that they express so much trueness and uniqueness. A Dyer senior said that the hardest thing for him was "just getting accepted and learning how to be myself. . . . You are forced to, because if you aren't yourself people don't like you. They act like, 'What an outcast!'" When asked how he knew what "being yourself" was, he answered, "I don't know. I guess you just know. I guess it has to do with what you feel comfortable with and what other people feel comfortable with—not having to put a mask on all the time." During his first year at Dyer, he felt that most people didn't like him. "This one guy who was my friend would say, 'You're so shallow, you've got to deepen your mind and be more considerate of other people.'" Now, three years later, he says he "feels okay talking to people one-on-one" but still gets "really quiet" in a group "because I'm afraid I'll say something stupid."

The Quaker philosophy of "being yourself" is also hard on those who seek the support of a typical teenage clique. At Mott, a girl felt that "they're always pushing you to be an individual, and that's not fair, because maybe you feel like being like someone else. . . . Cliques aren't just bad little groups; they're normal, even if Mott thinks they're wrong." For those, however, who have rejected (or been rejected by) cliques in their old schools, who are used to being different from everyone else, it is rather disconcerting to arrive at a place where everyone is a nonconformist. A freshman was shocked to realize that at Quaker school he could no longer take his specialness for granted. Although a part of him welcomed the company of like-minded people, he also resolved to be even more different, so as to avoid any taint of conformity:

I've kind of learned not to try to fit into regular society, and here it's odd, because a lot of other people are sort of like me. And here I am trying to be me, and he's me and he's me and he's me, but wait, *I'm* me! And it's never happened to me before—being with a bunch of kids who are like me to an extent and also unique in their own way. . . . I know that I'm different from them somehow. I figure I've got to be. I can't conform to society.

This pressure to be an individual is so great that many students (and some faculty) interpret it as a mandate to be odd. Said a Dyer girl disgustedly, "The big thing here is to be as different as you can; the norm is to be different. . . . But more than half the people are just being different to be different, they're not really being themselves." In addition, some ways of being different are not acceptable. A young, conservatively dressed Dyer student, insecure and eager for approval from adults and peers, had learned these unspoken rules the hard way. "This year has been very lonely," she said. "People tease me about being preppie and trendy." When asked what she thought people objected to, she said it had to do with the clothes and jewelry she wore, the "Top 40" music she listened to, and the fact that she never gets into trouble. Yet one of the most popular seniors at Dyer was a girl who dressed conventionally and was renowned for never breaking any rules. It was the younger girl's social anxiety that caused her personal style to be interpreted as "trendy"—a word that at Dyer was synonymous with phony—while the older girl was perceived as "just being herself." As Mott's Leah Brodsky observed, the most important quality that a true self must project is a sense of security and confidence.

The Dyer senior is also accepted despite her straightness because of her reputation for kindness. At Quaker school, the true self must be kind: that is why the Dyer boy whose friend called him shallow was told to be "more considerate of other people." Students try to act kind, and they look for that quality in others. In fact, the belief that Mott is a kind place is shared even by students who are not treated kindly. One boy insisted, as so many other students had, that "everybody here is close and cares about each other. In public school, certain people get singled out, but that doesn't happen here." As we continued to talk, however, it emerged that his roommate didn't like him and often made remarks that hurt his feelings, and that he had been labeled a narc by many of his dormmates because he had told the head of his dorm that he suspected a particular student of theft. From his stories, it was clear that this boy *was* singled out and was not treated kindly. Yet even as his problems surfaced, he never once stopped praising the school and his fellow students, who were "like a family" and "work[ed] together." For his own sense of self-worth, he needed to believe that the overall tolerance and friendliness that was, indeed, prevalent at Mott was also extended to him.

One of the most prominent examples of the kindness that is part of student identity is the popularity of Mott's Students Helping Students, or SHS. Seven girls and seven boys of different ages run this peer-counseling service with the help of two faculty advisors and also sponsor workshops on such topics as "Eating Disorders," "Children of

Alcoholics," "Date Rape," and "Racism and Stereotyping." One of SHS's most important goals is to discourage substance abuse. The organization "plays a very critical role in the school," one of its student members said. "Of all the student-run organizations, I think it's the one that gets the most recognition, the most respect." A central SHS service is the drop-in center, where no faculty are allowed. "It's a place for people who get drunk or high, and also a place to come if you feel lonely and want somewhere to feel at home. . . . There's a lot of family problems within the school; some people want to talk about that."

SHS members want to help fellow students—and they do—but they don't want to give up any aspect of "being themselves" in the process. By their code, it would be hypocritical to alter their behavior just because they have been chosen to be in SHS. However, this insistence on being true to their real selves involves them in a much greater hypocrisy, as a number of non-SHS students are quick to point out. One boy who has friends in the group said, "I know that several SHS members . . . drink and smoke dope and tobacco. And that's a real weird thing, because SHS is supposed to be an anti-drug group. . . . It's a weird double standard." Leah Brodsky was even more direct in her criticisms:

The kind of logic I see going on in SHS is like the lung surgeon who says, "Well, I used to smoke twelve packs of cigarettes a day and now that I'm a lung surgeon I only smoke one." I don't think that that's effective. Because if a student comes in and wants to be counseled about something involved with drugs, and if the person counseling them is rather involved with drugs themselves, how honest can the counselor be with the questioner, if they are not honest with themselves?

In spite of deploring the "irony and hypocrisy" that goes on in SHS, Leah strongly approves of the feelings of caring that make students want to be part of the peer-counseling service. This recognition of the centrality of concern exists at Fox and Dyer, too. "Here you care about everyone," said a girl at Fox, while, on Dyer's Alumni Day, graduate after graduate, male and female, young and old, stood up in Meeting for Worship and talked about how the school had taken them in as "lost souls," "misfits," and "rejects" and, in the words of one, "tapped all the goodness" in them. For Leah, this was the primary purpose of a Quaker school. She considered Mott to be a place where a very unstable person can develop into a strong, sensitive human being. I think Western society is generally pretty bad at accomplishing this. . . . At Mott, the difference is that they don't focus so much on the details but on the long-run product, the person as a whole. And so they produce very whole people.

This wholeness is, in the eyes of the students, the ideal outcome of the search for the true self. It grows out of self-examination in an environment that encourages experimentation but is quick to condemn certain types of insincerity and cruelty. As Mike Dugan said about Mott, "It provides a very, very powerful . . . environment for learning about yourself and experimenting with who you are. You learn how to interact with people and thereby discover a lot more about what you're all about. I'm so glad I've had the opportunity to learn about me."

The Military Adolescent Image:
The Heroic Survivor

It is a natural part of the adolescent identity-formation process to want to test oneself and others against dramatic (and often unrealistic) standards of worthiness, fidelity, and courage. At the academies, the emphasis in the moral tradition on pride, loyalty, and selflessness encourages this aspect of teenage behavior. Suffering is an offshoot of the virtue of selflessness; it is also crucial to adolescent experimentation with the image of heroic survivor. For cadets, military school is like baptism by fire: if one can endure the pain, one will emerge stronger and surer of oneself. A boy said how much he had hated Pershing his first year there but said he would send his children to it because "I have suffered a lot here . . . but I think it's worth it." Another cadet said that every time he felt too exhausted and burned out to continue at Pershing, "then I look back and I know it's good for me." A senior summed it up: "The main lesson you learn here is that you can accomplish anything. If you've been able to handle just being here, then you can survive anything."

Many teenagers at the academies say they are there "to prove something" to parents, stepparents, and teachers. But most of them are also trying to prove something to themselves. On top of the challenges the schools set them—to learn the military drill, become accepted by their unit, earn rank, and in the meantime keep up with their schoolwork—the cadets set challenges for themselves. They work hard to try to become first sergeants and captains, and those who achieve these ranks then sweat to make their particular unit the best in the school. In the process they learn how to handle leadership without becoming overly cocky and alienating their subordinates.

More often than success, however, students must learn how to handle failure, since only one cadet can become the battalion commander and only a few others will rise to the rank of captain. Hard-earned rank can also be taken away. I asked Erik Bergstrom, the lieutenant who was busted to private for something he says he didn't do, whether he was happy at Sherman. He paused a long time before answering. "Happiness for me has a lot of definitions," he said finally. "I feel that I need to go through this to reach my happiness. I'm trying to make the best of it. And I do think about tradition: about someday having my kid on my lap and telling him about this school, like my father did with me." It is important to Erik to pass on to his son the male tradition of courage and survival that he and his father both received at Sherman.

The worst ordeal cadets have to survive is being a plebe. As a Pershing senior said, "It really gives you confidence to get through something so tough." This boy's plebe experience four years earlier was particularly brutal: "Kids got hit over the head with chairs, got their ribs broken or their hands. We were taught that . . . if anyone asks, you just say you fell down the stairs. There were a lot of stair accidents among freshmen!" Most cadets spoke more positively about their plebe experiences, echoing the junior who said, "My plebe year . . . I learned about respect, I learned how to handle pressure, I learned how to rely on myself and my peers—not the people who are older than me but my class, the people I need to rely on." A senior captain said that he'd "never had to work so hard for anything in [his] life" as for his rank insignia at the end of the plebe period. Being "scared and . . . alone" taught him "that I could either be those things or take them and turn them into something positive. And I hope I have, because . . . I got Cs and Ds in grade school, and I had a 3.9 average last semester."

Learning to handle fear continues long after freshman year. One girl joked that the unofficial lessons of military school "are that you either learn to be a smart-mouth, if you don't like to take orders, or you learn to shut up because you're scared." Indeed, silence is often an important key to survival. A Pershing senior without rank described learning to swallow his anger at being ordered around by "a guy who's the same age as me":

When a junior first sergeant comes up and inspects you and tells you to go back and shine your shoes, oh boy, that is the worst. And there's nothing to say. . . . Either you go back or he'll write you up, he has the authority to do that. . . . So you just get angry and then you get over it.

Being obedient can also have its pitfalls, though, particularly if you are a plebe. A cadet sergeant said that "dorks who don't do what they are told" have to be disciplined, but so do "plebes who never screw up"—these "have to be humbled."

Some students survive their years at the academy by trying to minimize the intrusion of the military into their lives. But most want to be leaders. Winning recognition for leadership, the official lesson of military school, is by far the best method of proving to oneself that one has not only endured but grown. (It is also an excellent survival technique, as is shown by a Jackson student's statement that he decided to seek rank "because I was tired of being beat up.") Through leadership, a cadet proves to his or her fellow students that he or she has made it. The leader is then expected to help younger students to survive, through tough training that teaches respect and endurance. Leadership status helps adolescents meet their need for an audience before which to try out their different roles, by providing them with a set of subordinates for whom they are expected to set an example. High rank turns adolescents' obsession with self-presentation into a virtue; leaders are expected to be perfectly dressed, to speak in a commanding tone of voice, and to carry themselves proudly. The best of them are heroes to their subordinates. One senior still remembers with gratitude and awe the captain of his unit during freshman year:

When I came to Pershing, it was such a shock that I had to put my trust and my faith into something, and I put it into my captain. . . . There were some guys who just yelled and screamed and that's all they did, but Raúl really cared about the kids. He would come into my room when I had problems and we'd talk. . . . He was a big man, the captain of the football team, and he had such power. I never saw him hit a person . . . and I'm glad, because that would have tarnished my image of him.

Surviving as a leader doesn't require becoming a hero; sometimes it is sufficient just to keep up appearances. A leader's reputation with the adults depends in large part on the appearance of subordinates; if the company plays its role well, the leader is rewarded. Says Pershing's Kyle Bennett:

I don't ask for a lot from the people in my company, but when it comes time to look good, I want them to look good . . . or else they're going to lose some of the freedom I give them. . . . I'd like my lieutenants to be good people, but if they're not going to be good people, I at least want them to put up a good front!

Whether a student learns to keep quiet and take orders, like the senior private; or shows concern for people, like Raúl; or focuses on looking good, like Kyle, each one finds a system of survival that becomes part of his or her self-image. One of the Pershing counselors speculates that for some kids the process of "getting through the four years" is so important that it shapes their sense of themselves not only while they are at the school but also in adulthood. Interestingly enough, he thinks this is particularly true for the most rebellious students:

I have a theory that the ones who hate it the most while they are here are the first ones to come back [as alumni]. . . . They found meaning in their lives from hating the place, it gave them a reason to live—to fight the system. It gave them a sense of motivation and purpose or something, dodging and bending and manipulating and bitching and being with a group that did likewise. They had an identity here.

These cadets are the ones who fail to become leaders; rebellion becomes—and perhaps remains later in life—their way of surviving and making their mark. Some of the students who start as rebels, however, change during their years at the school. Jackson's Chip Lang, whom Major Sedgefield helped to turn around, is one example. Another is the senior private at Pershing who resents taking orders from juniors. He has a reputation as a BA, but he is convinced that the school has "made me a better person, more responsible. . . . When I go home, I can't even understand how some of my friends act and talk the way they do. My manners, my attitude . . . boy, I've really changed a lot, I think."

The rebels' attempts to survive with dignity, to try to endure and grow even as they strike out against the system, have at times a kind of heroism. One cadet at Jackson seemed particularly brave, as she struggled to shape and retain a positive image of herself in the face of contempt from her teachers and rejection by many of her peers. When we talked, she was in her sixth week of a nine-week restriction period, being punished for two separate offenses: smoking a joint, and being in the boys' dorm with her boyfriend. Week after week she was confined to the girls' dorm during evenings and weekends. "You go in your room some nights at seven when everyone else is outside having fun, and it really drives you insane. Day in, day out: it's like I'm in a closed prison." She said she was at Jackson because "my mom drinks a lot, and my dad kind of wanted me to get away from her." Asked how she thought she'd changed as a result of being at the school, she said that she was no longer quite as likely to go along with doing something "wrong." Instead, "I think about it first, and I think about what will happen to me afterwards. . . . I'm a troublemaker, though." I asked her why. "Rebelling against the school," she replied. "I'm tired of it. Some of the stuff that goes on makes you so mad. I don't want out of the school, I like to go here, but . . . actually, it's that I've got nowhere else to go, nowhere else to turn. I don't want to start over and go to a new school."

Sometimes, while "marching on D-squad [detention], thinking about all the trouble I've gotten into," she says to herself, "Golly, I'm at a *military* school. And then I think, 'I'm a really good person inside and how could I do this, how could I mess up?' It's like I've already messed up my life. But I'm coming back next year, I'm coming back till I graduate, because maybe it will straighten me out." Later she said, "It may look like I've done a lot of [bad] stuff, but I've also refused a lot of stuff." I asked her if there was anything at Jackson that made her feel happy. "I have a good boyfriend, and we have a good relationship, and I make good grades. And I talk to my dad on the phone. . . . I don't know. I haven't got too much to look forward to around here. I hate to say it, but I look forward to [going to] McDonald's on Friday nights. I'm allowed to do that. That's the highlight." Asked whom she respected most at Jackson, she answered immediately:

The people that are on restriction. Because they can handle it. They haven't broken loose yet, they haven't gone into a mental breakdown. The people on restriction! Because they are the strongest ones. . . . And the people who make it through restriction . . . without getting kicked out. Just the people who make it through.

Unlike the Quaker-school kids, who are searching to discover their true selves, students at military academies are trying to "straighten themselves out" or even transform themselves into "winners." The only real way to beat the system is to manage to come through it unbroken. Whether they decide to cope by being a rebel or by becoming a leader, their sense of self-worth will depend on making a show of toughness in the face of either success or failure. "Just the people who make it through": they are the heroes.

Throughout this tale of survival, endurance, and growth the threat of violence runs like a leitmotif. The ability both to withstand and to inflict suffering is central to the military-school adolescent's identity as a heroic survivor. This is part of male culture. At Foley's North Town High School, punching someone's bicep as hard as possible, a practice Foley remembered from his own high-school days in the late 1950s, "was still the common masculinity test, the other variations being pinching the forearm and rapping the knuckles." These "tests of pain thresholds" could be part of "joking, buddy relationships" or they could serve as "small, daily ritual degradations" directed at boys who were perceived as weak or effeminate.[27] Behavior like this is part of our way of "making men" by teaching young males to overcome "the universal urge to flee from danger."[28]

Such violence also plays a role in the adolescent development process as a whole, which can drive teenagers to test extremes and court danger in their search for stability.[29] Adolescents—male and female—inflict violence on themselves—depriving themselves of food or sleep, drinking or taking drugs to excess, getting tattoos, or exercising fanatically, for example—in order to test their endurance and self-control.[30] They inflict violence on others partially so as to test others' strength and worthiness, but also as part of the secret self-monitoring process that goes on in a teenager's mind. They may lash out at someone in anger without thought, but when they participate in an elaborate piece of cruelty—hanging a smaller boy out a window, for example, or cutting off great chunks of a roommate's hair—they are doing it as part of a silent experiment. "Am I the kind of person who does things like this?" they are thinking. "How far will I go?" "What will people think of me?" "What will I do next?" "How will I stop?" Military school, because it heightens the survival ethic, the desire to test and be tested, the need to appear strongest and best, encourages this kind of adolescent violence. Without the threat of violence, survival would lose its heroic dimensions and, as a result, much of its value as a symbol of maturity.

Jerome Kagan has said that, from about the age of two on, most people want to be considered good; throughout their lives, they "attempt continually to reassure themselves of their virtue." He argues that "schools are an essential instrument in each person's crusade to accumulate a personal sense of virtue, for they permit children to acquire some of the local signs that define personal worth."[31] At the boarding schools, students use the moral traditions to shape their sense of themselves as virtuous. For adolescents at a Friends school, to be a good person is to be true to oneself; key virtues are interpreted and practiced by adolescents as part of this greater goal, and choices about behavior—for example, whether to smoke marijuana as an SHS member—are made in service to it. To be a good person at military school is to be a heroic survivor; loyalty, competence, selflessness, integrity, and pride are interpreted by adolescents as survival techniques, and battles are fought against adults to defend the students' rights to impose on one another the initiation rites, punishments, and harsh conditions that give survival its significance. In the eyes of many adults at both sets of schools, the teenagers' ways of understanding and enacting the two moral traditions distort the traditions' meaning and damage their moral worth. Yet it is the students' ability, year after year, to adapt the traditions to their needs and infuse them with special meaning that in fact ensures their continuing viability and strength.

The Elusive Lesson of Sacredness

The adolescents' interpretations of the moral traditions ring false to adults because a crucial ingredient is missing from their vision of Quakerism as a search for the true self or of military professionalism as a code of heroic survival. What is missing is a grasp of the sacred element in each tradition. A sense of the sacred is not discussed by most members of the school communities, and particularly not by adolescents. Yet unless a moral tradition continues to offer its members an experience of sacredness, of being one with something greater than the self, it will stagnate. Thus one important problem school administrators face is how to communicate to the adolescents the sacred aspects of the traditions. This is a lesson that the students have particular trouble understanding.

Chapter Two has shown that one similarity between the two traditions is a commitment to service experienced as a sacred calling. Among devout Quakers, the experience of sacredness means "obedience to the Light," a merging of one's own will with the will of God. For Friends, this is usually a silent but not a solitary experience:

To be "joined to the Lord" results in being joined to one another, and being joined to one another results in being "joined to the Lord." . . . The same identical Spirit of Truth exists in all of us, and the more truly we are united with it the nearer we come to one another.[32]

Soldiers are also joined both to one another and to something greater than the self; for them, it is war that supplies comradeship and a sense of mystical enormity. Gray writes of "the feeling of freedom and power instilled in us by communal effort in combat" and "the assurance of immortality that makes self-sacrifice at these moments so relatively easy, . . . for the self has become indestructible in being united with a supreme reality."[33] To a pacifist Quaker the comparison may seem obscene, but participation in war, like Quaker worship, is a sacred ritual: an ecstatic union with others experienced as a oneness with something wholly apart from and greater than the self that generates an urge to sustain and serve the group.[34] When William Penn wrote that "true religion does not draw men out of the world but enables them to live better in it and excites their endeavors to mend it," he was recognizing the communal aspect of the sacred.[35] When Gabriel called soldiering a vocation requiring membership in a brotherhood, "a special sense of obligation," and devotion "to something beyond one's self, to the community and the profession," he, too, was talking about sharing a sacred experience.[36]

Swidler has written that bursts of collective enthusiasm among students and teachers at alternative schools reinforce commitment to school activities.[37] Lesko, writing about a small Catholic school,

showed how the tensions between "caring" and "contest" that dominated the school were temporarily resolved through the shared rituals
of assembly and mass.[38] If sacredness consists of these special moments of intense communal feeling, then students at the six schools
are acquainted with it, particularly during graduation ceremonies—
which are exactly the kind of liminal ritual or rite of passage most
conducive to feelings of unity.[39] In their ideal forms, however, the two
moral traditions promise not merely fleeting access to a sacred moment but the ability to tap at will a sacred source of strength. This
ongoing access to the sacred is something a number of the adults at
Quaker and military schools have experienced but which they find
extremely difficult to communicate to the adolescents. Nevertheless,
they try.

Quaker Schools: Silent Worship
and Serving Others

At the three Friends schools, students are required to attend Meeting
for Worship, and during their school careers they must do some form
of volunteer work for the school and, at Dyer and Mott, for the
community as well. Through silent worship—every morning and evening at Fox, twice a week at Mott, and once a week at Dyer—and
through service—whether it be cleaning bathrooms, traveling once a
week to a psychiatric hospital to do crafts with patients, or participating in a two-week work camp in Appalachia—the schools try to communicate to students a sense of spiritual union with one another and a
commitment to something greater than the self. For the most part,
however, students see these experiences as just another set of graduation requirements.

At all three schools, Meeting for Worship is portrayed as important
in the students' lives; Dyer's catalogue states that "most students find
it a valued opportunity to center, to listen, and to touch a deeper level
within themselves," while Fox's student handbook calls it "a major part
of the Fox experience." Students new to Quakerism are fascinated by
the idea of having to sit for an extended time in silence, and they use
the time in a way that seems meaningful to them. One Mott freshman
said, "The Meeting for Worship is different, 'cause you sit there for
half an hour and nothing happens. . . . But I've grown to like it. Sometimes I fall asleep, if I'm tired, but sometimes it's good to think about

what's happened to me. I get my thoughts together." Other students resent having to go to Meeting. Whether they like it or not, however, few students seem to consider Meeting a sacred experience.

A retired Mott teacher, a Quaker, suggested that Meeting for Worship comes to have a greater impact on students later in life. "There are so many kids who have gone on and done tremendous things; you read about them in the alumni magazine, and they . . . often will say that they miss Meeting for Worship, that this was a time that became valuable for them when they were students. And of course, when they were students, they were always saying, 'Oh, no, why do we have to go to Meeting; this is terrible, we should be free to do what we want to do!'" His contact with alumni has also convinced him that "there are lots of kids whose service work at Mott has triggered what they've done with their lives since that time."

While at school, however, most students have no suspicion that the two hours per week of menial or secretarial work that they do in the kitchen, classrooms, or library and the sixty-five to eighty-five hours of community service outside the school that they must perform to graduate might help to determine their future. Nor do they see anything sacred in these experiences. One boy poked fun at the idea of Mott's "future yuppies"—as he insisted students were, because of their wealth and ambitions—"going to Appalachia and spending two weeks squatting in the dirt learning how to be a person who's underprivileged." A sophomore girl, who found Meeting for Worship "peaceful" but with "little relevance to my daily life," thought the service projects artificial:

I understand what they are trying to do . . . but I just look at it as another requirement. . . . To me the whole principle behind charity and service work is that it comes from your feelings, your own thoughts, philosophy, and principles, so to force people to do a service project . . . takes away from the whole purpose of charity.

Or, as one of the non-Quaker teachers said bluntly, "For a lot of the kids, going on a work camp is just one more task they have to do, instead of spending the rest of their vacation in Hawaii." This is a far cry from the words of a staff member at Fox: "I want the students to leave here with a sense of belonging and with a willingness to be a servant without the fear of losing something of themselves, to know the rewards of serving." In the Quaker tradition, such service is most joyfully done when it is in answer to a concern. The vast majority of students at the Friends schools simply do not experience their service projects as spiritual concerns.

I attended almost every Meeting for Worship that was held during my weeks at the three schools, and only once, at Mott, did a number of students speak out movingly on topics of social and personal concern. The mood of the other meetings ranged from patiently silent to annoyed and restless. I participated in a Mott service project, joining four girls and a staff member on their weekly visit to an inner-city after-school program. There the girls played ball in a desultory way for under an hour with ten elementary-school children. They seemed not to know any of the children's names, and they brought no special games to engage their interest, made no plans beforehand for the hour of play, and did not discuss or evaluate the experience on the way home. Whenever their teacher's eye wandered from them, the girls tended to drift away from the children and talk among themselves. They were not sullen; they merely engaged themselves as little as possible with their surroundings and their young clients. There are better-organized service projects and more committed students at Mott than this one example indicates; nevertheless, this vignette gives evidence of how difficult it is to try to communicate a Quaker sense of concern to youngsters who are simply going through the motions of service. The girls at the after-school center apparently did not experience sacredness, or deeply felt commitment to others, or even a sense of personal responsibility.

Military Schools: Devotion to Subordinates and School

Friends schools try to communicate the sacred by teaching devotion to the Inner Light and the school community through Meeting for Worship, and devotion to needy others through service projects. Out of this combination of silent worship and social activism they hope to awaken an experience of concern as a spiritually motivated desire to "mend the world." Military academies avoid the depth and breadth of Quaker devotions, focusing instead on a commitment that is easier for students: one to their school and their peers. Such dedication to "the mission and the men" may not have the religious overtones of a Quaker Meeting, but for some, especially former military officers, it has a quality of sacredness nonetheless. For leaders trained in the military system, the phrase "Take care of the men" means as much as "mind the Light" does to a Quaker. A former naval captain at Pershing communicated the sacred quality of that care when he described what he called "the *agape* method of leadership" as "almost a religion" in the profession of arms. *Agape*, he explained, is the Greek word for love of one's fellow man, and that love was the best method of leadership he knew:

> If you want to lead someone, you have to give yourself to them, and you have to take a part of them to you, you have to hurt when they hurt, you have to laugh when they laugh. They don't have to see this, but you've got to be able to do it. You cannot go down to the mess decks of the ship and say to the crew, "Hey guys, I love you," because they'd immediately turn around and say, "What's the matter, you queer?" Because they don't understand the word *love*, don't understand what you mean by it. And you can't go down and say, "I *agape* you!" . . . But that's what you have to do, you have to lead that way.

The Pershing chaplain puts the same emphasis on "caring for the corps," which he describes as anything from "soldiers giving their lives in battle to officers in the dining room letting the rest of the unit eat first." He rejects the idea of leadership as a privilege, saying, "I'm not the least bit impressed with leadership unless it is in the context of servanthood."

Some of the cadets feel this kind of religious dedication, even if they do not voice it in obviously spiritual terms. When Sherman's Erik Bergstrom describes himself and his subordinates crying at his demotion to private, when Joe Novak at Jackson talks about turning his young glue-sniffers into two of the best cadets in his unit, when Sherman's Lamont Sandler delights in his unit's newly learned ability to bring their feet together in unison to make a loud noise at attention, they are showing the kind of devotion to their subordinates that gives leadership its sacred quality. The majority of student officers, however, do not have the capacity to lead so selflessly. Instead, as one Pershing senior put it, "there are a lot of hypocrites—people who expect everyone else to do things that they don't expect themselves to do."

Devotion to the school is an extension of devotion to the corps of cadets. At Pershing, the sacredness of this dual love is symbolized by a plaque on the administration building commemorating the graduates who have died in war. Cadets are required to salute this plaque whenever they pass it, as a sign of respect for the dead men and the school that produced them. Lamont expressed his devotion to Sherman another way: "There was this one kid who said, 'Sherman sucks,' and that upset me so much I pushed him down, and I said, 'This school is not a bunch of bull, this school is the people within it, and it's what you make it.'" But this devotion to the community as a whole remains elusive for many students at the three academies.

A teacher at Pershing offered his thoughts about this problem. His class was studying the People's Republic of China, and he found that the students couldn't seem to grasp "something not only Chinese but socialist in nature—the importance of the collective over the individual," a concept that "ran right square into the fierce individualism of the West and especially of America." Suddenly it occurred to him, he said, that the students' rejection of the idea of the collective must also extend to the way they interpreted the military system. "And I couldn't help but think of our commandant, who bangs his head up against the wall trying to model and teach and talk about the importance of the group over the individual to a society that is ferociously individualistic." Laughing affectionately, since he is fond of Duncan Graham, he calls him "a kind of a Mao Zedong of Pershing, watching the revolutionary spirit and in this case the military spirit die." Graham "so very much believes in this spirit—that you find yourself by being part of a group—he believes all of these things so intensely" because of his experience in Vietnam:

> What Duncan wants to reproduce for the cadets here is a wartime experience, a "moral equivalent of war." . . . But the problem with that is that it doesn't apply here, and life in the [boarding-school] barracks just isn't that way, and I don't think it can be. . . . That's why . . . there is this kind of sadness in him.

Students do recognize one aspect of leadership that seems to transcend the ordinary, and that is the power of charisma. They know that some of their fellows have an uncanny ability to make others follow them, and that ability doesn't seem to have much to do with following school rules and regulations about leadership. A junior remembered, "Last year we had a guy in our unit who was a BA, but he was such a leader. People listened to him. I can't explain it; it was really weird—

you just had to listen to the guy." Kyle Bennett thinks that Pershing's leadership courses are essentially useless:

You can work on being a leader, . . . but you're either going to command respect or not. Because someone who's five-foot-two and stays in his room all day could get [the rank of] captain, and keep his mouth shut, his room clean, memorize all 150 rules of leadership, and command no respect. Whereas the person who's the biggest BA walking around campus could say, "Hey, guys, let's do this," and everyone would say, "Hey, yeah, let's do that." But this school has problems recognizing that.

Kyle is wrong. The faculty recognize perfectly well the power of a charismatic student leader, and they are eager to harness that power in service to the school. But the idea of a leader as a servant is difficult for the majority of the adolescents to grasp—it remains a phrase in their Leadership I workbooks. It is also difficult for even the best-intentioned leaders to achieve, since their leadership responsibilities must share a place in their day with the time-consuming demands of teachers, coaches, and friends. Leadership is a requirement, and for many it is an honor, but rarely is it seen as a sacred experience.

The Adolescent Search for Identity

Why is sacredness, so central a feature of the two traditions, missing from the experience of most of the adolescents? The simplest answer is that to try to communicate the traditional meaning of the Inner Light and the importance of concern in the absence of a belief in God is impossible, and to try to teach the true importance of leadership, loyalty, and the responsibility for mission and men in the absence of war is impossible, too. The sacredness of the Quaker tradition is inseparable from the immensity of the idea of God, and that of the military tradition is equally bound up with the all-consuming passion of warfare. Equality, community, simplicity, and peace; loyalty, competence, selflessness, integrity, and pride: the key virtues of the two traditions exist not to help adolescents shape their identities but to serve God or win wars. The kind of passion and dedication to service that led a eighteenth-century Quaker like John Woolman to spend his life fighting slavery or caused a soldier like George C. Marshall to lead the United States through World War II as chief of staff is not appropriate at a boarding school. Nevertheless, students should be able to feel something of the devotion to principle and humanity that inspired these two men and other men and women like them. Why do they have so much trouble comprehending and articulating this feeling of the sacred?

The answer is that sacredness requires a stepping outside of one-self, an ability to lose oneself in the strength of something larger and more important than the psyche. Kanter calls this losing and reinvesting of the self "mortification" and "transcendence": experiences that are prerequisites for deep moral commitment to utopian communities.[40] The boarding schools are not utopian communities, however, much as they may resemble them in some ways. Nor is their purpose the same as that of a religious sect. Sects do indeed offer teenagers self-surrender and ecstatic union with others in the context of a highly structured community.[41] A fundamentalist Christian school, intent on teaching adolescents absolute obedience to God's Truth, can perform a similar function, inspiring at least some of its students to be "on fire for the Lord."[42] But Quaker and military boarding schools are trying to do something different and in some ways more difficult than fundamentalist schools are. They are trying to strengthen the individual in the context of the community, rather than strengthen the community through the absorption or indoctrination of individuals.

For students at the six schools to embrace the selflessness inspired by sacred devotion would be more destructive than inspiring. Their still-fragile identities need to be protected and nurtured, not lost in ecstatic union. Certainly, when they find something or somebody to be true to, they have the capacity to subordinate themselves in service to a cause. One can see this quality of fidelity in the devotion of several of the Mott student to their duties as members of Students Helping Students, and even more vividly in the wholeheartedness with which so many boys and girls adhere to and strive to enforce the requirements of the military system. For the most part, however, the adolescents at the six schools are concerned with themselves, and so they must be, if they are to get on with the business of identity formation that will eventually enable them to have, in Erikson's words, "the strength of disciplined devotion" to some of the values they have learned.[43] The schools must continue to try to communicate the importance of sacredness, however, even while the students' self-absorption continues to get in the way of their comprehending it, because without a sacred element the tradition is powerless to inspire the devotion Erikson describes. If the sacred is present at the schools, communicated through rituals and through the example of dedicated teachers, then it will be available for students to draw upon when they are ready to participate in it.

Conclusion

The Capacity for Reflective Living

This book has used the themes of order and conflict to explain how a moral tradition is taught and followed at six schools. It concludes by reviewing what membership in a moral tradition offers participants and by reexamining conflict as a crucial element of morality, using Emile Durkheim's vision of moral order as a foil. At the schools, most conflicts are caused by students and teachers wanting to be accepted by the community and, at the same time, seeking to interpret the requirements of communal life in their own way. This Conclusion discusses how the Quaker and military moral traditions help members to balance these contradictory desires. Finally, it summarizes the tools and skills that adolescents acquire as a result of practicing virtue at the schools.

Belonging to a Moral Tradition

People yearn for the return of a society based upon traditional values because they seek a life of harmony and order. At the boarding schools, however, daily life lived in service to the Quaker or the military moral tradition is actually full of dilemmas and impassioned debates. Yet there is a kind of order in it, too: order that comes above all from feeling that one belongs to something important to which one can contribute. To be part of a moral tradition means to be part of the history of a group of people and a set of ideas. The history has times of triumph to celebrate and times of disaster to mourn and ponder. It is full of saints and heroes to emulate, sayings to learn, and rituals to repeat. This shared narrative provides a context for one's personal history: one's life is not a lone thread unwinding into oblivion but is part of a complicated tapestry that existed before one was born and will continue to exist after one's death. To be part of a moral tradition also means to have a special language. Unlike an occupational jargon, this language deals not simply with day-to-day affairs but with responsibilities, relationships to other people, and feelings about oneself. Although it can be comforting, it is more often demanding. It describes virtues and imposes duties: it tells one what kind of person to be and what such a person should do. Using this language with other members of the moral community gives one a sense of belonging to the group and a feeling of superiority to those outside the group who do not use the same words.

A moral tradition also explains the source of the virtues that members must practice. God's grace, noble birth, hard work, harmony with nature, strict standards: different traditions offer different stories about the true origins of morality. But the idea that there is a wellspring of strength and guidance that one can tap into is essential to any moral tradition. Another feature of a moral tradition is that it does not simply lay down rules and demand unthinking obedience and commitment. Instead, it requires choice, since without choices one cannot experience a sense of personal responsibility for one's life.[1] A moral tradition binds one to the community, but it also recognizes independence, initiative, conscience, or some other force that can drive one to confront the demands of group membership. It provides ways of reconciling oneself with the group without losing one's sense of autonomy and one's self-respect.

Finally, a moral tradition gives access to an experience of the sacred. It grants its members a feeling of being at one with something greater than the self, an incentive to action that transcends the everyday and the personal and is experienced as service to some absolute good. In spite of all the ambiguities that may arise in the use of the tradition's language and all the contradictions that may lie just under the surface of its purest ideals, the sense of sacredness it imparts will continue to sustain its members during personal crises. Ultimately, it is the tradition's ability to communicate this sacredness that will keep it alive and capable of attracting new adherents.

This is an idealized portrait of what membership in a moral tradition provides. Many people who call themselves Quakers or military professionals do not feel truly a part of the community to which they lay claim. A sense of community requires a sense of commitment and a desire to serve. In addition, some people's past histories give them special access to the communities. Certainly the majority of teachers and students at the Quaker schools are not as deeply committed to the Friends tradition as Fox's Andrew Henley, who descends from generations of Friends, nor are most teachers and students at the academies as involved in the military tradition as Jackson's Major Sedgefield and some of the other retired officers and NCOs. Yet even those who do not, or cannot, identify completely with Quakerism or the military gain something by their attempts to fulfill the tradition's requirements. One suggestion of what it is they gain comes from Emile Durkheim. The structure that a moral tradition imparts to daily life, the sense of unity members feel in sharing their tradition's language and ideals, the personal commitment and responsibility the traditions demand: these correspond to Durkheim's three elements of morality, which are the spirit of discipline, attachment to social groups, and autonomy.

Fitting Conflict into Durkheim's Vision of Moral Order

Durkheim was interested in the forces that cause people to act for the common good—to do what one might call their societal duty. For him, morality is the source of social unity. Society (which in his writings took on the quality of a powerful and almost living force) produces morality and is also regenerated by it; he wrote that "when our conscience speaks, it is society speaking within us" and argued that "to act morally is to act in terms of the collective interest." In order to be effective, a moral system must involve three things. First, "morality . . . is basically a discipline," and "all discipline has a double objective: to promote a certain regularity in people's conduct, and to provide them with determinate goals that at the same time limit their horizons." Second, morality must serve to attach people to their society, persuading them "to go beyond [themselves], to go beyond the circle of self-interest," and act for the good of the group. Finally, if morality is not to be merely a slavish obedience to rules or a mindless self-sacrifice, it must offer the opportunity for reflection, allowing people to understand the reasons for its requirements and to choose freely to act as discipline and devotion to the group indicate that they should.[2]

Durkheim's vision of morality is a vision of order. Members of society accept the limits placed on them as being for the good of society, and their understanding of the reasons for these limits gives them autonomy even as they obey. Life at the six schools sometimes resembles this orderly picture. Some school rules—the dress code at the military academies, for example, or the family-style seating arrangements in the Quaker-school dining halls—are understood as concrete expressions of important values. People obey the rules not only because they must but because they believe they are right; to defy the rules would be to reject the community and the virtues it teaches. The limits imposed by the tradition—the choices it filters out, the opportunities it fails to bring into focus—are perceived to be for the individual's own good and for the good of the community.

This is not the image of morality that predominates at the schools, however, since traditions that are strong enough to inspire such passionate allegiance also lead to conflict. In the morally charged world of Mott Friends School or Pershing Military Academy, a difference of opinion over student discipline, grading methods, or the damming of a stream can become a crusade. Then the moral language, the set of special words and phrases that carry so much meaning and so much ambiguity, comes into its own. In conflict, members of the communities are forced to use the language they have learned, in order to explain to themselves and others what is important about the traditions, what the virtues mean, what actions must follow as a consequence of their beliefs. These inner monologues, vehement conversations, and heated meetings are the signs of a living morality. At times the talk can serve to reinforce loyalties; at other times, to bring about much-needed changes. Frequently it leads nowhere. But if feelings about the moral traditions are strong—and do not turn to bitterness and cynicism as conflicts remain unresolved—then the same problems will surface again and again, stimulating discussion and commitment and eventually, perhaps, agreement.

Thus conflict, too, is a product of discipline, attachment, and autonomy; it is as much a part of morality as is order. Durkheim paints a harmonious picture of human beings' need for the three elements of morality, implying that these needs are smoothly coordinated, but in real life the everyday demands of discipline, attachment, and autonomy frequently clash.[3] Autonomy depends not simply on reason but on reflection, discussion, and debate—in other words, on language, which Durkheim does not consider. With language come reinterpretations, criticisms, misunderstandings. Under these circumstances, autonomy does not necessarily lead to an acceptance of discipline; it frequently leads instead to rebellion. Yet rebellion can also be a sign of attachment to the group and can have the good of the society at heart. Much of what seems to be rebellion at the schools, for example—by teachers against administrators at the Quaker schools, by cadets against counselors and tactical officers at the military academies—is produced not by a rejection of the moral tradition but by a different understanding of its demands. Such rebellions prove that the traditions' requirements are taken seriously.

Seeking Virtue Through Balance

For insight into morality as lived at the schools, Durkheim's orderly vision must be supplemented with the views of his contemporary Simmel, who wrote, "Contradiction and conflict not only precede . . . unity but are operative in it at every moment of its existence. . . . An absolutely centripetal and harmonious group, a pure 'unification,' not only is empirically unreal, it could show no real life process."[4] Yet even though the schools' vitality as moral communities is strengthened by the contentiousness of students and faculty, there must also be balance. The attempt to reconcile discipline, attachment, and autonomy is part of the process of trying to live a virtuous life.

For a person of character, a difficult decision becomes a moral dilemma when he or she is forced to weigh the relative claims of the three elements of morality, instead of being able to take their harmonious conjunction for granted. When Pershing's battalion commander, Tom Hurd, has to choose whether to enforce school rules as discipline requires, relax into being "just one of the boys" in response to his need for attachment, or deal with his friends' misbehavior in a way that demonstrates his independence from the adults, his dilemma is clearly the result of a clash between the three aspects of morality. The same is true for the Mott teacher who has to decide what to do about the dam that he believes is against school principles, or for Charlie McDowell as he responds to the idea of a military recruiter visiting Mott. This book has shown that the process of trying to translate moral belief into everyday action throws up countless dilemmas like these, dilemmas that involve balancing the demands of conscience against the expectations of the community. It has also shown that the moral traditions provide ways of finding this balance. Here, in conclusion, are some final thoughts about the effectiveness of the concepts of concern and leadership in mediating extreme responses to the two traditions.

The Quaker moral tradition clearly emphasizes the individual. Each person's conscience is his or her best source of the Inner Light that constitutes that of God within. Obedience to conscience is therefore a moral mandate. In any group's attempt to practice such an individualistic tradition, one would expect to see incoherence, excess, and schisms, and, indeed, these problems have plagued Quakers off and on since the religion was founded. But when one looks at the practice of Quakerism at the schools, and particularly at Mott, one sees that in spite of the tradition's emphasis on the individual, one of the most important lessons it tries to teach is how to function and make decisions as a collective. People trying to live a Quaker life work at listening to each other's ideas and explaining their own opinions in ways that others can understand. This ability to see moral issues and dilemmas as problems to be addressed by the group, rather than mere personal crises, is due in part to the strength of the concept of concern. A person who belongs to the Friends tradition cannot be concerned in solitude; he or she must explain the concern to others, seeking their approval and their advice, before making a decision about what action to take. A concern that arises out of the shared silence in Meeting for Worship becomes in a sense the property of the Meeting as a whole, to be considered and weighed by all its members. At the schools, staff and students voice the majority of their concerns not in Meeting for Worship but in informal conversations, in faculty or community meetings, or during special retreats. The religious nature of the discussions is often nonexistent, but the commitment to the community and its members is as strong as that found in many religious gatherings. Through the sharing of concerns, the tendency toward extreme individualism that lies within the tradition is mitigated.

The military moral tradition emphasizes the collective. Everyone obeys a single set of rules and tries to live according to one set of standards. One would expect the result to be conformity and lack of initiative, and, indeed, many officers are afraid to speak up and take risks for fear of receiving on their Officer Efficiency Report a black mark that will destroy their career. But a glance at the military tradition in the schools shows that it inspires individuals to do extraordinary things: to shoulder enormous responsibilities, to tackle problems single-handedly, and to break rules right and left if necessary, all in the name of leadership. At the schools, the military tradition is not used to build an army but, rather, to build individual character. The potential for extreme conformity is there, and attempts to enforce unity can lead to the sort of violence that takes place in the dorms. But this tendency within the tradition is balanced by the idea of leadership as personal accountability. The most striking thing about the military academies is not the dominance of the collective but the strength, courage, maturity, and forbearance of many individual students.

Despite the Quaker vision of tolerance toward the individual conscience, we have seen that the tradition contains the potential for intolerance toward those who are not secure enough to project a "real" self that rings true. The military tradition, despite its vision of discipline, hides a potential for anarchy, "a delight in destruction" and hurting others that emerges in the barracks as well as on the battlefield.[5] These sides of the traditions need to be acknowledged in order for their dangers to be recognized. Yet despite their painful consequences at the schools, these impulses toward censure within the tradition of tolerance and toward license within the tradition of discipline are a part of the same search for balance between extremes that produces the reconciling concepts of concern and leadership.

The lessons the Quaker tradition teaches about consensual decision-making have a greater impact on the adult members of the school communities than on the adolescents, whereas the lessons of the military academies about the importance of assuming responsibility have a greater impact on the cadets. The distinct visions of change predominating at the two sets of schools provide a partial explanation for this difference. At Quaker schools, teachers and administrators feel that part of their job is to shape the community to the needs of the students. The students, passing through, for the most part accept the community as a given and are not called upon to contribute to its perpetual remaking. As a result, many of them miss an important lesson in collective problem-solving. At military academies, on the other hand, teachers and administrators are expected to be the system's supporters rather than its critics. The school is an institution they are bound to uphold; they do not have to learn its lessons about character, because they themselves are the representatives of character. Students come to the schools to be transformed, to acquire certain values, to become leaders. Adults contribute to this process, but they do not take part in it. Learning to handle problems alone, without the help of adults, is one of the most important lessons that cadets learn in military school.

The Quaker emphasis on the Inner Light and on transforming the environment and the military emphasis on standards and on transforming the individual are interesting not only for their own sakes, but because they provide a new way to think about the contrasts between liberal and conservative expectations for American society. On the issue of social welfare, for example, liberals are Quaker-like in their desire to improve the environment of the poor, while conservatives resemble the military in their focus on improving character: that is why liberals talk about supporting social services and conservatives talk about fighting drugs, promoting stable families, and instilling a work ethic. How can people with two such different visions of virtue find the grounds for agreement that will allow them to address the problems of our society? Even at their best, when the vision of tolerance is braced with accountability and the vision of discipline tempered with compassion, the liberal and conservative perspectives seem to lack a meeting point. A thoughtful look at schools where the Quaker and military traditions are practiced shows that the answer may lie in the idea of service. For all their differences, Quakers and military professionals share a calling to serve. Charlie McDowell, the head of Mott's religion department, and Lieutenant Duncan Graham, the Vietnam veteran who is Pershing's commandant of cadets, are good men with very different ideas about what it means to be good. Yet they are surprisingly alike: intense, committed, full of integrity, worried about the future, and dedicated to serving the tradition they believe in, the school they work for, and the adolescents they teach. If liberals and conservatives who care about solving the problems of American society and taking a responsible stand toward the rest of the world could find in each other the common need to serve, perhaps they could also find the mutual respect and trust that would enable them to work together for the common good.

Growing Up at the Schools

The adolescents at the six boarding schools do not devote much thought to liberal or conservative politics or the problems of the world. Caught up in the process of building a sense of identity, they think mostly about themselves. The moral traditions contribute to this process of identity formation by providing the adolescents with a vocabulary for discussing and determining which qualities of character to emulate, which rules to obey, and which choices to worry about. Never simply absorbing, constantly adapting, redefining, and sometimes rejecting the interpretations passed on by administrators, teachers, alumni, and fellow students, each adolescent works on the material of the traditions to form a picture of the world outside the school and of the kind of role he or she wants to play in it.

Gerald Grant has written that education involves "being inducted into some set of standards, beliefs, and values about what it means to be a human being," and that "schools, even in democratic and pluralistic societies, have had the responsibility for teaching . . . a provisional morality," which should be communicated in such a way that it can be questioned freely and responsibly by children in adulthood.[6] The adolescents at the six schools do question; they do not wait for adulthood to voice their skepticism and trumpet the inconsistencies they uncover in the values they are taught. Yet they also have the opportunity to observe and grow close to a few men and women who practice the values that they preach. Observing these adult exemplars, students gather material to forge an identity in which the concepts of goodness and rightness have a place.

Lightfoot says that the good high school is a place where

ideology, authority, and order combine to produce a coherent institution that supports human interaction and growth. These institutional frameworks and structures are critical for adolescents, whose uncertainty and vulnerability call for external boundary setting. In their abrupt shift from childishness to maturity, they need settings that are rooted in tradition, that will give them clear signals of certainty and continuity.[7]

The Quaker and the military boarding schools try to provide this kind of structure and, through the moral traditions, to give adolescents ideals around which they can shape and order their lives. Yet the purpose of the six schools is not to indoctrinate students or remove them from mainstream American life, but, rather, to prepare them to face the world as strong and responsible adults. Thus, even as the schools provide ideals to give structure to students' lives, they also give students the right to interpret these ideals for themselves and to make choices. The inevitable result is that adolescents and adults sometimes disagree. The moral traditions shape the contexts of many of these battles and give them a weight and a meaningfulness that they might not otherwise have. Students clash with teachers over drugs, alcohol, sex, schoolwork, dormitory responsibilities, dress, their whereabouts, and all the other usual points of adolescent/adult conflict. But at Quaker schools they also challenge adults about the meaning of concern and the limits placed on the equality between teachers and students, while at military schools they question adult definitions of loyalty and demand more authority as leaders.[8]

The moral traditions make the adolescents feel part of a history that provides a meaningful context and a goal for their actions. Ideally, however, the traditions do not bind them, but, rather, provide "the linguistic, emotional, and rational skills that give [students] the strength to make [their] decisions and [their] life [their] own."[9] Using the language and the ideas provided by the traditions, they question the rightness of their own actions and those of their friends and teachers. It is through inner turmoil and conflict with others, more than through mere acceptance, that the adolescents form a sense of themselves as moral people and learn to take responsibility for their actions. The traditions help them acquire "skills of discernment and distancing,"[10] since having the vocabulary to think about and discuss their actions in a moral context allows them eventually to acquire the distance from themselves that they lack at the height of the identity-formation process. "For," as Stanley Hauerwas says:

it is certainly a skill to be able to describe my behavior appropriately and to know how to "step back" from myself so that I might better understand what I am doing. The ability to step back cannot come by trying to discover a moral perspective abstracted from all my endeavors, but rather comes through having a narrative that gives me critical purchase on my own projects.[11]

The Quaker and military moral traditions provide such narratives.

All of this may take place as the adolescents grow up at the schools—or it may not. Some adolescents seem to pass through the schools untouched by the moral environment that surrounds them, like the boy who insisted that Mott was merely a training ground for yuppies. Others do not grow and acquire a judicious distance from the moral messages they receive and from their own actions, but seem instead to shrink and harden, becoming willing apologists for the narrowest and most destructive interpretations of the traditions, as was the Jackson battalion commander, who talked about the "niggers and low-life scum" among his fellow cadets getting in the way of the school's "mission."

This book is about life at the schools, not life after the schools. It cannot show that the students' adult lives are affected by their exposure to the traditions. Yet surely many of them carry away a sense of belonging and self-respect and a clearly defined image of what it means to be a good person that will strengthen whatever moral identity they continue to build in adulthood. Even the adolescents' elusive and unsuccessful contact with the sacred aspects of the traditions may acquire more meaning when they come to seek a life's work to which they can dedicate themselves. One indication of this effect came from a Mott alumnus who has returned in his late twenties to teach at the school after initial success in another career. He said:

When it came time to decide what to do, I felt that I was losing touch with the things I'd learned here [at Mott]. I was afraid I wasn't a good person anymore. I felt like all the time I'd spent here and all the good things I'd learned were being worked out of me—and those were the things that made me me. . . . There's a spiritual fulfillment in being here. I feel like I give more of myself here than I would in another job.

Only research among graduates of the two sets of schools could uncover the ways that their lives continue to be influenced by the moral traditions they were exposed to in boarding school. However, I anticipate that at least two qualities will be present in greater abundance in graduates of Quaker and military boarding schools than in their counterparts who attended other types of schools: kindness, among the Quaker-school graduates, and courage, among former cadets. Kindness and courage are everyday distillations of the heady brew of virtues poured forth at the six schools. They are useful possessions for someone beginning adult life. One must only hope that those who have learned kindness at Quaker schools go on to learn more about facing difficult challenges, and that those who have learned courage as cadets eventually acquire more tolerance and concern for others. The traditions, even at their best, can give only so much. It is up to the graduates, as men and women whose schooling has helped them achieve a sensitivity to moral language and belief, to continue to grow as moral people by building on what they have learned through a combination of fidelity and skepticism or, as Bernard Williams says, "truthfulness to an existing self or society . . . combined with reflection, self-understanding, and criticism."[12] This capacity for reflective living, for critical examination of both self and society within the narrative context of a moral tradition, is the most important virtue the schools can teach.

Appendix A

Doing Fieldwork

Choosing the Schools

In 1987, the Friends Council on Education identified twenty-eight Quaker secondary schools in the United States; the Association of Military Colleges and Schools, thirty-five military secondary schools. To choose six schools as research sites, I consulted *Peterson's Annual Guide to Independent Secondary Schools* and ordered catalogues from seventeen Quaker schools and sixteen military academies. After four months of reading about the Religious Society of Friends and the United States Armed Forces, I narrowed the search to eight boarding schools, four of each type. My primary criterion was commitment to the moral traditions. About the Quaker schools, I considered: What percentage of the staff and students were Friends? Was the school under the care of a Friends Yearly Meeting? Did the admissions catalogue emphasize the teaching of Quaker principles and the importance of Meeting for Worship? Did the values listed coincide with those I had encountered in Quaker materials? Questions about the military academies were similar: What percentage of the staff were former military professionals? Did the admissions catalogue stress the importance of the military system in students' lives? Were the values listed similar to those emphasized in professional military training materials?

Headmasters at six of the eight schools agreed to a preliminary visit during the summer of 1987. Afterwards, it was arranged that I would spend two to three weeks during the 1987–88 school year at each of the three Quaker schools and at two of the military academies. One military-school headmaster refused to participate. Looking for a third academy to study, I was encouraged by staff at other military schools to contact Pershing, which I had rejected because the girls were not cadets. When I spoke with Pershing's headmaster, he accepted my proposal immediately, without a preliminary get-acquainted visit.

The six schools finally chosen for the study were all coeducational, included small (150 or fewer students) and large (500 or more students) schools in both categories, and were located in four different regions of the United States and in rural, suburban, and urban areas. The three Quaker schools were four-year high schools; although two of the three military academies also accepted younger pupils, these children were not included in the study.

Interviewing Quakers and Army Officers About the Traditions

In July 1987 I attended an annual meeting of Quakers in Oberlin, Ohio, sponsored by the Friends General Conference, an association of approximately 500 Meetings from all over the United States. At Oberlin I put notices on a prominent bulletin board and in the daily conference newsletter describing my interest in Quaker and military moral traditions and requesting volunteers who would be interested in answering questions about their values. I received fifteen responses to this request, thirteen from Quakers and two from men who had served in Vietnam and now attended a Meeting. I spoke with these fifteen people—eight men and seven women—for between one and two hours each, using the questions in Appendix B as a basis for the interview. I also conducted an informal two-hour discussion about Quaker values with two more Friends, both men. All of these exchanges were tape-recorded and later transcribed.

In August 1987 I was able to send out a similarly worded request for volunteers over the computer network at an army base; since all officers were expected to check the computer mail system daily, this was an excellent way of reaching potential subjects. I also placed a notice on the officers' club bulletin board. These requests led to interviews with nine officers—six captains, one a woman; two majors; and a lieutenant colonel—in which I also used the Appendix B questionnaire. These interviews, too, were taped and transcribed.

In September, drawing on these interviews and my reading, I outlined descriptions of the ideal Quaker and the ideal military officer. I also made lists of Quaker and military keywords, identifying concepts that had come up repeatedly in the interviews. These lists helped to focus my research at the schools and aided later in the analysis of interviews with faculty and students.

Observation at the Schools

My visits to all six schools had the written approval of the headmaster, but that did not mean that students and teachers knew about the research. Introducing myself and explaining the study was no problem at the Quaker schools; within a day or two of my arrival I was able to stand up in an all-school assembly or community meeting and explain the purpose of my visit. Since the three military academies had no such gatherings, I simply introduced myself to as many adults and adolescents as possible, explained my presence, and hoped they would spread the word with relative accuracy.

I was fortunate in that I was able to live at the schools during my visits, either in a guest room, a teacher's house, or a girls' dormitory room. I ate in the school cafeteria, where I sat sometimes with teachers and sometimes with students. At each school I attended at least one class in American history, global history, American literature, a science, a foreign language, health, and art or music. Where they were offered, I also audited a class in government, economics, or current events. At the Quaker schools, I went to classes in Quakerism; at the military schools, in leadership. I also observed a great many other school activities: administrative staff meetings at all six schools; faculty meetings at the three Friends schools (none were held during my stays at the three military academies); meetings with members of the school board at two Quaker schools; student-council meetings; all-school or student assemblies; religious services, which were mandatory at all six schools; student plays and performances; team practice and games in a variety of sports; and student dances. At the academies I observed parades and military events. Another useful source of information was school documents: admissions catalogues, departmental reading lists, yearbooks, literary magazines, and publications for alumni.

When I wasn't conducting interviews, auditing classes or meetings, reading yearbooks, or watching dramatic or sporting events, I was usually "hanging out." I drank coffee in the teachers' lounge or the student snack bar; talked to whoever was sitting next to me on the bleachers during soccer or baseball practice; spent time in the Fox kitchen, where students helped out; played pool and pinball in the student lounge at Jackson; went for walks on campus and chatted with the people I found along the way; visited with administrators' secretaries; stood with the cadet guards who were on duty at the military schools; watched TV with students on weekend evenings; and dropped in on girls in their dorm rooms. To my relief, people seemed to accept my intrusive friendliness. Boarding schools can be lonely places for both adults and adolescents, and a new face is a welcome diversion. My hanging out paid off: it allowed me to observe a great deal in an informal way, and I was told things that probably would not have emerged in an interview.

At each school a few adults invited me home for a meal or agreed to speak with me a number of times. They served as special sources of information, because they were willing to reflect at length about school goals and values and comment on the communities' serious problems.

Identifying and Contacting
Interview Partners

I formally interviewed between sixty and seventy-five people at each school, approximately half adults and half students.[1] Among adults, I arranged appointments with top administrators: headmaster, academic dean, business manager, admissions director, and dean of students or its military equivalent, commandant of cadets. I also interviewed heads of academic departments and at least one teacher from each department. I met with at least one secretary, one nurse, and one kitchen or grounds worker at each school. At Quaker schools, I interviewed the dormitory heads and several dormitory residents, and, at military academies, a selection of the tactical officers or counselors in charge of the various cadet companies. Also at the military schools, I met with active-duty or retired army sergeants involved in the JROTC program. Beyond these choices, other factors determining whom I asked for an interview were length of employment, sex, race, reputation, and Quaker or military background. For example, I made sure I interviewed at least one new faculty member and one old-timer at each school; men and women in proportion to their numbers on the staff; adults who were especially praised *or* condemned by students or colleagues; many of those who were either committed Quakers or former military professionals; and those who were known to be particularly critical of their school's tradition. I also asked everyone I interviewed if there were any adults on campus whom they especially respected or considered in some way representative of the school, and then sought out the people who were named repeatedly.

Among students, I sought out seniors and juniors, officers and NCOs at the military academies and prefects at the Quaker schools and Pershing girls' school, and leaders of extracurricular activities, such as the captain of the football team, the newspaper editor, and the yearbook editor. I made sure, however, that I also included a number of troublemakers and problem students among my interview partners. At the Quaker schools, I divided my list about equally between boys and girls; at the military schools, where boys outnumbered girls, I interviewed a disproportionately high number of girls, because I wanted to be sure that their perspective was represented. I also interviewed foreign students and members of minority groups at all six schools and made sure some students from Quaker families were included at the Quaker schools and students from professional military families, at the academies. Although I emphasized boarders, I also spoke with day students at each school, and at least one boy and one girl freshman and several sophomores. I made a point of noticing loners and eccentrics among the students and met with several at each place, and I tried to interview at least one member of each of the most obvious cliques. At military schools I divided my interviews among the different units (Band, Troop A, Company B, and so forth). In addition, as I had done with the adults, I asked students and teachers to identify students they especially respected, and I met with those who were mentioned frequently.

Conducting the Interviews

Although I used the questions in Appendix C to stimulate discussion, the interviews were flexible. Occasionally, with people who were not very forthcoming, I asked every single question on the list. In other cases, five or six questions generated two hours of interesting discussion. I opened the interview by explaining the topic of my research, encouraging the person to ask any questions he or she had, and discussing the issue of confidentiality. Although most people agreed to let me tape the interviews, a few did not; whether I taped or not, I always took notes. Adults were usually interviewed in their office or classroom. At four schools I was assigned a little-used room to serve as a place for interviewing students; at the other two schools I used the guest-house. I considered privacy an important factor in the interviews. On four occasions, however, students asked if they could be interviewed in groups of two or more, and this proved useful in a different way, since the teenagers compared stories and commented on one another's statements, giving me different insights on the same information. I also talked with many groups of students informally, as part of hanging out.

Interviews lasted from thirty minutes to two hours or more; the average length was about forty-five minutes. Students often set up appointments during a free class period, which was forty to fifty minutes long. In cases where our time together seemed too short, I scheduled a second appointment. Many teachers also talked to me during free periods, but we tried to set up interviews that ran into lunch or study hall to give us more time.

The Fieldwork Experience

My visits to the schools were short, and during those weeks I was attempting to familiarize myself with the community; observe classes, meetings, and activities; hang out; interview between sixty and seventy-five people; and still find time to write up my observations and read through each day's notes. In her study of six high schools, Lightfoot describes returning from all-day and all-evening sessions and sitting down to review her notes and write up an interpretive summary of the day. Coming in between ten and midnight most nights and knowing that I had a breakfast meeting at seven o'clock the next morning, I could not always keep my eyes open long enough to reread all my scribbled notes on the day's interviews and flesh out my field notes. Lightfoot also finished analyzing each school and wrote an essay on it before she went on to the next one. This was a luxury I could not afford, since I needed to complete all six field visits during the 1987–88 school year. By the time I got to the sixth school in May I was battling exhaustion.

I mention this growing fatigue in order to counteract the intimidating portrait sometimes painted in sociological field studies of the tireless participant-observer. For me, fieldwork at the schools meant being "on" with strangers for as much as sixteen hours a day, day after day; continuously attempting to be an alert listener and observer; and, then, after only a short break, repeating the whole process in a new environment with a new set of people. On the one hand, it was exhilarating. I was learning constantly, I was stimulated every day to think and rethink about the Quaker and military values that fascinated me, and each person I met was a new source of stories, ideas, and often warm interest in my work. On the other hand, there were times when I was fed up, depressed, and lonely. It is an irony of fieldwork that one can be tired of being with people and yet be lonely, because almost all human contact is so constrained by the demands of the research. At five of the six schools I managed to find at least one adult with whom I allowed myself to step out of the researcher role and have "normal" conversations about everyday things. These little interludes of simple companionship made an enormous difference in my ability to keep up my spirits.

Although most adults and adolescents at the six schools were kind to me, I also encountered some distrust and hostility. At Sherman in particular many of the adults seemed unsure of my purpose (in spite of my repeated explanations) and uncomfortable in my presence. Several faculty members set up interviews over and over, only to cancel them; others, when asked for an interview, would breezily say, "Any time," and then refuse to be pinned down to an appointment. Only at Sherman did I have the sense that I was being watched and even avoided by some teachers and that my presence in a room had a pronounced effect on the conversation. By the end of the second week the atmosphere had improved, and a tactical officer confided that a rumor had circulated that I was a spy, sent either by the board of directors or by a wealthy alumnus considering making a donation to the school. To my relief I never sensed a similar fear from the Sherman cadets, who were eager to meet with me.

Jackson was the only school where I had a bad experience with students. Toward the end of my stay, a teacher told me she had overheard a boy advise his classmates not to talk to me, because I was a narcotics agent. I asked several cadets—including two who'd discussed their drug use with me— about this rumor, and they dismissed it as a joke and told me not to worry. Nor did I sense any hostility from the last few teenagers I interviewed. Nevertheless, the rumors at Sherman and Jackson bothered me, and I tried to understand what lay behind them. One thing I noticed was that the whispers seemed to be among people who had not spoken with me at any length and were forced to invent explanations for my presence that made more sense to them than my own claim to be a sociologist doing research on morality. It is even possible that these people I did not interview felt slighted. However, I believe the chief cause of these rumors was the teachers' and students' sense of vulnerability, which was greatest at the two schools where teachers had the least say in self-government and students had the most antagonistic relationships with adults. There was good reason for them to feel vulnerable, since at small private schools teachers really can be, and are, fired between one semester and the next (and those who live on campus are evicted from their homes in the process); students really can be, and are, expelled overnight for drug use. In their insecure world, it was not so improbable that a spy could be planted by the school board to report on teachers' indiscretions or by the police to report on students' use of drugs. As Eckert said about her fieldwork at Belten High, "Drugs are the one thing that many adolescents have to feel paranoid about, and the danger of being suspected of being a narc is real and great." [2] My experience at Jackson proves her point; I was lucky that the rumor was not taken more seriously.

The Interactive Observer Among Adolescents

Throughout the year, I was faced with the delicate task of interacting in a friendly way with adolescents without stepping out of my place as an adult. I was not a twenty-two-year-old right out of college (as some of their teachers were), whom they could view as a slightly older peer; instead, I was closer in age to some of their parents. I am familiar with adolescents' contempt for adults who curry favor with them, pretend to share their interests, offer them embarrassing confidences, and pry into their personal lives on the pretext of advising them. But at the same time, teenagers dislike being talked down to, lectured at, or treated as children. In general, I tried to be as matter-of-fact and informal as possible—but not intimate. I never acted disapproving of anything I was told, but I also tried not to seem to condone behavior that was clearly against school rules, such as smoking, drinking, sneaking out with one's boy- or girlfriend, or manhandling plebes. I encouraged teenagers to talk about personal matters, but I was careful not to probe too much, particularly about sexual relationships, because I did not want them to feel that their privacy was being invaded. I found that almost all the students, once they got over some initial shyness, were interested in the questions I was asking and delighted to have a chance to talk about themselves and their friends and give their opinions about life at school. Some of the cadets, especially at Sherman, seemed almost desperate to tell me things, perhaps because their relationships with teachers and tacs were so distant.[3]

I decided early in the research not to hang out with students in the woods and fields around the schools where many of them smoked cigarettes, drank alcohol, met the opposite sex, and dealt and used marijuana, LSD, and occasionally heavier drugs. It did not seem right to share in activities, even if only as an observer, which I knew were so heartily condemned by the faculty, especially when I was trying to build a relationship with teachers and administrators. I was touched when, at Fox, two girls and a boy invited me (with the seriousness of those conferring a great honor) to join them at their hideout about half a mile from school, where they met to smoke cigarettes; I accepted the invitation and spent half an hour crouched in some bushes, talking. Apart from this incident, I found that students did not expect me to engage in their unofficial activities, although they welcomed me as an observer at such school-sanctioned social events as dances, picnics, and games.

In *With the Boys*, Fine has included an interesting essay on participant observation with children.[4] His situation was different from mine: he worked with small groups of boys between the ages of ten and twelve for months at a time. He too had some problems with his role among young people and was at one point suspected of being, not a narcotics agent, but a drug dealer. Fine describes his role as that of friend and even "honorary kid." I, however, never had any intention of becoming an "honorary teenager." Whereas Fine's primary focus was preadolescent culture, mine was the school culture as a whole, and it would have hurt my relationship with the faculty had I been perceived as allied with the students. The best I could hope for was trust from both age groups, and this I believe I had in most cases.

Analyzing the Data

Throughout the research year and during the summer that followed, I snatched time whenever I could to read through field and interview notes from the six schools and note important themes, similarities, and differences. In the fall of 1988, sitting down in earnest to the process of data analysis, I made a decision to focus on Mott Friends School and Pershing Military

Academy and to check conclusions drawn from my findings at these two schools against observations and interview data from Sherman, Jackson, Fox, and Dyer. Mott and Pershing were the largest, most stable, and most respected schools in their categories, with the best academic programs. In that sense, they were similar. If I found strong contrasts between these two schools, I could feel confident that they were attributable to the two moral traditions and not to a vast difference in the quality of teaching or leadership. Only after I had transcribed the Mott and Pershing data and used it as the basis for a detailed outline of this book did I reread all the notes from the other four schools, noting similarities to and differences from the two key schools and marking passages to be transcribed. This is the reason that there are more references to Mott and Pershing in the book than to Fox, Dyer, Jackson, and Sherman.

The Difficulty of Honoring Both Subjects and Subject Matter

When people consent to participate in a sociological study, they make themselves vulnerable. They give the researcher personal information about themselves and their colleagues; they use the opportunity of an interview to voice their gripes and worries; they say things for a written record that, later, they may regret. Although they are fully aware that anything they say may appear in print, their pleasure at having a chance to talk about what is important to them may overcome their caution. Knowing that this is the case, I feel protective toward my interview partners at the six schools. They did me a great service in allowing me to be part of their lives for several weeks and in speaking with me so frankly. As I reread what I have written about them and the communities in which they live, I fear I have repaid these people who were so kind to me with descriptions and conclusions that may sometimes wound them. Yet, to present the schools other than as I have done would be dishonest, not only to my own observations but to the confidences with which faculty and students entrusted me. I hope that the respect and affection I have for so many of the people I interviewed shines through what I have written.

Appendix B

Questions Used in Interviews with Quakers and Military Officers

Part I

1. I would like you to think of the best Quaker/military officer you know: the person who best lives up to the most important Quaker/military values. It can be someone whom you know personally or know of—or even a historical figure. Please tell me about this person.

2. Now I would like you to think of the worst Quaker/military officer you know: someone who utterly fails to live up to Quaker/military values, or who you think has betrayed those values. I'd like you to tell me about this person, too.

3. I want to ask you about your view of human nature. If you had to describe human beings in general, what would you say most people are like?

4. If you had the power to assign everyone on earth five moral qualities—five virtues, you could say—when they were born, what would these be? Can you give them to me in order of priority?

5. I'd like you to tell me about a time in your life when you felt your beliefs or values were greatly tested. This could be a time when you had to make a very difficult decision and couldn't decide what to do. Or it could be a time when you felt in conflict with yourself about what was right and what was wrong. Could you describe this crisis to me? What values were in conflict?

6. I'd like you to tell me about a good deed you have done.

7. Now I'd like you to tell me about something you have done that you think is a bad deed.

8. What qualities about yourself are you proud of? I'd like you to think of ethical qualities and others, as well.

9. What are the traits you have that you are not proud of, that you would most like to change?

10. Do you feel that in your life right now you have certain major obligations to live up to, both in your work life and your personal life? If yes, what are they? Can you prioritize them?

11. Now I'd like you to list what you think are your most important identities. By that I mean the roles you fill in life—in your work, at home, in your community, as a man/woman—that best fit your image of yourself and are most meaningful to you. Can you put them in a priority order?

12. Have you ever been told to do something by a boss or superior that you thought was wrong? Describe the situation to me.

Part II

1. I'd like you to tell me what you think of the following statements by famous people. Do they make sense to you? Do you agree with them? Disagree? Why?

a. Be sure you are right, then go ahead.

b. Religion is built on humility, honor on pride.

c. The right is more precious than peace.

d. There is no duty we so much underrate as the duty of being happy.

e. Let us have faith that right makes might; and in that faith let us to the end dare to do our duty as we understand it.

f. All service ranks the same with God.

2. What would you do in the following situations? Please try to tell me what you honestly think you would do, even if the answer is that you think you'd do nothing.

a. You are in a dime-store and you see a girl of about twelve or thirteen pick up an item from the counter and put it in her pocket.

b. You realize that a colleague of yours at work, not a best friend but someone you like, has a drinking problem that you are afraid is going to get him in trouble with his boss. Certainly it is affecting his job. As far as you can tell, you are the only person who is aware of the problem.

Appendix C

Questions Used in Interviews with Faculty and Students at the Six Schools

1. Tell me how you came to be here. (Find out Quaker or military associations.)

2. What is distinctive about the school?

3. What are some of the good things about being here?

4. What are some of the bad things about being here?

5. Who are some people who seem to best represent the school? whom you particularly respect? Why?

6. What lessons would you like people to leave here with? Are there any negative lessons you think the school teaches? (For students: What lessons do you think the school teaches? Official lessons? Unofficial lessons?)

7. Tell me about the role of the Quaker religion/military system here. What are some of the things that make this a Quaker/military school?

8. Tell me a moral dilemma you've faced while you've been here. (If probe is needed: Tell me about a crisis you've had to deal with.)

9. How have you changed while you've been here?

10. How do you feel you fit in here? Are there ways in which you don't fit?

11. Do you see any gaps between what the school preaches and what it practices?

12. What would you change about the school, if you ran it?

13. What are some of the hot topics that get discussed? Things people complain about?

14. What groups do the adults fall into?

15. Are there tensions between different groups of adults: academic, (military), athletic, counseling, etc.? Between administrators and teachers?

16. What are some generalizations you think you could make about the teachers? the students?

17. What are some key traits students should have to be happy here?

18. What groups do students fall into?

19. How do boarders and day students get along?

20. How do people around here communicate? How are decisions made?

21. Talk to me about some of the rules and methods of discipline.

22. What does the school do about sexual relationships, birth control?

23. At some schools, students have their own special set of rules, like a code against narcing. Is that true here?

24. What has changed here over the years? What has not changed?

25. Can you tell me some important school traditions?

For Students Only

26. What was your first year like?

27. (If appropriate) What are your responsibilities as an officer/prefect?

28. Is it important to be in a couple here? Tell me about the school's attitude toward couples.

Questions Asked Only at Fox, Dyer, Pershing, and Jackson

29. Are there certain words that are used at the school a lot, words that come up again and again in conversation?

30. Who is the most powerful person at the school? Why?

31. Can you think of an important decision affecting the school as a whole and tell me how it was made?

32. What happens when students get picked on or get into fights?

Additional Questions for Headmasters and Academic Deans

33. How have you changed the school while you've been here?

34. Are there certain types of problems that come up over and over again?

35. What experiences do you think are the best direct sources of values at the school?

36. Are there any ways in which you think the school fails?

Notes

Introduction

1. See Ann Swidler, *Organization Without Authority: Dilemmas of Social Control in Free Schools* (Cambridge: Harvard University Press, 1979), 6.

2. Some books and essays about this process of socialization include: Basil Bernstein, "Social Class and Pedagogic Practice," in *The Structuring of Pedagogic Discourse* (London: Routledge, 1990), 63–93; Pierre Bourdieu and Jean-Claude Passeron, *Reproduction in Education, Society, and Culture* (Beverly Hills: Sage Publications, 1977); Samuel Bowles and Herbert Gintis, *Schooling in Capitalist America: Educational Reform and the Contradictions of Economic Life* (New York: Basic Books, 1976); Douglas E. Foley, *Learning Capitalist Culture: Deep in the Heart of Tejas* (Philadelphia: University of Pennsylvania Press, 1990); Shirley Brice Heath, *Ways with Words: Language, Life, and Work in Communities and Classrooms* (Cambridge: Cambridge University Press, 1983); Paul Willis, *Learning to Labor: How Working Class Kids Get Working Class Jobs* (New York: Columbia University Press, 1977).

3. Alan Peshkin, for example, in his study of Riverview High School, a large, ethnically mixed public school in a relatively poor California town, finds that teachers and pupils agree that the school's general purpose is to teach students to be "ordinary Americans." Yet none of the teachers experiences this goal as a "shared mission." Unlike teachers at the small fundamentalist-Christian school Peshkin had studied earlier, who are sustained by a sense of mission that is strongly encouraged by the school's principal, Riverview teachers "are not compelled to articulate the general ends for which their instruction is the means. . . . They readily acknowledge that those purposes they do express are personal: they made them up themselves" (Alan Peshkin, *The Color of Strangers, the Color of Friends: The Play of Ethnicity in School and Community* [Chicago: University of Chicago Press, 1991], 166, 115, 113).

4. Gerald Grant, "The Character of Education and the Education of Character," *Daedalus* 110 (Summer 1981): 146.

5. Immanuel Kant is the most important representative of the universal view of morality; Aristotle, of the particular view. Lawrence Kohlberg and John Rawls are universalists; Alasdair MacIntyre and Bernard Williams, particularists. For a short analysis of the two viewpoints, written by a particularist, see Evan Simpson, *Good Lives and Moral Education*, Studies in Moral Philosophy 4 (New York: Peter Lang, 1989), 1–37.

6. Alan Wolfe, *Whose Keeper? Social Science and Moral Obligation* (Berkeley: University of California Press, 1989), 225.

7. John P. Hewitt, *Dilemmas of the American Self* (Philadelphia: Temple University Press, 1989), 237.

8. For a fascinating description of the mission of a fundamentalist school, see Alan Peshkin, *God's Choice: The Total World of a Fundamentalist Christian School* (Chicago: University of Chicago Press, 1986).

9. Robert N. Bellah, Richard Madsen, William M. Sullivan, Ann Swidler, and Steven M. Tipton, *Habits of the Heart: Individualism and Commitment in American Life* (Berkeley: University of California Press, 1985), 154.

10. Alasdair MacIntyre, *After Virtue: A Study in Moral Theory*, 2d edition (Notre Dame, Ind.: University of Notre Dame Press, 1984), 222.

11. For summaries of early Quaker history and religious practice, see Margaret Hope Bacon, *The Quiet Rebels: The Story of the Quakers in America* (Philadelphia: New Society Publishers, 1985), 9–24, and William Wistar Comfort, *Just Among Friends: The Quaker Way of Life* (Philadelphia: American Friends Service Committee, 1968), 1–23.

12. There are still a few American Friends who use "plain speech," or "thee" rather than "you," in everyday conversation.

13. Bellah et al., *Habits of the Heart*, 32–35.

14. Ralph H. Turner, "The Real Self: From Institution to Impulse," *American Journal of Sociology* 81 (March 1976): 991–95.

15. Joseph Anthony Amato II, *Guilt and Gratitude: A Study of the Origins of Contemporary Conscience*, Contributions in Philosophy 20 (Westport, Conn.: Greenwood Press, 1982), xvi.

16. James Davison Hunter, *Culture Wars: The Struggle to Define America* (New York: Basic Books, 1991).

17. Carol Gilligan, *In a Different Voice: Psychological Theory and Women's Development* (Cambridge: Harvard University Press, 1982); Deborah Tannen, *You Just Don't Understand: Men and Women in Conversation* (New York: Ballantine Books, 1990).

18. Quakerism has been called a feminine religion because its adherents "perceive truth and social harmony as extensions of concrete, personal experience" and "project the personal, affective relationships of everyday existence into the public sphere" (Phyllis Mack, "Feminine Symbolism and

Feminine Behavior in Radical Religious Movements: Franciscans, Quakers, and the Followers of Gandhi," in *Disciplines of Faith: Studies in Religion, Politics, and Patriarchy,* ed. Jim Obelkevich, Lyndal Roper, and Raphael Samuel [London: Routledge and Kegan Paul, 1987], 123). In addition, Friends have always preached (and, up to a point, practiced) the equality of men and women. The macho elements of the military code, perhaps above all its concern with personal and national honor and its use of violence when honor is affronted, are the products of traditional definitions of manliness. For more on this relationship among honor, violence, and manhood see J. G. Peristiany, ed., *Honor and Shame: The Values of Mediterranean Society* (London: Weidenfeld and Nicolson, 1966), and Bertram Wyatt-Brown, *Southern Honor: Ethics and Behavior in the Old South* (Oxford: Oxford University Press, 1982).

19. In their discussion of the dangers of both laissez-faire liberalism and authoritarianism, Michael A. Wallach and Lise Wallach (*Rethinking Goodness* [Albany: State University of New York Press, 1990]) use the phrase "ethical minimalism" to identify the tendency to "link . . . tolerance and respect for differences with asking little ethically of others (and of ourselves)" (p. vii). I hesitate to call even the most secular and liberal of Quakers "ethical minimalists," since, even when they ask little ethically of others, they still tend to demand much of themselves. Nevertheless, the Wallachs' liberals and my Quakers have traits in common.

20. MacIntyre, *After Virtue,* 222–23.

21. Hewitt, *Dilemmas of the American Self,* 71.

22. MacIntyre, *After Virtue,* 222.

23. See Mary Haywood Metz, *Classrooms and Corridors: The Crisis of Authority in Desegregated Schools* (Berkeley: University of California Press, 1978), for a study of "the twin tasks of pursuing education and maintaining . . . order" in conventional schools (p. ix). Swidler's *Organization Without Authority* shows how free schools handle the same problem.

24. Wolfe, *Whose Keeper?* 216.

1. School Life Through the Lens of Moral Tradition

1. For a description of the traditional college-preparatory boarding-school environment, see Peter W. Cookson, Jr. and Caroline Hodges Persell, *Preparing for Power: America's Elite Boarding Schools* (New York: Basic Books, 1985), esp. 27–30, 45–48.

2. The schools cost between $8,000 and $13,000 per year in 1987; by 1993 the highest fee was $18,600.

3. Cookson and Persell, *Preparing for Power*, 27.

4. Sara Lawrence Lightfoot, *The Good High School: Portraits of Character and Culture* (New York: Basic Books, 1983), 225.

5. Erving Goffman, *Asylums: Essays on the Social Situation of Mental Patients and Other Inmates* (reprint New York: Anchor Books, Doubleday, 1961).

6. Ibid., 116–18.

7. Metz, *Classrooms and Corridors*, 26–29.

8. The Inner Light "is the central concept of Quakerism. Friends may differ on almost any other issue, but they are united in their belief in the presence of an inward source of inspiration and strength . . . [or] that of God within" (Warren Sylvester Smith, *One Explorer's Glossary of Quaker Terms* [Philadelphia: Friends General Conference, 1985], 26).

9. These names for different student groups are not unique to Quaker schools. "Punkers" favor heavy-metal music and adolescent nihilism. "Deadheads," whose name is derived from a rock group formed in the 1960s, the Grateful Dead, adopt a hippie style of dress and speech and may use hallucinogenic drugs. The epithet "mall rats" refers to giggly freshman and sophomore girls (and some boys) who like to spend their leisure time together at shopping malls.

10. In order to facilitate comparisons, I call the heads of all six schools *headmaster*, whether they supervise a staff of thirty or three hundred, and the person directly under the headmaster, *academic dean*.

11. Smith, *One Explorer's Glossary*, 8.

12. Each of these three quotes is from a different admissions handbook: respectively, Fox, Dyer, Mott.

2. The Quaker and Military Moral Traditions Compared

1. Military professionals are men and women who make a career of the army, navy, marine corps, or coast guard. In the army, they are either noncommissioned officers (NCOs), warrant officers, or commissioned officers. A sergeant major, for example, is an NCO, while a major is a commissioned officer. Similar distinctions exist in the other branches of the service.

2. Sydney V. James, *A People Among Peoples: Quaker Benevolence in Eighteenth-Century America* (Cambridge: Harvard University Press, 1963), 263–85.

3. Samuel P. Huntington, *The Soldier and the State: The Theory and Politics of Civil-Military Relations* (Cambridge: The Belknap Press of Harvard University Press, 1957), 14–15, 156–57.

4. Friends were exhorted by George Fox to "be patterns, be examples in all countries . . . that your carriage and life may preach among all sorts of people, and to them" (quoted in Howard H. Brinton, *Friends for 300 Years: The History and Beliefs of the Society of Friends Since George Fox Started the Quaker Movement* [Wallingford, Penn.: Pendle Hill Publications, 1952], 29). Morris Janowitz found that "professional officers think of themselves as bearers of the positive values of American society and as subject to higher standards of behavior than civilians" (*The Professional Soldier: A Social and Political Portrait*, 2d edition [New York: Free Press, 1971], xxxix).

5. Because the purpose of this chapter is to present Quaker and military values in their ideal forms, I have drawn almost exclusively on the writings of Friends and those with experience in the military (primarily the army). Seeking more personal information about the impact of the two traditions on members today, I also interviewed fifteen Quakers, two Vietnam veterans with Quaker sympathies, and nine army officers.

6. Ralph H. Turner, "The Role and the Person," *American Journal of Sociology* 84 (July 1978): 1.

7. Roger C. Wilson, *Authority, Leadership, and Concern: A Study in Motive and Administration in Quaker Relief Work* (London: Friends Home Service Committee, [1949] 1970), 9–10.

8. On the army as a religious order, see Huntington, *Soldier and the State*, 465; Richard A. Gabriel, *To Serve with Honor: A Treatise on Military Ethics and the Way of the Soldier* (Westport, Conn.: Greenwood Press, 1982), 147. On hazing, see Edward Tabor Linenthal, *Changing Images of the Warrior Hero in America: A History of Popular Symbolism*, Studies in American Religion 6 (New York: Edwin Mellen Press, 1982), xiii–xv. And on the battlefield as a sacred world, see J. Glenn Gray, *The Warriors: Reflections on Men in Battle*, 2d edition (New York: Harper and Row, 1970), 47.

9. Brinton, *Friends for 300 Years*, 35.

10. The first sentence of the army's basic field manual emphasizes that the army's primary function is to deter war and to fight only when deterrence fails (U.S. Department of the Army, Headquarters [Army], *The Army*, Field Manual 100-1 [Washington, D.C.: Government Printing Office, 1991], i, 3). This perception is shared by most professional soldiers. "The military man . . . wants to prepare for war. But he is never ready to fight a war. . . . It is the people and the politicians . . . who start wars" (Huntington, *Soldier and the State*, 69–70).

11. Thomas S. Brown, *When Friends Attend to Business* (Philadelphia: Philadelphia Yearly Meeting of the Religious Society of Friends [PYM], 1986), n.p.

12. Anthony E. Hartle, *Moral Issues in Military Decision Making* (Lawrence: University Press of Kansas, 1989), 37.

13. Bacon, *Quiet Rebels*, 123.

14. Brinton, *Friends for 300 Years*, 131.

15. Thomas R. Kelly, *Eyes on the Border* (Philadelphia: American Friends Service Committee, 1985), 8.

16. Quoted in PYM, *Faith and Practice: A Book of Christian Discipline* (Philadelphia: PYM, 1972), 16.

17. Michael J. Sheeran, *Beyond Majority Rule: Voteless Decisions in the Religious Society of Friends* (Philadelphia: PYM, 1983), 6.

18. Thomas R. Kelly, *The Gathered Meeting* (Philadelphia: The Tract Association of Friends, n.d.), n.p.

19. James, *People Among Peoples*, 316–34.

20. For example, see PYM, *Faith and Practice*, 192.

21. Comfort, *Just Among Friends*, 54.

22. These descriptions of simplicity come from PYM, *Faith and Practice*, 19; Gray Cox, *Bearing Witness: Quaker Process and a Culture of Peace*, Pamphlet 262 (Wallingford, Penn.: Pendle Hill Publications, 1985), 12–13; and Frances Irene Taber, "Finding the Taproot of Simplicity: The Movement Between Inner Knowledge and Outer Action," in *Friends Face the World: Continuing and Current Quaker Concerns*, ed. Leonard S. Kenworthy (Philadelphia: Friends General Conference, 1987), 63.

23. Thomas Kelly, *A Testament of Devotion*, quoted in Taber, "Finding the Taproot," 70.

24. Quoted in Bacon, *Quiet Rebels*, 18–19.

25. Quoted in Bacon, *Quiet Rebels*, xi.

26. Cox, *Bearing Witness*, 17–21.

27. On soldiers' reasons for fighting, see S. L. A. Marshall, *Men Against Fire: The Problem of Battle Command in Future War* (New York: William Morrow, 1947). The quotation is from Studs Terkel, *"The Good War": An Oral History of World War Two* (New York: Ballantine Books, 1984), 57.

28. Gray, *Warriors*, 44.

29. Terkel, *"Good War,"* 159.

30. Richard A. Gabriel, "Modernism versus Pre-modernism: The Need to Rethink the Basis of Military Organizational Forms," in *Military Ethics and Professionalism: A Collection of Essays*, ed. James Brown and Michael J. Collins (Washington, D.C.: National Defense University Press, 1981), 71.

31. Martin E. Dempsey, "Repose: A Forgotten Factor in Leadership Development," *Military Review* 68 (November 1988): 30.

32. The oath goes as follows: "I will not lie, cheat, or steal, nor tolerate those who do." West Point cadets who are caught violating this honor code

are tried by a court of their peers and, if found guilty, are usually expelled from the academy. Most military colleges and high schools in the United States share this code.

33. D. M. Malone, "The Trailwatcher," in U.S. Military Academy, Department of Military Instruction, *Professional Notebook 1986* (West Point: U.S. Military Academy, 1986), T-13.

34. Lewis S. Sorley, "Competence as Ethical Imperative: Issues of Professionalism," in *Military Ethics and Professionalism*, ed. Brown and Collins, 39, 52.

35. John P. Lovell, *Neither Athens nor Sparta? The American Service Academies in Transition* (Bloomington: Indiana University Press, 1979), 246.

36. Army, *The Army*, 16.

37. Terkel, *"Good War,"* 304.

38. Gray, *Warriors*, 125.

39. Quoted in Linenthal, *Changing Images*, 37, 234.

40. Army, *Values: A Handbook for Soldiers*, Pamphlet 600-71 (Washington, D.C.: Government Printing Office, 1987). This pamphlet, which is based on the fourth chapter of the army's basic Field Manual 100-1, was distributed to all soldiers in honor of the army's "year of values," 1987.

41. Gray, *Warriors*, 45.

42. Army, *Values*, 1-3.

43. Quoted in Lovell, *Neither Athens nor Sparta?* 248.

44. Army, *The Bedrock of Our Profession*, Pamphlet 600–68, White Paper (Washington, D.C.: Government Printing Office, 1986), 9–10.

45. Cited in Francis B. Galligan, *Military Professionalism and Ethics* (Newport, R.I.: Naval War College Center for Advanced Research, 1979), 89–91.

46. Linenthal, *Changing Images*, 35.

47. Lawrence B. Radine, *The Taming of the Troops: Social Control in the United States Army*, Contributions in Sociology 22 (Westport, Conn.: Greenwood Press, 1977), 55.

48. Janowitz, *Professional Soldier*, 129.

49. Hugh A. Kelley, "A Proposal for the United States Army Ethic," microfiche of a U.S. Army War College study project, Carlisle Barracks, Penn., 1984, 21.

50. Lovell, *Neither Athens nor Sparta?* 264.

51. Pat Conroy, *The Lords of Discipline* (New York: Bantam Books, 1980), 129.

52. Terkel, *"Good War,"* 172.

53. For a extended discussion of this military dilemma, see Hartle, *Moral Issues*.

54. Richard Bauman, *Let Your Words Be Few: Symbolism of Speaking and Silence Among Seventeenth-Century Quakers*, Cambridge Studies in Oral and Literate Culture 8 (Cambridge: Cambridge University Press, 1983), 120–36.

55. Quoted in Leonard S. Kenworthy, *Quaker Quotations on Faith and Practice* (Philadelphia: Friends General Conference, 1983), 57.

56. From a 1888 speech by Haverford President Isaac Sharpless, quoted in Douglas H. Heath, *The Peculiar Mission of a Quaker School*, Pamphlet 225 (Wallingford, Penn.: Pendle Hill Publications, 1979), 29.

57. Jack Kirk, "Creaturely Activities or Spiritually Based Concerns?" in *Friends Face the World*, ed. Kenworthy, 14.

58. Wilson, *Authority, Leadership, and Concern*, 63.

59. Cox, *Bearing Witness*, 15.

60. Quoted in Howard H. Brinton, *Quaker Journals: Varieties of Religious Experience Among Friends* (Wallingford, Penn: Pendle Hill Publications, 1972), 86.

61. Sheeran, *Beyond Majority Rule*, 89.

62. Ibid., 81, 87.

63. George A. Selleck, quoted in Leonard S. Kenworthy, *Quakerism: A Study Guide on the Religious Society of Friends* (Kennett Square, Penn.: Quaker Publications, 1981), 82.

64. Heath, *Peculiar Mission*, 9.

65. Harold D. Yow, "The Ethical Bases for Leadership," *Military Review* 40 (September 1960): 51.

66. The major is referring to the events that led to the My Lai massacre in Vietnam, which was carried out under the direct orders of Lieutenant William L. Calley.

67. See Sorley, "Competence," 41–46; Thomas E. Kelly III, "Ethics in the Military Profession: The Continuing Tension," in *Military Ethics and Professionalism*, ed. Brown and Collins, 27–33; Galligan, *Military Professionalism*, 50–56.

68. Sorley, "Competence," 43.

69. Anna M. Young, "Points of Honor," microfiche of a U.S. Army War College study project, Carlisle Barracks, Penn., 1986, 3.

70. Maxwell Taylor, "A Professional Ethic for the Military?" reprinted in *Ethics and the Military Profession* (August 1978): 8.

71. Quoted in Galligan, *Military Professionalism*, 50.

72. Sorley, "Competence," 42.

73. Marshall, *Men Against Fire*, 41–42.

74. Robert E. Potts, "Professional Military Ethics: Are We on the Right Track?" microfiche of a U.S. Army War College study project, Carlisle Barracks, Penn., 1986, 35.

75. Charles W. Ricks, "The Non-Toleration Clause: A Chance for Misperception," *Ethics and the Military Profession* (April 1982): 3–4.

76. Hewitt, *Dilemmas of the American Self*, viii.

77. Ibid., 85–86.

78. Stanley Hauerwas, *A Community of Character: Toward a Constructive Christian Social Ethic* (Notre Dame, Ind.: University of Notre Dame Press, 1981), 115.

3. Virtue as a Source of Order

1. This kind of easy give-and-take also existed between adolescents and adults at alternative high schools in the 1970s. See Swidler, *Organization Without Authority*, 23–24, and Robert B. Everhart, *Practical Ideology and Symbolic Community: An Ethnography of Schools of Choice* (New York: Falmer Press, 1988), 85–87.

2. An emphasis on equality does not prevent Mott from assigning students with different academic abilities to different scholastic tracks.

3. Smith, *One Explorer's Glossary*, 51.

4. Rolf E. Muuss, *Theories of Adolescence*, 5th edition (New York: Random House, 1988), 91–92.

5. Quakers distinguish between "convinced Friends," or converts, and "birthright Friends," who are born into Quaker families.

6. It is important to take into account that when the speaker was mistreated by her former classmates she was in junior high school, whereas now she is a senior and has attended Mott for four years. Cliques, rigid categories, and intolerance toward peers who are different tend to be much more prominent in the middle-school years—grades six through eight or nine—than in high school (Muuss, *Theories of Adolescence*, 71; Penelope Eckert, *Jocks and Burnouts: Social Categories and Identity in the High School* [New York: Teachers College Press, 1989], 95–96; David A. Kinney, "From 'Dweeb' to 'Normal': Identity Change During Adolescence," paper presented at the annual meeting of the American Sociological Association, 1989), and Mott begins in the ninth grade. However, since even students who had come to Mott from another high school agreed that people were exceptionally nice to one another, Mott's reputation for kindness does seem to be more than just an artifact of students' ages.

7. Pershing, Jackson, and Sherman are permitted to nominate four candidates each to the service academies, but the academic standards at the academies are high and competition for entry is fierce. At Jackson, for example, out of the twenty-nine students graduating in 1987, one went on to

the United States Military Academy, one to the United States Naval Academy, one to The Citadel, and one to North Georgia Military College.

8. Hazing is not simply a military-school phenomenon; accounts of English and American boarding-school life are filled with descriptions of cruel pranks and beatings. For example, see Louis Auchincloss, *The Rector of Justin* (Boston: Hill and Company, 1964), 239–47; David Nobbs, *Second from Last in the Sack Race* (London: Methuen, 1983), 139–84; and Roald Dahl, *Boy: Tales of Childhood* (London: Penguin Books, 1984), 141–43, 154–59.

9. This is a reference to a 1985 movie about five teenagers from different high-school cliques who come to accept one another after a spending a day in Saturday detention together.

10. Bellah et al., *Habits of the Heart*, 333–34. Such language was also common in the alternative schools of the 1970s. In *Practical Ideology*, Everhart focuses on what he calls "the ethos of openness," which dominated beliefs and behavior in the alternative schools he studied and eventually became so firmly entrenched that it prevented critical analysis of the education teenagers received. Similarly, students at Midwest Seminary were socialized to use "the rhetoric of community" (Sherryl Kleinman, *Equals Before God: Seminarians as Humanistic Professionals* [Chicago: University of Chicago Press, 1984], 11–12, 63–84, 102).

11. Fox and Dyer also held regular meetings to discuss problem students, but those I observed were not as well organized or as goal-oriented.

12. The flexible boundaries between student groups described here present a contrast to the rigid distinctions between "Jocks" and "Burnouts" observed by Penelope Eckert (*Jocks and Burnouts*) in a Michigan public high school. One reason for this difference is size: Eckert's Belten High has four times more students than Mott. A more important reason is class: at Belten, the Jock/Burnout distinction echoes and reinforces the students' middle- and working-class backgrounds, while at Mott, students overwhelmingly belong to the same class. In addition to these structural factors, I believe the Quaker virtues of equality and community play an important role in Mott students' apparent rejection of rigid categories.

13. This stoicism is heightened by the military system, but it is prominent in other male subcultures as well. Foley considers it an important part of male socialization through high-school sports (*Learning Capitalist Culture*, 54–55), and Gary Alan Fine describes in detail how Little Leaguers learn to show toughness, control their emotions, and endure pain (*With the Boys: Little League Baseball and Preadolescent Culture* [Chicago: University of Chicago Press, 1987], 79–89). At all three military academies, these typically male values are also shared by many of the girls, even those who are not cadets.

14. On the difference between real self and role self and the emphasis on the former at Midwest Seminary, see Kleinman, *Equals Before God*, 24–48.

15. Rosabeth Moss Kanter, *Community and Commitment: Communes and Utopias in Sociological Perspective* (Cambridge: Harvard University Press, 1972), 74.

4. Conflict as a Source of Strength

1. A case could be made for classifying Fox as a utopian community until it began to admit non-Quaker children in the 1940s. This is one of the reasons that older members of the staff and Yearly Meeting are loath to treat Fox as a business that has to attract customers if it is to survive.

2. Kanter, *Community and Commitment*, 32–57.

3. Ibid., 71.

4. Ibid., 84.

5. Ibid., 174–75.

6. Education as crusade is a dominant theme at the Christian fundamentalist school described by Peshkin. Although its students are "lambs" and "babes in Christ" who must be sheltered from the world, they are also "warriors" whose duty it is to defy the world's temptations and "present . . . the path of salvation to the unsaved" (*God's Choice*, 54). A crusader spirit is also present, although to a lesser extent, among teachers and students at the two alternative high schools studied by Swidler (*Organization Without Authority*, 100).

7. Georg Simmel, *Conflict*, trans. Kurt H. Wolff (New York: Free Press, 1955), 18.

8. Hewitt, *Dilemmas of the American Self*, 195.

9. Ibid., 11, 71.

10. On April 14, 1986, U.S. warplanes bombed Tripoli and Benghazi, officially in retaliation for the Libyan bombing of a West Berlin discotheque.

11. Hewitt, *Dilemmas of the American Self*, 17–18.

12. Boys were treated for each of these injuries during my visit to Jackson. I did not hear of girl plebes being beaten up or hung out of windows; their superiors apparently punish by yelling, assigning push-ups and cleaning tasks, and giving demerits. Girls do get into fights, however. At Jackson, one girl attacked several dorm mates with a broomstick; at Sherman, I was told of girls cutting off hunks of another girl's hair and destroying one another's property.

13. Students at Quaker schools, like most adolescents, also tend not to tell on their peers. There are two factors, however, that keep the no-narcing code from causing as much conflict at Quaker schools as it does at military academies. First, more adults are willing to listen to students' confidences without

taking disciplinary action, so students can talk to teachers without being labeled narcs. Second, most Quaker-school adults don't expect kids to tell on their peers and only ask them to do so in cases of threatened suicide, severe drug or alcohol usage, and major thefts.

14. I quote what the headmaster told me he said in the assembly, which was held weeks before my stay at Pershing.

15. There may well be racial or ethnic prejudice at Mott and Pershing, but nothing that I observed or was told in an interview provided evidence of it. However, the fact that the Pershing student body is less than 5 percent African-American suggests that the school does not actively recruit black students. As for sexism at the Quaker schools, although incidents occur the problem is not integral to the moral tradition, as it is at the academies. In fact, the Quaker tradition is, in theory, one of equality between men and women, and Quaker history is filled with activist women.

16. Army, *The Army*, 17.

17. David D. Gilmore, *Manhood in the Making: Cultural Concepts of Masculinity* (New Haven: Yale University Press, 1990), 11.

18. Although a distorted sense of military pride exacerbates prejudice at Jackson and Sherman, it doesn't cause it. Bigotry at the two schools is simply a part of life. Words like *nigger, hebe, gook, spic,* and *camel jockey* are common, particularly at Sherman. There I heard a white girl say to a black classmate, in a hostile voice, "Hey, nigger, why don't you go wash some of that black off with soap?" and no one reacted; a black cadet told me of tactical officers using racial slurs. Yet at Sherman there were also black and white cadets who were best friends, and at Jackson, mixed-race cadet couples—a reminder of what a complicated phenomenon racism is. As Alan Peshkin discovered at Riverview High School, people's statements and behavior regarding racial and ethnic differences are often paradoxical, resisting "all-or-none type labels. . . .We lack a vocabulary that would allow easy summation, and it may be just as well that we do" (*Color of Strangers*, 234–35).

19. Peshkin found that both blacks and whites at Riverview made a distinction between blacks with middle-class values and "niggers," who were "thugs" with "no hopes, no dreams, no aspirations." He also found that the word "nigger," even when used by whites, Mexicans, or Asians, was largely "defanged" (*The Color of Strangers*, 47, 239–42). When whites at Jackson used the word, however, the hostility was palpable.

20. Kleinman, *Equals Before God*, 64.

21. Ibid., 106.

22. Ibid., 66.

23. Ibid., 120.

24. Ibid., 109.

25. Wolfe, *Whose Keeper?* 231–32.
26. MacIntyre, *After Virtue*, 222.

5. Making, Breaking, and Enforcing the Rules

1. Any seasoned Friend reading this description of Fox faculty meetings would immediately think, "Bad clerking," since a good clerk does not permit even a weighty Friend to make or block every decision. Fox faculty meetings had no clerk, and the headmaster who ran them was inexperienced. It is nonetheless true that the possibilities for manipulation in a Quaker Meeting for Business are myriad; see Sheeran, *Beyond Majority Rule*, 104–6, for examples.

2. Tensions between teachers and administrators at Fox and Dyer were exacerbated by the lame-duck status of their headmasters, both of whom were resigning at the end of the semester and therefore lacked the energy and authority to resolve heated discussions among staff members.

3. Joyce Rothschild-Whitt, "The Collectivist Organization: An Alternative to Rational-Bureaucratic Models," *American Sociological Review* 44 (August 1979): 519–21.

4. Ibid., 521.

5. Bauman, *Let Your Words Be Few*, 126–36.

6. Mike's statement is supported by surveys indicating that, in spite of their idealism, most adolescents "are simply too preoccupied with personal concerns" to be politically active (Roberta S. Sigel and Marilyn B. Hoskin, *The Political Involvement of Adolescents* [New Brunswick, N.J.: Rutgers University Press, 1981], 15).

7. One reason for this "apathy" could be adolescents' discouragement: adults' positive attitude toward student involvement and students' occasional success in influencing school policy do not mean that changes are usually made in response to their wishes. At Mott, for example, the senior girls presented a petition to be allowed to close their doors during evening study hall; the request was turned down.

8. Cadet officers at all three schools have the power to assign demerits without asking adult permission. But since demerits are communicated to tacs or counselors, and since punishments based on demerits are determined by the commandant's office, most cadets still perceive this form of discipline as a reinforcement of adult authority.

6. The Adolescent Moral Worldview

1. Cookson and Persell, *Preparing for Power*, 3.

2. Erik H. Erikson, "Youth: Fidelity and Diversity," in *Adolescence: Contemporary Studies*, ed. Alvin E. Winder and David L. Angus (New York: Van Nostrand Reinhold, 1968), 35.

3. Lyn Mikel Brown, "When Is a Moral Problem Not a Moral Problem? Morality, Identity, and Female Adolescence," in *Making Connections: The Relational Worlds of Adolescent Girls at Emma Willard School*, ed. Carol Gilligan, Nona P. Lyons, and Trudy J. Hanmer (Cambridge: Harvard University Press, 1990), 106–7.

4. Willis, *Learning to Labor*, 18–19.

5. Nancy Lesko, *Symbolizing Society: Stories, Rites, and Structure in a Catholic High School* (New York: Falmer Press, 1988), 40–43; Everhart, *Practical Ideology*, 141–42.

6. James Macpherson, *The Feral Classroom* (Melbourne: Routledge and Kegan Paul, 1983), 11.

7. Anna Freud, "Adolescence," *Psychoanalytic Study of the Child* 13 (1958): 260, 275.

8. Sharon Rich, "Daughters' Views of Their Relationships with Their Mothers," in *Making Connections*, ed. Gilligan et al., 260.

9. Eckert, *Jocks and Burnouts*, 149.

10. Foley, *Learning Capitalist Culture*, 76.

11. Lesko, *Symbolizing Society*, 88.

12. In schools as different as the tiny, fundamentalist Bethany Baptist Academy and the large, ethnically mixed Riverview public high school, Peshkin found that teenagers' main creed for themselves and advice to one another was "Don't act phony" (*God's Choice*, 151–53) and "Don't ever deny who you are" (*Color of Strangers*, 173).

13. Lesko, *Symbolizing Society*, 74.

14. James S. Coleman, *The Adolescent Society: The Social Life of the Teenager and Its Impact on Education* (New York: Free Press, 1961), 221.

15. Cookson and Persell, *Preparing for Power*, 20.

16. Lightfoot, *Good High School*, 265.

17. According to Planned Parenthood, approximately half of the young women and two-thirds of the young men in the United States have had intercourse by the time they are eighteen. It thus seems realistic to assume that many of the students at the six schools are sexually active.

18. The themes of justice and care and the importance of relationships to teenage girls are discussed throughout the book. See, for example, Nona P. Lyons, "Listening to Voices We Have Not Heard: Emma Willard Girls' Ideas About Self, Relationships, and Morality," in *Making Connections*, ed. Gilligan et al., 30–72.

19. Erik H. Erikson, *Identity: Youth and Crisis* (New York: W. W. Norton, 1968), 50.

20. Fine, *With the Boys*, 104.

21. Foley, *Learning Capitalist Culture*, 62, 98.

22. Ann Swidler, "Culture in Action: Symbols and Strategies," *American Sociological Review* 51 (April 1986): 273.

23. Wolfe, *Whose Keeper?* 214.

24. Kleinman, *Equals Before God*, 25–28.

25. Swidler, *Organization Without Authority*, 114–15.

26. Ibid., 97–98.

27. Foley, *Learning Capitalist Culture*, 32.

28. Gilmore, *Manhood in the Making*, 223.

29. Erikson, "Youth," 35, 44.

30. It should be cautioned that this explanation is too simplistic to apply to the more extreme forms of adolescent self-destruction, such as anorexia, drug addiction, and attempted suicide.

31. Jerome Kagan, "The Moral Function of the School," *Daedalus* 110 (Summer 1981): 151–52.

32. Howard H. Brinton, *Friends and Their Spiritual Message* (Philadelphia: Friends General Conference, 1985), 3, 7.

33. Gray, *Warriors*, 46–47.

34. This is a Durkheimian view of sacredness. See Emile Durkheim, *The Elementary Forms of the Religious Life* (New York: Free Press, [1915] 1965), 253–62, for a classic description of the sacred as "an eternal truth that outside us there exists something greater than us, with which we enter into communion" (257).

35. From Kenworthy, *Quaker Quotations*, 116.

36. Gabriel, *To Serve with Honor*, 167–68.

37. Swidler, *Organization Without Authority*, 86–87.

38. Lesko, *Symbolizing Society*, 114–17.

39. Victor Turner, *The Ritual Process: Structure and Anti-Structure* (Ithaca, N.Y.: Cornell University Press, 1969), 96–97.

40. Kanter, *Commitment and Community*, 67–74.

41. For example, see the description of the Living World Fellowship in Steven M. Tipton, *Getting Saved from the Sixties: Moral Meaning in Conversion and Cultural Change* (Berkeley: University of California Press, 1982), 31–94.

42. Peshkin, *God's Choice*, 210.

43. Erikson, "Youth," 49.

Conclusion

1. Even at fundamentalist Bethany Baptist Academy, where students are taught that "there is right conduct and wrong conduct, without qualification,"

faculty believe that "you are never made to do [God's] bidding; the choice remains yours" (Peshkin, *God's Choice*, 61, 45).

2. Emile Durkheim, *Moral Education: A Study in the Theory and Application of the Sociology of Education* (New York: Free Press, [1925] 1961), 86, 90, 59, 47, 83, 120.

3. On Durkheim's failure to recognize the interactive and conflictive nature of morality, see Jean Piaget, *The Moral Judgment of the Child* (New York: Free Press, 1965), 353–371; Lewis A. Coser, "Durkheim's Conservatism and Its Implications for Sociological Theory," in *Continuities in the Study of Social Conflict*, 153–80 (New York: Free Press, 1967); and Wolfe, *Whose Keeper?* 220.

4. Simmel, *Conflict*, 15.

5. Gray, *Warriors*, 51.

6. Grant, "Character of Education," 146.

7. Lightfoot, *Good High School*, 350.

8. Bethany Baptist Academy differs greatly from both the Quaker and the military schools, in part because BBA faculty are more concerned with claiming students for Christ than they are with preparing them for roles in mainstream society. Yet although BBA's adolescents are taught unquestioning obedience to the rules, students note the double standards and inconsistencies in teachers' behavior and claim the right to interpret Christian doctrine for themselves. The teenagers "ascrib[e] . . . to themselves the prerogative of defining the boundaries of the sacred." Thus, for example, although the school requires students to tell an adult when they see a fellow student misbehaving, model senior and devout Christian Mary Becker refuses to do so, arguing that "tattling is just as much of a sin as cheating," because "in the Bible it says that you aren't supposed to tell on your brothers" (Peshkin, *God's Choice*, 245, 196).

9. Hauerwas, *Community of Character*, 115.

10. Ibid., 144.

11. Ibid., 144–45.

12. Bernard Williams, *Ethics and the Limits of Philosophy* (Cambridge: Harvard University Press, 1985), 200.

Appendix A

1. At Mott and Sherman, the first two schools I studied, I interviewed almost twice as many teachers as students, partially because students didn't keep appointments. At the other four schools I had more practice in working with adolescents, and I made sure that I met with approximately the same number of teenagers as adults. In addition, as a result of reading through the

data collected at Mott and Sherman, I added several questions to my interview guide for use at the other four schools.

2. Eckert, *Jocks and Burnouts*, 35.

3. Eckert comments on being unprepared for "the number of adolescents who desperately need an adult to talk to" (ibid., 34).

4. Fine, *With the Boys*, 222–44.

Bibliography

Alexander, Jeffrey C. 1987. *Twenty Lectures: Sociological Theory Since World War II*. New York: Columbia University Press.

Amato, Joseph Anthony, II. 1982. *Guilt and Gratitude: A Study of the Origins of Contemporary Conscience*. Contributions in Philosophy 20. Westport, Conn.: Greenwood Press.

Anderson, Jeffrey W. 1986. "Military Heroism: An Occupational Definition." *Armed Forces and Society* 12 (Summer): 591–606.

———— 1987. "The Warrior Spirit." *Military Review* 67 (July): 73–81.

Arendt, Hannah. 1956. "What Is Authority?" and "What Is Freedom?" *Between Past and Future: Eight Exercises in Political Thought*, 91–171. New York: Viking.

Aristotle. 1976. *The Nicomachean Ethics*. Trans. J. A. K. Thomson. Revised edition. Harmondsworth, England: Penguin Books.

Auchincloss, Louis. 1964. *The Rector of Justin*. Boston: Hill and Company.

Bacon, Margaret Hope. 1985. *The Quiet Rebels: The Story of the Quakers in America*. Philadelphia: New Society Publishers.

Bauman, Richard. 1971. *For the Reputation of Truth: Politics, Religion, and Conflict Among the Pennsylvania Quakers, 1750–1800*. Baltimore: Johns Hopkins University Press.

———— 1974. "Speaking in the Light: The Role of the Quaker Minister." In *Explorations in the Ethnography of Speaking*, edited by Richard Bauman and Joel Sherzer, 144–60. Cambridge: Cambridge University Press.

———— 1983. *Let Your Words Be Few: Symbolism of Speaking and Silence Among Seventeenth-Century Quakers*. Cambridge Studies in Oral and Literate Culture 8. Cambridge: Cambridge University Press.

Bellah, Robert N. 1970. "Civil Religion in America." In *Beyond Belief: Essays on Religion in a Post-Traditional World*, 168–89. New York: Harper and Row.

Bellah, Robert N., Richard Madsen, William M. Sullivan, Ann Swidler, and Steven M. Tipton. 1985. *Habits of the Heart: Individualism and Commitment in American Life*. Berkeley: University of California Press.

———— 1991. *The Good Society*. New York: Alfred A. Knopf.

Benson, Peter L., Michael J. Donahue, and Joseph A. Erikson. 1989. "Adolescence and Religion: A Review of the Literature from 1970 to 1986." In *Research in the Social Scientific Study of Religion*, vol. 1, edited by Monty L. Lynn and David O. Moberg, 153–81. Greenwich, Conn.: JAI Press.

Berger, Peter. [1970] 1983. "On the Obsolescence of the Concept of Honor." Reprinted in *Revisions: Changing Perspectives in Moral Philosophy*, edited by Stanley Hauerwas and Alasdair MacIntyre, 172–81. Notre Dame, Ind.: University of Notre Dame Press.

Bernstein, Basil. 1990. "Social Class and Pedagogic Practice." In *The Structuring of Pedagogic Discourse*, 63–93. *Class, Codes and Control*, vol. 4. London: Routledge.

Bietz, Charles A., Jr. 1985. "Introduction." *Ethics: A Selected Bibliography*. Carlisle Barracks, Penn.: U.S. Army War College.

Bourdieu, Pierre, and Jean-Claude Passeron. 1977. *Reproduction in Education, Society, and Culture*. Beverly Hills: Sage Publications.

Bowles, Samuel, and Herbert Gintis. 1976. *Schooling in Capitalist America: Educational Reform and the Contradictions of Economic Life*. New York: Basic Books.

Brinton, Howard H. 1952. *Friends for 300 Years: The History and Beliefs of the Society of Friends Since George Fox Started the Quaker Movement*. Wallingford, Penn.: Pendle Hill Publications.

———— 1972. *Quaker Journals: Varieties of Religious Experience Among Friends*. Wallingford, Penn.: Pendle Hill Publications.

———— 1985. *Friends and Their Spiritual Message*. Philadelphia: Friends General Conference.

Brown, James, and Michael J. Collins, eds. 1981. *Military Ethics and Professionalism: A Collection of Essays*. Washington, D.C.: National Defense University Press.

Brown, Lyn Mikel. 1990. "When Is a Moral Problem Not a Moral Problem? Morality, Identity, and Female Adolescence." In *Making Connections*, 88–109. See Gilligan, Lyons, and Hanmer.

Brown, Thomas S. 1986. *When Friends Attend to Business*. Philadelphia: Philadelphia Yearly Meeting of the Religious Society of Friends.

Callahan, Sidney deShazo. 1983. "In Defense of Honor: A Misunderstood Moral Resource." *Cross Currents* 33 (Summer): 171–80.

Cohen, David K. 1976. "Loss as a Theme in Social Policy." *Harvard Educational Review* 46 (November): 553–71.

Coleman, James S. 1961. *The Adolescent Society: The Social Life of the Teenager and Its Impact on Education*. New York: Free Press.

Coleman, James S., Thomas Hoffer, and Sally Kilgore. 1982. *High School Achievement: Public, Private, and Catholic Schools Compared*. New York: Basic Books.

Comfort, William Wistar. 1968. *Just Among Friends: The Quaker Way of Life*. 5th and revised edition. Philadelphia: American Friends Service Committee.

Conroy, Pat. 1980. *The Lords of Discipline*. New York: Bantam Books.

Cookson, Peter W., Jr., and Caroline Hodges Persell. 1985. *Preparing for Power: America's Elite Boarding Schools*. New York: Basic Books.

Coser, Lewis A. 1956. *The Functions of Social Conflict*. London: Routledge and Kegan Paul.

——— 1967. "Durkheim's Conservatism and Its Implications for Sociological Theory." In *Continuities in the Study of Social Conflict*, 153–80. New York: Free Press.

Cox, Gray. 1985. *Bearing Witness: Quaker Process and a Culture of Peace*. Pamphlet 262. Wallingford, Penn.: Pendle Hill Publications.

Crocker, Lawrence P. 1985. *The Army Officer's Guide*. 43d edition. Harrisburg, Penn.: Stackpole Books.

Cunliffe, Marcus. 1968. *Soldiers and Civilians: The Martial Spirit in America, 1775–1865*. Boston: Little, Brown.

Dahl, Roald. 1984. *Boy: Tales of Childhood*. London: Penguin Books.

Dempsey, Martin E. 1988. "Repose: A Forgotten Factor in Leadership Development." *Military Review* 68 (November): 28–33.

Dornbusch, Sanford M. 1989. "The Sociology of Adolescence." *Annual Review of Sociology* 15:233–59.

Dorrance, Christopher A., ed. 1982. *Reflections from a Friends Education*. Philadelphia: Friends Council on Education.

Douglas, Mary. 1966. *Purity and Danger: An Analysis of Concepts of Pollution and Taboo*. Harmondsworth, England: Penguin Books.

Durkheim, Emile. [1925] 1961. *Moral Education: A Study in the Theory and Application of the Sociology of Education*. New York: Free Press.

——— [1915] 1965. *The Elementary Forms of the Religious Life*. New York: Free Press.

——— 1973. *On Morality and Society*. Selected writings edited and with introduction by Robert N. Bellah. Chicago: University of Chicago Press.

Eckert, Penelope. 1989. *Jocks and Burnouts: Social Categories and Identity in the High School*. New York: Teachers College Press.

Elkin, Frederick, and Gerald Handel. 1984. *The Child and Society: The Process of Socialization*. 4th edition. New York: Random House.

Erikson, Erik H. 1968a. *Identity: Youth and Crisis*. New York: W. W. Norton.

———— 1968b. "Youth: Fidelity and Diversity." In *Adolescence: Contemporary Studies*, edited by Alvin E. Winder and David L. Angus, 13–52. New York: Van Nostrand Reinhold.

Everhart, Robert B. 1988. *Practical Ideology and Symbolic Community: An Ethnography of Schools of Choice.* New York: Falmer Press.

Fine, Gary Alan. 1987. *With the Boys: Little League Baseball and Preadolescent Culture.* Chicago: University of Chicago Press.

Foley, Douglas E. 1990. *Learning Capitalist Culture: Deep in the Heart of Tejas.* Philadelphia: University of Pennsylvania Press.

Foot, Philippa. 1978. "Virtues and Vices." In *Virtues and Vices and Other Essays in Moral Philosophy*, 1–18. Berkeley: University of California Press.

Fox, George. [1694] 1985. *The Journal of George Fox.* Revised edition by John L. Nickalls. Philadelphia: Philadelphia Yearly Meeting of the Religious Society of Friends.

Frankena, William K. 1980. *Thinking About Morality.* Ann Arbor: University of Michigan Press.

Freud, Anna. 1958. "Adolescence." *Psychoanalytic Study of the Child* 13:255–78.

Friends Council on Education. 1983. *Religious Education in Friends Elementary Schools.* Revised edition. Philadelphia: Friends Council on Education.

———— 1984. *Making Sense Out of Consensus.* Philadelphia: Friends Council on Education.

———— 1985a. *The Friends Meeting for Worship: The Purpose, Process, and Potential of a Religious and Educational Experience in Friends Schools.* Philadelphia: Friends Council on Education.

———— 1985b. *Occasional Papers on the Meeting for Worship for Friends Schools.* Philadelphia: Friends Council on Education.

Gabriel, Richard A. 1981. "Modernism vs. Pre-modernism: The Need to Rethink the Basis of Military Organizational Forms." In *Military Ethics and Professionalism*, 55–74. See Brown and Collins.

———— 1982. *To Serve with Honor: A Treatise on Military Ethics and the Way of the Soldier.* Westport, Conn.: Greenwood Press.

Galligan, Francis B. 1979. *Military Professionalism and Ethics.* Newport, R.I.: Naval War College Center for Advanced Research.

Gilligan, Carol. 1982. *In a Different Voice: Psychological Theory and Women's Development.* Cambridge: Harvard University Press.

Gilligan, Carol, Nona P. Lyons, and Trudy J. Hanmer, eds. 1990. *Making Connections: The Relational Worlds of Adolescent Girls at Emma Willard School.* Cambridge: Harvard University Press.

Gilmore, David D. 1990. *Manhood in the Making: Cultural Concepts of Masculinity*. New Haven: Yale University Press.

Goffman, Erving. 1961. *Asylums: Essays on the Social Situation of Mental Patients and Other Inmates*. Reprint. New York: Anchor Books, Doubleday.

Grant, Gerald. 1981. "The Character of Education and the Education of Character." *Daedalus* 110 (Summer): 135–49.

Gray, J. Glenn. 1970a. *On Understanding Violence Philosophically and Other Essays*. New York: Harper Torchbooks.

——— 1970b. *The Warriors: Reflections on Men in Battle*. 2d edition. New York: Harper and Row.

Gusfield, Joseph R. 1989. Introduction to *On Symbols and Society*, by Kenneth Burke, 1–49. Chicago: University of Chicago Press.

Hammersley, Martyn, and Peter Woods, eds. 1984. *Life in School*. Milton Keynes: Open University Press.

Hartle, Anthony E. 1989. *Moral Issues in Military Decision Making*. Lawrence: University Press of Kansas.

Hauerwas, Stanley. 1981. *A Community of Character: Toward a Constructive Christian Social Ethic*. Notre Dame, Ind.: University of Notre Dame Press.

Hays, Kim. 1986. "The Voices of Justice and Care: Socio-economic Power and Moral Worldview." Department of Sociology, University of California, Berkeley. Photocopy.

Heath, Douglas H. 1969. *Why a Friends School?* Pamphlet 164. Wallingford, Penn.: Pendle Hill Publications.

——— 1979. *The Peculiar Mission of a Quaker School*. Pamphlet 225. Wallingford, Penn.: Pendle Hill Publications.

Heath, Shirley Brice. 1983. *Ways with Words: Language, Life, and Work in Communities and Classrooms*. Cambridge: Cambridge University Press.

Hewitt, John P. 1989. *Dilemmas of the American Self*. Philadelphia: Temple University Press.

Hunter, James Davison. 1991. *Culture Wars: The Struggle to Define America*. New York: Basic Books.

Huntington, Samuel P. 1957. *The Soldier and the State: The Theory and Politics of Civil-Military Relations*. Cambridge: The Belknap Press of Harvard University Press.

Hutchinson, Dorothy H. 1985. *Friends and Service*. Revised edition. Philadelphia: Friends General Conference.

James, Sydney V. 1963. *A People Among Peoples: Quaker Benevolence in Eighteenth-Century America*. Cambridge: Harvard University Press.

James, William. [1910] 1982. "The Moral Equivalent of War." In *Essays in Religion and Morality*, 162–73. Cambridge: Harvard University Press.

Janowitz, Morris. 1971. *The Professional Soldier: A Social and Political Portrait*. 2d edition. New York: Free Press.

Jonas, Gerald. 1971. *On Doing Good.* New York: Charles Scribner's Sons.

Kagan, Jerome. 1981. "The Moral Function of the School." *Daedalus* 110 (Summer): 151–65.

Kanter, Rosabeth Moss. 1972. *Community and Commitment: Communes and Utopias in Sociological Perspective*. Cambridge: Harvard University Press.

Kelley, Hugh A. 1984. "A Proposal for the United States Army Ethic." Microfiche of a U.S. Army War College study project. Carlisle Barracks, Penn.

Kelly, Thomas E., III. 1981. "Ethics in the Military Profession: The Continuing Tension." In *Military Ethics and Professionalism*, 23–38. See Brown and Collins.

Kelly, Thomas R. 1985. *Eyes on the Border*. Philadelphia: American Friends Service Committee.

————— N.d. *The Gathered Meeting*. Philadelphia: The Tract Association of Friends.

Kenworthy, Leonard S. 1981. *Quakerism: A Study Guide on the Religious Society of Friends*. Kennett Square, Penn.: Quaker Publications.

—————1983a. *The Meaning of Membership in the Religious Society of Friends*. Kennett Square, Penn.: Quaker Publications.

————— 1983b. *Quaker Quotations on Faith and Practice*. Philadelphia: Friends General Conference.

—————, ed. 1987. *Friends Face the World: Continuing and Current Quaker Concerns*. Philadelphia: Friends General Conference.

Kinney, David A. 1989. "From 'Dweeb' to 'Normal': Identity Change During Adolescence." Paper presented at the annual meeting of the American Sociological Association.

Kirk, Jack. 1987. "Creaturely Activities or Spiritually Based Concerns?" In *Friends Face the World*, 5–21. See Kenworthy 1987.

Kleinman, Sherryl. 1984. *Equals Before God: Seminarians as Humanistic Professionals*. Chicago: University of Chicago Press.

Labov, Teresa. 1989. "Social and Language Barriers Among Adolescents." Paper presented at the annual meeting of the American Sociological Association.

Lakoff, George, and Mark Johnson. 1980. *Metaphors We Live By*. Chicago: University of Chicago Press.

Lasch, Christopher. 1984. *The Minimal Self: Psychic Survival in Troubled Times*. New York: W. W. Norton.

Lesko, Nancy. 1988. *Symbolizing Society: Stories, Rites and Structure in a Catholic High School*. New York: Falmer Press.

Lightfoot, Sara Lawrence. 1983. *The Good High School: Portraits of Character and Culture.* New York: Basic Books.

Linenthal, Edward Tabor. 1982. *Changing Images of the Warrior Hero in America: A History of Popular Symbolism.* Studies in American Religion 6. New York: Edwin Mellen Press.

Lovell, John P. 1979. *Neither Athens nor Sparta? The American Service Academies in Transition.* Bloomington: Indiana University Press.

Lyons, Nona P. 1990. "Listening to Voices We Have Not Heard: Emma Willard Girls' Ideas About Self, Relationships, and Morality." In *Making Connections*, 30–72. See Gilligan, Lyons, and Hanmer.

McDonough, James R. 1988. "Leadership for the New Lieutenant." *Military Review* 68 (November): 62–68.

MacIntyre, Alasdair. 1966. *A Short History of Ethics.* New York: Collier Books.

——— 1984a. *After Virtue: A Study in Moral Theory.* 2d edition. Notre Dame, Ind.: University of Notre Dame Press.

——— 1984b. *Is Patriotism a Virtue?* The Lindley Lecture, University of Kansas.

Mack, Phyllis. 1987. "Feminine Symbolism and Feminine Behavior in Radical Religious Movements: Franciscans, Quakers, and the Followers of Gandhi." In *Disciplines of Faith: Studies in Religion, Politics, and Patriarchy*, edited by Jim Obelkevich, Lyndal Roper, and Raphael Samuel, 115–30. London: Routledge and Kegan Paul.

Macpherson, James. 1983. *The Feral Classroom.* Melbourne: Routledge and Kegan Paul.

Maginnis, Robert L. 1987. "The Warrior Spirit." *Military Review* 67 (April): 69–79.

Malone, D. M. [1981] 1986. "The Trailwatcher." Reprinted in U.S. Military Academy, Department of Military Instruction, *Professional Notebook 1986*, T8-13. West Point: U.S. Military Academy.

Marshall, S. L. A. 1947. *Men Against Fire: The Problem of Battle Command in Future War.* New York: William Morrow.

Metz, Mary Haywood. 1978. *Classrooms and Corridors: The Crisis of Authority in Desegregated Schools.* Berkeley: University of California Press.

Mills, Eugene S. 1987. "Creating Centers of Contagion: Quaker Education in the United States." In *Friends Face the World*, 73–83. See Kenworthy 1987.

Moskos, Charles C. 1984. "The Citizen-Soldier and the All-Volunteer Force. In *The Military, Militarism, and the Polity: Essays in Honor of Morris Janowitz*, edited by Michel Louis Martin and Ellen Stern McCrate, 139–54. New York: Free Press.

Moulton, Phillips P. 1973. *The Living Witness of John Woolman.* Pamphlet 187. Wallingford, Penn: Pendle Hill Publications.

Muuss, Rolf E. 1988. *Theories of Adolescence*. 5th edition. New York: Random House.

Narel, James L. 1981. "Values and the Professional Soldier." *Ethics and the Military Profession* (March): 3–9.

Nelson, Marjorie. 1982. *Friends and Violence*. Philadelphia: Friends General Conference.

Nobbs, David. 1983. *Second from Last in the Sack Race*. London: Methuen.

Peristiany, J. G., ed. 1966. *Honor and Shame: The Values of Mediterranean Society*. London: Weidenfeld and Nicolson.

Peshkin, Alan. 1978. *Growing Up American: Schooling and the Survival of Community*. Chicago: University of Chicago Press.

———— 1986. *God's Choice: The Total World of a Fundamentalist Christian School*. Chicago: University of Chicago Press.

———— 1991. *The Color of Strangers, the Color of Friends: The Play of Ethnicity in School and Community*. Chicago: University of Chicago Press.

Philadelphia Yearly Meeting of the Religious Society of Friends. 1972. *Faith and Practice: A Book of Christian Discipline*. Philadelphia: Philadelphia Yearly Meeting of the Religious Society of Friends.

Piaget, Jean. 1965. *The Moral Judgment of the Child*. New York: Free Press.

Pitkin, Hanna Fenichel. 1981. "Justice: On Relating Public and Private." *Political Theory* 9 (August): 327–52.

Potts, Robert E. 1986. "Professional Military Ethics: Are We on the Right Track?" Microfiche of a U.S. Army War College study project. Carlisle Barracks, Penn.

Radine, Lawrence B. 1977. *The Taming of the Troops: Social Control in the United States Army*. Contributions in Sociology 22. Westport, Conn.: Greenwood Press.

Reitz, John W. 1981. "Hidden Assumptions of the Honor Concept." *Ethics and the Military Profession* (November): 3–8.

———— 1982. "Values and the Non-Toleration Clause." *Ethics and the Military Profession* (April): 8–11.

Rich, Sharon. 1990. "Daughters' Views of Their Relationships with Their Mothers." In *Making Connections*, 258–73. See Gilligan, Lyons, and Hanmer.

Ricks, Charles W. 1982. "The Non-Toleration Clause: A Chance for Misperception." *Ethics and the Military Profession* (April): 2–4.

Rosenberg, Morris. 1989. *Society and the Adolescent Self-Image*. Revised edition. Middletown, Conn.: Wesleyan University Press.

Rothschild-Whitt, Joyce. 1979. "The Collectivist Organization: An Alternative to Rational-Bureaucratic Models." *American Sociological Review* 44 (August): 509–27.

Sarkesian, Sam C. 1981a. *Beyond the Battlefield: The New Military Professionalism.* New York: Pergamon Press.

———— 1981b. "Moral and Ethical Foundations of Military Professionalism." In *Military Ethics and Professionalism*, 1–22. See Brown and Collins.

———— 1984. "Two Conceptions of Military Professionalism." In *The Military, Militarism, and the Polity*, 155–68. See Moskos.

Savage, Paul L., and Richard A. Gabriel. [1976] 1980. "Cohesion and Disintegration in the American Army: An Alternative Perspective." Reprinted in *The Military in America from the Colonial Era to the Present*, edited by Peter Karsten, 399–430. New York: Free Press.

Schaar, John H. 1981. "Legitimacy in the Modern State" and "The Case for Patriotism." In *Legitimacy in the Modern State*, 15–51 and 285–311. New Brunswick, N.J.: Transaction Books.

Sheeran, Michael J. 1983. *Beyond Majority Rule: Voteless Decisions in the Religious Society of Friends.* Philadelphia: Philadelphia Yearly Meeting of the Religious Society of Friends.

Sigel, Roberta S., and Marilyn B. Hoskin. 1981. *The Political Involvement of Adolescents.* New Brunswick, N.J.: Rutgers University Press.

Simmel, Georg. 1955. *Conflict.* Translated by Kurt H. Wolff. New York: Free Press.

Simpson, Evan. 1989. *Good Lives and Moral Education.* Studies in Moral Philosophy 4. New York: Peter Lang.

Skelly, James M. 1984. "The Minuteman Is a Missile, Not a Soldier: The Legitimation of American Military Service." Ph.D. dissertation, Department of Sociology, University of California, San Diego.

Smith, Warren Sylvester. 1985. *One Explorer's Glossary of Quaker Terms.* Philadelphia: Friends General Conference.

Sorley, Lewis S. 1981. "Competence as Ethical Imperative: Issues of Professionalism." In *Military Ethics and Professionalism*, 39–54. See Brown and Collins.

———— 1987. "Beyond Duty, Honor, Country." *Military Review* 67 (April): 2–13.

Steere, Douglas V. 1972. *On Speaking Out of the Silence: Vocal Ministry in the Unprogrammed Meeting for Worship.* Pamphlet 182. Wallingford, Penn.: Pendle Hill Publications.

Stockdale, James B. 1987. "Education for Leadership and Survival: The Role of the Pressure Cooker." Reprinted in *Military Ethics*, edited by Malham Wakin, Kenneth Wenker, and James Kempf, 223–51. Washington, D.C.: National Defense University Press.

Swidler, Ann. 1979. *Organization Without Authority: Dilemmas of Social Control in Free Schools.* Cambridge: Harvard University Press.

———— 1986. "Culture in Action: Symbols and Strategies." *American Socio-logical Review* 51 (April): 273–86.

Taber, Frances Irene. 1987. "Finding the Taproot of Simplicity: The Movement Between Inner Knowledge and Outer Action." In *Friends Face the World*, 59–72. See Kenworthy 1987.

Tannen, Deborah. 1990. *You Just Don't Understand: Men and Women in Conversation*. New York: Ballantine Books.

Taylor, Maxwell. 1978. "A Professional Ethic for the Military?" Reprinted in *Ethics and the Military Profession* (August): 4–11.

Terkel, Studs. 1984. *"The Good War": An Oral History of World War Two.* New York: Ballantine Books.

Thompson, John B. 1987. "Language and Ideology: A Framework for Analysis." *Sociological Review* 35 (August): 516–36.

Tipton, Steven M. 1982. *Getting Saved from the Sixties: Moral Meaning in Conversion and Cultural Change*. Berkeley: University of California Press.

Turner, Ralph H. 1976. "The Real Self: From Institution to Impulse." *American Journal of Sociology* 81 (March): 989–1016.

———— 1978. "The Role and the Person." *American Journal of Sociology* 84 (July): 1–23.

Turner, Victor. 1969. *The Ritual Process: Structure and Anti-Structure*. Ithaca, N.Y.: Cornell University Press.

U.S. Department of the Army, Headquarters. 1986. *The Bedrock of Our Profession*. Pamphlet 600-68, White Paper. Washington, D.C.: Government Printing Office.

———— 1987a. *Leadership and Command at Senior Levels*. Field Manual 22-103. Washington, D.C.: Government Printing Office.

———— 1987b. *Values: A Handbook for Soldiers*. Pamphlet 600-71. Washington, D.C.: Government Printing Office.

———— 1988. *Army Regulation 600-50*. Washington, D.C.: Government Printing Office.

———— 1990a. *Military Leadership*. Field Manual 22-100. Washington, D.C.: Government Printing Office.

———— 1990b. *Military Qualification Standards I Manual (Precommissioning Requirements)*. Soldier Training Publication 21-I-MQS. Washington, D.C.: Government Printing Office.

———— 1991. *The Army*. Field Manual 100-1. Washington, D.C.: Government Printing Office.

U.S. Military Academy, Department of Military Instruction. 1986. *Professional Notebook 1986*. West Point: U.S. Military Academy.

Vagts, Alfred. 1959. *A History of Militarism: Civilian and Military*. Revised edition. New York: Free Press.

Varenne, Hervé. 1982. "Jocks and Freaks: The Symbolic Structure of the Expression of Social Interaction Among American Senior High School Students." In *Doing the Ethnography of Schooling: Educational Anthropology in Action*, edited by George Spindler, 210–35. New York: Holt, Rinehart, and Winston.

———— 1983. *American School Language: Culturally Patterned Conflicts in a Suburban High School*. New York: Irvington Publishers.

Wallach, Michael A., and Lise Wallach. 1990. *Rethinking Goodness*. Albany: State University of New York Press.

Wilkinson, Rupert. 1988. *The Pursuit of American Character*. New York: Harper and Row.

Williams, Bernard. 1972. *Morality: An Introduction to Ethics*. New York: Harper and Row.

———— 1985. *Ethics and the Limits of Philosophy*. Cambridge: Harvard University Press.

Williams, Christine L. 1989. *Gender Differences at Work: Women and Men in Non-Traditional Occupations*. Berkeley: University of California Press.

Willis, Paul. 1977. *Learning to Labor: How Working Class Kids Get Working Class Jobs*. New York: Columbia University Press.

Wilson, Roger C. [1949] 1970. *Authority, Leadership, and Concern: A Study in Motive and Administration in Quaker Relief Work*. London: Friends Home Service Committee.

Wolfe, Alan. 1989. *Whose Keeper? Social Science and Moral Obligation*. Berkeley: University of California Press.

Woolman, John. [1774] 1961. *The Journal of John Woolman*. The John Greenleaf Whittier Edition Text. Reprint. Secaucus, N.J.: Citadel Press.

Wuthnow, Robert. 1987. *Meaning and Moral Order: Explorations in Cultural Analysis*. Berkeley: University of California Press.

Wyatt-Brown, Bertram. 1982. *Southern Honor: Ethics and Behavior in the Old South*. Oxford: Oxford University Press.

Young, Anna M. 1986. *Points of Honor*. Microfiche of a U.S. Army War College student essay. Carlisle Barracks, Penn.

Yow, Harold D. 1960. "The Ethical Bases for Leadership." *Military Review* 40 (September): 50–53.

Zuckerman, Michael. 1977. "The Fabrication of Identity in Early America." *William and Mary Quarterly* 34 (April): 183–214.

Index

Academies. *See* Military boarding schools

Activism, 62–63, 169–70, 171–73

Adolescent identity: and ambivalent feelings about adults, 185–87; developed through association with peers, 187; formation of, incompatible with sacredness, 216–17; importance of fidelity to development of, 184, 216–17; influence of moral traditions on, 10, 196–208, 227–30; and judging self, 194–95; and self-presentation, 194–208; and testing self through violence, 207–8

Adolescents: and excess, 75; importance of acceptance by peers to, 187–90; importance of consistency and sincerity to, 184–87, 260n.12; judging adult behavior by standards of moral tradition, 227, 262n.3; Mott tolerance for experimentation by, 126; and need for adult confidantes, 263n.3; and self-destructive behavior, 261n.30; surveys of political activity by, 259n.6; working with, as researcher, 237–38. *See also* Adolescent identity; Military-school students; Quaker-school students; Students

African-Americans: at Dyer, 134–36; at Fox, 133–34; at Pershing, 258n.15; at Sherman and Jackson, 14. *See also* Racism

Agape, as method of leadership, 213

Amato, Joseph, 7

Ambiguity: of Quaker and military virtues, 60–61; as unifier, 112; as vehicle for compromise, 48, 143

American Friends Service Committee, 50, 52, 155

Amish, 75

Annapolis. *See* United States Naval Academy

Anti-Semitism, 138–40

Apathy, 169–70

Appearance, 45, 100. *See also* Clothing

Aristotle, 248n.4

Army. *See* Military

Attachment: vs. autonomy, 3–4, 8, 47–48, 60–68, 113–14, 118–32, 209–10, 216–17, 223–26; as Durkheimian element of morality, 221–23

Austerity, 13, 41, 77, 114–18

Authority: contrasting Quaker and military positions on, 45–47, 145–47; for military professionals, 46; for Quakers, 45–46; in schools, 10

Autonomy: vs. attachment to groups, 3–4, 8, 47–48, 60–68, 113–14, 118–32, 209–10, 216–17, 223–26; as Durkheimian element of morality, 221–23

Background: students', 181–83; teachers', 181

Bad attitude (BA), 91, 99, 139–40, 214–15

Baker, Newton, 58

Barclay, Robert, 50

Battalion commander (BC), 24, 101, 176. *See also* Hurd, Tom

Bennett, Kyle (Pershing): on advantages of rank, 24; on control over his company, 37; defending hazing, 128; on difficulty of teaching leadership, 215; on keeping up appearances, 205; on narcing in his company, 74

Bergstrom, Erik (Sherman): criticizing narcs, 129–30; devotion to subordinates, 213; on how to beat the system, 107;

Compositor: Printed Page Productions
Text: 11/13 Caledonia
Display: Caledonia
Printer: BookCrafters, Inc.
Binder: BookCrafters, Inc.